# Ancient

# American Civilizations

*The Untold Story of Pre-Columbian Cities,*
*Impossible Stonework, and Lost Empires*

Theresa G. Bryan

# Table of Contents

# Preface

Something extraordinary occurred in the summer of 1997. Dr. Tom Dillehay stood in a laboratory at the University of Kentucky, inspecting radiocarbon test results. The figures on the paper before him could not be accurate. The samples from Monte Verde, Chile, are dated to 14,800 years ago. This discovery shattered every accepted timeline about when humans first arrived in the Americas.

Dillehay had spent twenty years defending his excavation work against fierce academic criticism. Colleagues dismissed his evidence. Peer reviewers rejected his papers. Conference presentations faced hostile questions. The archaeological establishment had invested decades in developing theories around the Clovis-first model. Humans crossed the Bering Land Bridge 13,000 years ago. They created the distinctive fluted spear points found across North America. They were the first Americans.

Monte Verde challenged this comfortable certainty. The Chilean site contained house foundations, preserved food remains, and even twisted plant fibers used for rope. People had lived there for 1,800 years before the Clovis culture supposedly began. The implications reached far beyond academic debates. If Monte Verde was real, then everything taught in textbooks about ancient America would need rewriting.

Ruth Shady faced similar resistance when she started excavating mysterious mounds in Peru's Supe Valley during the 1990s. Local farmers told her the hills contained nothing of interest. Government officials refused to fund her work. International archaeologists ignored her efforts. Shady persisted with a small team and limited resources. What she uncovered changed our understanding of civilisation itself.

Beneath the desert sand lay Caral, a massive stone city dating back to 2600 BCE. Its construction rivaled early Egyptian pyramids. Its urban planning surpassed anything seen in contemporary Mesopotamia. Most astonishingly, Caral showed no signs of warfare — no weapons, no fortifications, no defensive walls. Instead, Shady's team discovered musical instruments, astronomical alignments, and evidence of peaceful trade networks stretching hundreds of miles.

These discoveries share a common thread. They challenge fundamental assumptions about human achievement in the ancient Americas. They reveal civilizations that are more advanced, ancient, and sophisticated than conventional history allows. They suggest our ancestors possessed knowledge and capabilities we have consistently underestimated.

My journey into this hidden history started with a simple question. Why do discoveries that challenge established timelines face such strong resistance? The answer took me through several years of archaeological research, peer-reviewed papers, and firsthand accounts from researchers willing to challenge academic orthodoxy.

This book shares their stories. It investigates the evidence they found. It follows the human drama behind discoveries made of stone and bone, preserved in mud and ice, hidden beneath jungle canopies and desert sands. The truth about ancient America has been waiting thousands of years to be revealed. The moment has finally arrived to listen.

# Introduction

The footprints appeared like ghosts stepping out of time. Dr. Matthew Bennett knelt beside the ancient trackway in White Sands National Park, New Mexico. His brush carefully cleared away centuries of sediment. What he uncovered changed everything we believed about the first Americans.

The prints belonged to a child, perhaps around ten years old. Nearby tracks showed an adult, likely the mother, carrying a toddler. Behind them walked other family members. The sequence told a story of people hurrying across wet, muddy playas during the Pleistocene epoch. Seeds embedded in the sediment layers above and below the tracks provided precise dating. These humans had walked this path between 21,000 and 23,000 years ago.

The Bering Land Bridge is thought to have opened for human migration about 13,000 years ago. Ice sheets had blocked southern routes until then. Humans could not have reached New Mexico during the peak of the last Ice Age. The White Sands footprints should not be there. Yet, they were, perfectly preserved, impossible to ignore.

Bennett's team recorded over 400 individual prints across various trackways. They discovered evidence of children playing, adults carrying heavy loads, and entire groups moving in coordinated patterns across the ancient landscape. Mammoth and giant ground sloth tracks intersected with human paths, offering a vivid snapshot of Ice Age life more striking than any museum display.

The discovery followed a familiar pattern in American archaeology. Evidence appears. Academic institutions resist. Years pass before official recognition arrives. Sometimes recognition never comes at all.

Consider Valsequillo, Mexico. Archaeologist Virginia Steen-McIntyre spent her career studying volcanic ash layers around this ancient lake bed. Her dating techniques consistently placed human artifacts at 250,000 years old. The U.S. Geological Survey dismissed her from the project. Colleagues avoided her research. Grant applications faced rejection. Steen-McIntyre's findings disappeared from the official record.

Similar stories repeat across the Americas. At Pedra Furada in Brazil, archaeologist Nède Guidon uncovered stone tools in rock shelters dating back 32,000 years. Critics claimed the tools were naturally broken rocks. They never visited the site. They refused to examine the evidence firsthand. Guidon's discoveries remain controversial three decades later.

These patterns reveal more than scientific caution. They expose institutional unwillingness to confront paradigm-shifting discoveries. American archaeology built its reputation on specific models of human migration and cultural development. Evidence that contradicts these models poses a threat to more than just theories. It challenges careers, funding sources, and academic hierarchies.

The resistance has deeper origins. European colonisation of the Americas needed justification. If indigenous peoples had independently developed advanced civilizations, colonial claims to "empty" or "unused" lands would have been harder to justify. If Native Americans had occupied the continent for tens of thousands of years, their ties to the land would have gained more legitimacy. Historical stories that downplayed indigenous achievements served political purposes.

This context shapes how archaeological evidence gets interpreted. Sites that suggest advanced ancient cultures face heightened skepticism. Dating methods that push back human presence timelines receive intense scrutiny. Researchers who publish contradictory findings encounter career obstacles. The scientific method becomes subordinated to institutional inertia.

Breaking through this resistance requires more than new evidence. It demands fundamental changes in how we approach the past. Instead of forcing discoveries to fit existing models, we must allow discoveries to reshape our understanding. Instead of dismissing anomalous findings, we must investigate why they seem anomalous.

The ancient Americas were home to extraordinary civilizations. They built cities rivaling any in the ancient world. They developed writing systems, calendar technologies, and astronomical knowledge that exceeded European achievements of the same periods. They created architectural marvels that modern engineers struggle to replicate. They established trade networks spanning entire continents.

These accomplishments were not isolated achievements by scattered tribes. They resulted from sophisticated societies with complex social organization, advanced technical knowledge, and a deep understanding of their environments. The evidence exists in stone monuments, precision metalwork, mathematical calculations carved in temple walls, and urban ruins hidden beneath jungle canopies.

The story begins with footprints in New Mexico mud. It leads through peaceful cities in Peru, massive earthworks in Ohio, underwater temples in Maya cenotes, and precision stonework in the high Andes. Each discovery adds pieces to a puzzle that reveals human capability, ingenuity, and achievement far beyond what conventional history teaches.

This book follows that evidence wherever it leads. It tells the stories of researchers who dedicated their careers to uncovering the truth, even when the truth contradicted academic orthodoxy. It examines civilizations that rose and vanished, leaving behind monuments that continue to puzzle modern observers. It explores technologies that seem impossible for their supposed time periods.

Most importantly, it restores human agency to ancient history. These were not primitive peoples waiting for outside contact to achieve civilization. They were innovative societies that solved complex problems, adapted to challenging environments, and created lasting achievements that continue to inspire wonder thousands of years later.

The footprints at White Sands tell us something profound. Humans have been shaping the American landscape for over twenty millennia. Their descendants built some of history's most remarkable civilizations. The time has come to give them the recognition they deserve.

*Ancient American Civilizations*

# PART I

# THE UNTOLD STORY OF PRE-COLUMBIAN CITIES

# Chapter 1: Footprints in Time - The Evidence That Changes Everything

## White Sands: 23,000-Year-Old Human Tracks

The morning sun cast long shadows across the white gypsum dunes of southern New Mexico. Dr. Matthew Bennett walked slowly across the hardpan surface, his eyes scanning for anything unusual. Park rangers had reported strange depressions in the dried lake bed. Bennett had seen similar formations before. Most turned out to be animal tracks or natural erosion patterns.

This time felt different. The depressions followed clear patterns. They displayed the unmistakable signs of human movement. Bennett knelt beside the clearest impression. The heel strike was easy to see. The toe push-off was perfectly preserved. The spacing aligned with human walking patterns. Someone had walked this very path thousands of years ago.

Bennett's team began systematic excavation the next day. They removed sediment grain by grain, photographing each layer. The prints appeared in sequence, one after another, telling a story frozen in time. A child's small feet pressed into the mud. Larger adult prints overlapped the smaller ones. The adult had been carrying something heavy, possibly a toddler, as indicated by the deeper heel impressions.

The excavation revealed entire family groups moving across the ancient playa. Children had run ahead of their parents, their playful steps captured forever in the hardened mud. Adults followed more deliberately, their prints showing the weight of carrying supplies or small children. Some trackways showed people walking in a single file. Others revealed groups spreading out across the landscape.

Mammoth tracks crossed the human paths at several locations. Giant ground sloths had lumbered through the same area. Dire wolves had hunted here. The human footprints appeared alongside these Pleistocene megafauna, creating a vivid snapshot of Ice Age life in North America.

Dr. Kathleen Springer joined the team to analyze the geological context. Seeds and plant fragments embedded in the sediment layers above and below the tracks provided material for radiocarbon dating. The results shocked everyone involved. The plant remains dated to between 21,000 and 23,000 years ago. The human footprints were the same age.

The implications hit like a thunderbolt. Conventional archaeology taught that humans first reached the Americas around 13,000 years ago. The Bering Land Bridge connected Asia and Alaska during the last glacial maximum. Ice sheets blocked southern migration routes until around 12,000 years ago. People could not have reached New Mexico during the height of the Ice Age.

Bennett contacted colleagues across the country. He shared the preliminary findings with experts in geochronology, human locomotion, and Pleistocene ecology. Every specialist confirmed the same conclusion. These were definitely human footprints. The dating was accurate. The geological context was sound.

The White Sands discovery documented over 400 individual human footprints across multiple trackways. The prints showed remarkable preservation detail. Researchers could identify specific individuals based on foot size and gait characteristics. They tracked family groups across hundreds of meters. They observed children playing games, jumping and running in circles.

One trackway told a particularly compelling story. A woman walked in a straight line across the playa, carrying a heavy load. Her footprints showed the characteristic deep heel strikes of someone bearing extra weight. The spacing between prints indicated a hurried pace. She was traveling to a specific destination with purpose and urgency.

Hours later, the same woman walked back along nearly the identical path. This time her prints showed normal depth and spacing. She was no longer carrying the heavy load. She moved at a relaxed pace, occasionally stepping sideways or pausing. The return journey told a story of task completion and leisure travel.

Toddler prints appeared throughout the trackways. The tiny feet created the most detailed impressions, with clear toe marks and arch patterns. Many appeared alongside adult tracks, showing parents carrying small children. Some toddler prints formed independent sequences, revealing moments when children walked on their own feet.

*Ancient American Civilizations*

The preservation resulted from perfect environmental conditions. The humans had walked across wet playa mud during a brief period when the lake level dropped. New sediments quickly covered the tracks, protecting them from erosion. The arid climate of southern New Mexico prevented decay. The prints remained undisturbed for over 20,000 years.

Bennett's team expanded the excavation across several square kilometers. They found trackways in all directions. Some led toward distant mountains. Others headed toward vanished water sources. The patterns suggested a substantial human presence in the area, not just occasional visitors passing through.

The discovery fundamentally changed the understanding of early human presence in the Americas. People had not only reached North America during the Last Glacial Maximum, but they had also established communities and traveled extensively across the landscape. They coexisted with Pleistocene megafauna. They raised families and pursued daily activities in environments scientists previously thought uninhabitable for humans.

# Monte Verde: Chile's 18,000-Year Settlement

Dr. Tom Dillehay's boots squelched through the boggy ground of southern Chile. Chinchihuapi Creek meandered through dense forest, creating wetlands that were perfect for preserving organic materials. Local residents had reported finding strange wooden objects in the creek banks. Dillehay hoped to discover evidence of Chile's earliest inhabitants.

The first artifact appeared in the creek bed itself. A wooden stake, sharpened to a point, protruded from waterlogged sediments. The wood showed clear signs of human modification. Tool marks scarred the surface. The tip had been deliberately shaped for a specific purpose.

Dillehay began systematic excavation in 1977. The waterlogged conditions had preserved organic materials that would typically be lost to decay. Wooden tools, plant fibers, and even food remains survived in the oxygen-free environment. The site offered a unique window into Pleistocene life in South America.

The excavation revealed structures unlike anything found at other early American sites. Wooden frameworks formed the foundation for tent-like dwellings. The builders had driven stakes into the ground, then stretched animal hides over the framework. Hearths provided warmth and cooking areas. Storage pits held food supplies and tools.

Plant remains told remarkable stories about the inhabitants' lives. Seeds from distant coastal areas showed that these people traveled long distances to gather specific foods. Medicinal plants from various ecological zones indicated sophisticated knowledge of natural remedies. Food preparation areas contained remains of fruits, nuts, and tubers from across the region.

The stone tools differed dramatically from the familiar Clovis points found throughout North America. Monte Verde inhabitants created simple cutting implements and scrapers. They preferred wooden tools for most tasks. Their technology emphasized efficiency and portability over elaborate craftsmanship.

One dwelling yielded extraordinary discoveries—twisted plant fibers formed rope and cord. The inhabitants had woven baskets and mats from local materials. Seeds and berries filled storage containers. Animal bones showed evidence of careful butchering and processing.

A child's footprint preserved in clay provided the most human connection to these ancient people. The small foot had pressed into soft mud near a hearth area. The impression captured individual toe marks and arch details. Someone's child had played near the family fire 18,000 years ago.

Radiocarbon dating confirmed the site's antiquity—charcoal from hearths dated to approximately 18,500 years ago. Plant materials from the same layers provided consistent dates. Monte Verde was 5,000 years older than the earliest accepted Clovis sites.

The discovery faced immediate skepticism from the archaeological establishment. Clovis-first proponents questioned every aspect of Dillehay's evidence. They challenged the dating methods. They disputed the interpretation of artifacts. They demanded additional evidence that other sites could not provide.

Dillehay invited critics to examine the site firsthand. He shared artifact collections with skeptical colleagues. He published detailed reports in peer-reviewed journals. Some critics gradually accepted the evidence. Others maintained their opposition despite the mounting proof.

The controversy raged for nearly two decades. Archaeological conferences became battlegrounds between Clovis-first defenders and pre-Clovis advocates. Careers suffered on both sides. Graduate students avoided the topic to protect their futures. The scientific process became subordinated to academic politics.

Independent verification finally settled the debate. Multiple laboratories confirmed the radiocarbon dates. Geological analysis supported Dillehay's stratigraphic interpretations. Microscopic examination verified the human manufacture of stone tools. Monte Verde gained acceptance as genuine pre-Clovis evidence.

The site revealed sophisticated adaptation to South American environments. The inhabitants knew which plants provided nutrition during different seasons. They understood animal migration patterns and hunting opportunities. They selected camp locations for access to water, shelter, and raw materials.

Monte Verde demonstrated that early Americans possessed complex knowledge systems. They traveled extensively across diverse landscapes. They maintained cultural traditions across generations. They adapted successfully to challenging environments using simple but effective technologies.

The settlement showed evidence of social organization beyond simple family groups. Different areas served specific functions: tool manufacturing, food preparation, storage, and living spaces. The inhabitants divided labor and shared resources. They maintained their community for extended periods in the exact location.

Dillehay's work opened new possibilities for understanding early American colonization. If people had reached southern Chile 18,000 years ago, they must have entered the Americas much earlier. The migration process was more complex than a simple Bering Land Bridge crossing. Multiple entry routes and earlier arrival times became plausible.

# Pedra Furada: Brazil's 32,000-Year Stone Tools

The red sandstone cliffs of Serra da Capivara rose like ancient fortresses from the Brazilian caatinga. Dr. Nième Guidon climbed the narrow trail leading to Pedra Furada rock shelter, her backpack loaded with excavation tools. Local guides had shown her cave paintings deep within the shelter. Guidon suspected the site contained much older evidence of human presence.

The rock shelter stretched back into darkness, its walls covered with thousands of painted figures. Animals, humans, and geometric designs decorated every surface. The artwork clearly showed great antiquity, but Guidon sought older evidence buried in the shelter floor.

Her team began excavation in 1978, working through successive layers of sediment. The upper levels contained pottery fragments and recent indigenous artifacts. Deeper layers yielded older stone tools and animal bones. At a depth of three meters, they encountered something extraordinary.

Crude stone implements appeared in sediment layers far below any expected human occupation. The tools showed clear signs of human manufacture. Sharp edges had been knapped from quartz cobbles. Flakes removed from cores displayed the characteristic patterns of intentional stone working.

Guidon examined each artifact under magnification. Impact scars showed where stones had been struck with hammers. Edge wear indicated use for cutting and scraping. The tools demonstrated human cognitive ability and motor skills. Natural processes could not have created such modifications.

The geological context seemed secure. Undisturbed sediment layers contained the tools in their original positions. No evidence of later intrusion appeared anywhere in the deposits. The stratigraphic sequence showed a clear temporal progression from bottom to top.

Charcoal samples from the tool-bearing layers provided material for radiocarbon dating. The results exceeded all expectations. The deepest levels are dated to 32,000 years ago. Stone tools appeared throughout the sequence, with the oldest specimens reaching potential ages of 50,000 years.

International reaction ranged from skepticism to outright hostility. North American archaeologists dismissed the findings without examination. They claimed natural rockfall had created the supposed tools. They questioned Guidon's experience and methodology. They refused to consider evidence that contradicted established theories.

Guidon invited critics to visit Pedra Furada and examine the evidence firsthand. Few accepted the invitation. Those who did often arrived with predetermined conclusions. They spent minimal time at the site before declaring the tools to be naturally broken rocks.

The rejection had devastating effects on Guidon's career. International journals refused to publish her research. Conference organizers excluded her from symposiums. Funding agencies denied grant applications. The archaeological establishment effectively ostracized one of Brazil's most distinguished researchers.

Despite the opposition, Guidon continued excavating at Pedra Furada and nearby sites. Additional rock shelters yielded similar evidence of extreme antiquity. The tools showed consistent manufacturing techniques across different locations. The pattern suggested sustained human presence over thousands of years.

Microscopic analysis supported Guidon's interpretations. The stone tools displayed use-wear patterns identical to experimentally produced implements. Residue analysis revealed the presence of organic materials on the cutting edges. Refitting studies demonstrated how knappers reduced cores to produce the desired tool forms.

Geological investigation confirmed the site's integrity. The sediment layers had accumulated gradually over millions of years without disturbance. Dating of multiple samples from each layer produced consistent ages. Independent laboratories verified the radiocarbon chronology.

New discoveries at other South American sites began supporting Guidon's claims. Monte Verde in Chile provided evidence of human occupation dating back 18,000 years. Sites in Argentina and Peru yielded pre-Clovis dates. The pattern suggested a much earlier human arrival than previously accepted.

Technological analysis revealed a sophisticated understanding of stone tool production. The Pedra Furada inhabitants carefully selected raw materials. They planned reduction strategies to maximize tool production from each core. They maintained and resharpened implements to extend their useful life.

The tools served diverse functions in daily activities. Cutting implements are used to process plant foods and animal materials. Scrapers prepared

*Ancient American Civilizations*

hides and wooden implements. Gravers created decorative patterns and functional notches. The assemblage reflected complex technological systems.

Environmental reconstruction showed challenging conditions during the site's occupation. Climate fluctuations caused repeated droughts and forest expansions. Animal populations shifted with changing vegetation patterns. Successful human adaptation required extensive knowledge of the environment.

The rock art added cultural dimensions to the archaeological evidence. Painted figures showed hunting scenes, ceremonial activities, and daily life. The artistic tradition continued for thousands of years, suggesting cultural continuity across generations. Humans had not only survived in this environment, but they had also created lasting cultural expressions.

Guidon's work demonstrated that scientific progress requires courage to challenge established paradigms. Her persistence, despite professional isolation, advanced the understanding of early American prehistory. The evidence from Pedra Furada forced reconsideration of human capabilities and chronologies.

# Topper Site: Pre-Clovis Cultures in South Carolina

Dr. Al Goodyear knelt in the red Carolina clay beside the Savannah River. His trowel scraped carefully through sediment layers that had accumulated over thousands of years. The Topper site had already yielded beautiful Clovis points from the upper levels. Goodyear suspected much older evidence lay deeper in the deposits.

The site occupied a strategic location on the river bluff. Ancient peoples had repeatedly returned here to manufacture stone tools from high-quality chert. Thousands of artifacts littered the ground surface. Systematic excavation had documented continuous occupation spanning thousands of years.

Goodyear decided to probe below the established Clovis horizon. Conventional wisdom suggested sterile soil lay beneath the 13,000-year-old artifacts. Most archaeologists would have stopped excavating at the Clovis level. Goodyear's curiosity drove him to dig deeper.

The first pre-Clovis artifact appeared at 50 centimeters below the accepted horizon. A small blade fragment showed clear human manufacture. The technology differed from Clovis traditions but displayed sophisticated knapping skills. More tools appeared as excavation continued deeper.

The pre-Clovis layer contained thousands of stone artifacts. Blades, scrapers, and cores filled systematic excavation units. The technology emphasized the production of sharp cutting implements from carefully prepared cores. The knappers possessed an advanced understanding of stone fracture mechanics.

Radiocarbon dates from the pre-Clovis layer shocked the archaeological community. Charcoal associated with the stone tools is dated to 16,000 years ago—additional samples from the same level produced similar ages. The Topper site contained human occupation 3,000 years before the Clovis culture appeared.

Academic reaction followed predictable patterns. Clovis-first advocates questioned every aspect of Goodyear's evidence. They challenged the stratigraphic associations. They disputed the human manufacture of artifacts. They demanded impossible levels of proof while accepting lesser evidence for Clovis sites.

Goodyear invited critics to examine the evidence directly. He provided detailed stratigraphic profiles showing a clear separation between Clovis and pre-Clovis levels. He demonstrated the human manufacture of stone tools through technological analysis. Independent experts confirmed his interpretations.

The site's integrity remained beyond question—undisturbed sediment layers contained artifacts in their original positions. No evidence of mixing between levels appeared anywhere in the deposits. The stratigraphic sequence demonstrated clear temporal separation between cultural components.

Additional excavation revealed even older evidence. Stone tools appeared in levels dating to 20,000 years ago. The deepest artifacts might be even older, pushing human presence back to the Last Glacial Maximum. The implications challenged fundamental assumptions about American prehistory.

*Ancient American Civilizations*

The pre-Clovis inhabitants displayed remarkable skill in stone tool production. They selected raw materials from sources dozens of miles away. They transported finished tools and manufacturing debris across the landscape. They established quarry workshops at optimal locations near high-quality stone sources.

Technological analysis revealed complex reduction strategies. The toolmakers produced standardized blade forms through systematic core preparation. They understood how to control fracture patterns to create specific tool shapes. They maximized the number of cutting implements produced from each stone core.

Use-wear analysis showed how these tools functioned in daily activities. Microscopic examination revealed residues from plant processing, hide working, and wood cutting. The implements served diverse functions in hunting, gathering, and camp maintenance activities.

The Topper discovery coincided with similar finds across the southeastern United States. Sites in Virginia, Tennessee, and Florida yielded pre-Clovis evidence. The pattern suggested widespread human presence thousands of years before conventional timelines allowed.

Environmental reconstruction provided context for early human adaptation. The Southeast remained habitable during glacial periods when ice sheets covered northern regions. Rivers provided transportation routes and abundant resources. The landscape supported both humans and the animals they hunted.

Goodyear's work demonstrated the importance of looking beyond established chronological boundaries. His willingness to excavate below the Clovis horizon revealed unexpected evidence of much earlier human presence. Scientific progress sometimes requires challenging conventional wisdom and exploring unlikely possibilities.

The site contributed crucial evidence to the growing pre-Clovis database. Combined with Monte Verde, Meadowcroft, and other early sites, Topper helped establish human presence in the Americas thousands of years before previously accepted. The evidence forced reconsideration of migration routes, timing, and early cultural adaptations.

# Gault: Texas Evidence of Early Human Presence

The Gault site sprawled across central Texas hills north of Austin. For decades, artifact collectors had gathered beautiful stone tools from the eroding creek banks. Dr. Michael Collins recognized the site's scientific potential and began systematic excavation in the 1990s.

The upper levels yielded spectacular Clovis artifacts. Perfectly fluted projectile points demonstrated the highest levels of prehistoric craftsmanship. Tool caches contained dozens of finished implements and manufacturing debris. The site ranked among North America's richest Clovis localities.

Collins decided to investigate deposits below the Clovis horizon. Previous experience at other Texas sites suggested earlier occupations might exist. His team carefully excavated through the interface between Clovis and the underlying sediments.

The first pre-Clovis artifacts appeared just centimeters below the established Clovis layer. Stone tools showed different manufacturing techniques but a clear human origin. The technology emphasized the production of thin bifaces and small cutting implements. Knapping debris indicated tool manufacture at the site.

Systematic excavation revealed extensive pre-Clovis occupation. Thousands of artifacts filled excavation units across multiple areas of the site. The inhabitants had repeatedly returned to this location over extended periods. Discrete tool concentrations suggested specific activity areas within the broader occupation zone.

The pre-Clovis technology differed dramatically from later Clovis traditions. The earlier inhabitants produced thin bifaces through sophisticated reduction techniques. They created standardized blade tools from carefully prepared cores. Their knapping methods displayed an advanced understanding of stone fracture mechanics.

Radiocarbon dating placed the pre-Clovis occupation between 16,000 and 20,000 years ago. Multiple samples from secure contexts produced consistent ages. Independent laboratories confirmed the chronology. Gault contained some of the oldest reliably dated human occupation in North America.

The site's exceptional preservation allowed detailed behavioral reconstruction. Discrete activity areas showed where inhabitants performed specific tasks. Knapping areas contained tool manufacturing debris. Hearth areas preserved evidence of food preparation and consumption.

One excavation unit yielded remarkable evidence of symbolic behavior. A limestone slab contained incised lines forming geometric patterns. The engravings required deliberate planning and execution. They demonstrated cognitive abilities associated with fully modern humans.

Tool production at Gault revealed sophisticated planning and execution. The inhabitants transported raw materials from quarries up to 100 kilometers away. They selected specific stone types for different tool categories. They maintained standardized production methods across generations.

Use-wear analysis showed how Gault tools functioned in daily activities. Microscopic examination revealed residues from plant processing, hide working, and bone modification. The implements served diverse functions supporting hunter-gatherer lifestyles in Ice Age Texas.

The environmental context provided insights into early human adaptations. The site location offered access to diverse ecological zones within a day's travel. Springs provided reliable water sources. Stone outcrops supplied raw materials for tool production. The landscape supported both human occupation and abundant game animals.

Gault inhabitants demonstrated remarkable technological continuity over thousands of years. The pre-Clovis and Clovis occupations showed evolution in tool forms and manufacturing techniques. Cultural traditions are adapted to changing environmental conditions and resource availability.

The discovery added crucial evidence to the growing pre-Clovis database. Combined with evidence from Monte Verde, Topper, and other sites, Gault helped establish human presence in the Americas much earlier than previously accepted. The pattern suggested multiple migration episodes and complex population histories.

Academic reception of the Gault evidence followed familiar patterns. Initial skepticism gradually gave way to acceptance as supporting evidence accumulated. The site's excellent preservation and rigorous excavation methods made the evidence difficult to dismiss.

Collins's work demonstrated the importance of investigating beyond established cultural horizons. Many significant discoveries remain buried beneath accepted chronological boundaries. Scientific progress requires a willingness to challenge established paradigms and explore unexpected possibilities.

The Gault site transformed the understanding of early human adaptations in North America. The evidence showed sophisticated technological traditions thousands of years before the Clovis culture appeared. Early Americans possessed advanced skills and complex cultural systems from their earliest presence on the continent.

# Chapter 2: The Carbon Dating Deception - When Science Becomes Ideology

## Atmospheric Carbon-14 Fluctuations Through History

Dr. Minze Stuiver sat in his University of Washington laboratory in 1982, staring at ice core data from Greenland. The numbers defied everything he had been taught about radiocarbon dating. Carbon-14 levels in the atmosphere had not remained constant over time. They fluctuated wildly.

Stuiver's ice cores revealed dramatic spikes during periods of intense cosmic radiation. Solar flares bombarded Earth's atmosphere, creating excess carbon-14. Volcanic eruptions released ancient carbon dioxide, diluting atmospheric ratios. Major climate shifts altered ocean circulation patterns, changing how carbon moved between air and water. Each event skewed the cosmic clock scientists trusted to date ancient artifacts.

The implications struck Stuiver immediately. Every radiocarbon date calculated using standard curves could be wrong by hundreds or thousands of years. Artifacts dated to 10,000 years ago might actually be 8,000 or 15,000 years old. The entire framework of archaeological chronology rested on false assumptions.

Stuiver began documenting these fluctuations. He published correction curves based on tree ring data going back 8,000 years. His work revealed that carbon-14 dating worked reasonably well for recent periods. Beyond that, uncertainty increased dramatically. For samples older than 20,000 years, the method became nearly unreliable.

The scientific community responded with quiet hostility. Archaeological institutions had built reputations on radiocarbon chronologies. Museum displays, textbook timelines, and grant applications all depended on these dates. Admitting fundamental uncertainty would undermine decades of published research.

Stuiver's colleague, Gordon Schlolaut, discovered even more troubling patterns in lake sediment cores from Japan. During the Late Glacial period, atmospheric carbon-14 levels spiked by 12 percent in less than two centuries. Any organic material from this period would appear artificially young by several thousand years. Archaeological sites from this crucial period of human development contained systematic errors.

The Laschamp Event, identified in volcanic rocks from France, showed the most significant fluctuation of all. Around 41,000 years ago, Earth's magnetic field weakened to 25 percent of its normal strength. Cosmic rays penetrated the atmosphere with unprecedented intensity. Carbon-14 production increased fourfold. Organic materials from this period displayed impossible dates, sometimes appearing 10,000 years younger than their actual age.

Dr. Pieter Grootes expanded this research using ice core samples from Antarctica. His data covered 50,000 years of atmospheric chemistry. The results devastated confidence in radiocarbon dating for prehistoric periods. Carbon-14 levels varied by factors of two or three during critical periods of human migration and cultural development.

These discoveries reached beyond academic circles. Legal cases involving indigenous land rights often relied on archaeological dates to establish occupation timelines. Radiocarbon uncertainty could shift these dates by millennia. Museum exhibitions labeled artifacts with specific ages based on problematic calculations. Educational materials taught students precise chronologies built on unstable foundations.

The response from archaeological institutions proved predictable. Rather than acknowledging uncertainty, they refined calibration curves using selective data. They excluded problematic samples from calculations. They developed statistical methods to smooth out inconvenient fluctuations. The illusion of precision continued despite growing evidence of systematic errors.

Independent researchers began questioning why specific periods showed more variation than others. The answer pointed to catastrophic events in Earth's history. Supernovae within 300 light-years of Earth could trigger massive carbon-14 spikes. Asteroid impacts might alter atmospheric chemistry for centuries. Major volcanic eruptions released carbon trapped in ancient rocks for millions of years.

Archaeological samples from these periods carried embedded false signals. A wooden artifact buried during high carbon-14 periods would appear artificially young. Conversely, materials deposited during low production phases would seem older than their actual age. These systematic biases made reliable dating nearly impossible for crucial periods in human prehistory.

The implications for American archaeology were staggering. Most evidence for early human presence fell within periods of maximum atmospheric instability. The Clovis-first model relied heavily on radiocarbon dates from 13,000 years ago. This period coincided with major climate transitions and possible cosmic ray events. The dates supporting orthodox chronologies might be systematically incorrect.

Dr. Paula Reimer's team at Queen's University Belfast created the most comprehensive calibration curves available. Their IntCal database incorporated tree rings, coral growth bands, lake sediments, and ice cores from around the world. The data revealed carbon-14 dating to be far more complex and uncertain than most archaeologists acknowledged.

Reimer discovered that standard error calculations vastly understated actual uncertainty. Published dates typically showed margins of plus or minus 50 to 100, yet the real uncertainty could exceed 500 years. This difference transformed archaeological interpretation. Sites supposedly separated by centuries might actually be contemporary. Cultural sequences might be compressed or extended beyond recognition.

The atmospheric data also revealed regional variations in carbon-14 levels. Ocean currents, wind patterns, and local vegetation affected atmospheric chemistry. Samples from different geographic regions showed systematic age offsets even when collected simultaneously. Global calibration curves failed to account for these local effects.

Archaeological laboratories began encountering samples with internal contradictions. Wood from the same tree trunk produced different ages depending on which rings were tested. Bone collagen and bone carbonate from the same skeleton yielded dates separated by millennia. Charcoal fragments from the same fire pit were scattered across thousands of years when subjected to analysis.

These anomalies pointed to contamination, but not the kind typically assumed. Instead of modern carbon infiltrating ancient samples, the problem involved ancient carbon with altered isotopic signatures. Natural processes could reset radiocarbon clocks in unpredictable ways. Groundwater dissolved and redeposited organic carbon. Bacterial action

*Ancient American Civilizations*

could introduce carbon from different time periods. Chemical processes could fractionate isotopes, creating false age signals.

# Valsequillo: The 250,000-Year-Old Wood Fragments

Virginia Steen-McIntyre arrived at Valsequillo in 1966 as a young geologist eager to apply new dating methods to Mexican prehistory. The U.S. Geological Survey had assigned her to determine the age of volcanic deposits around this ancient lake bed—archaeological artifacts scattered throughout the sediment layers promised to anchor human occupation in precise geological time.

Steen-McIntyre collected volcanic ash samples from multiple stratigraphic layers. Her laboratory used potassium-argon dating to determine when the volcanic eruptions occurred. The method measured radioactive decay in volcanic minerals, providing absolute ages independent of carbon-14 problems. The results shocked everyone involved in the project.

The volcanic layers containing human artifacts are dated to 250,000 years ago. Stone tools lay embedded in ash deposits from the Middle Pleistocene. The geological evidence was unambiguous. Humans had occupied central Mexico during a period when orthodox archaeology placed them still confined to Africa.

Steen-McIntyre returned to collect additional samples. She used multiple dating techniques to confirm her results—fission track dating of volcanic glass produced similar ages. Uranium series analysis of associated minerals supported the potassium-argon findings. Independent laboratories verified her measurements. The geological evidence consistently pointed to the same impossible conclusion.

Project leaders asked Steen-McIntyre to recalculate her dates. Perhaps contamination had affected the samples. Maybe volcanic processes had reset the isotopic clocks. Could laboratory procedures have introduced systematic errors? Steen-McIntyre checked and rechecked her work. The dates remained unchanged.

Dr. Harold Malde, her supervisor at the U.S. Geological Survey, began facing pressure from archaeological colleagues. The Valsequillo dates threatened fundamental theories about human evolution and migration. If humans had reached the Americas 250,000 years ago, the entire model of human dispersal from Africa needed revision. The implications extended far beyond American prehistory.

Steen-McIntyre submitted her findings to major archaeological journals. Reviewers rejected the papers without considering the geological evidence. They cited the impossibility of the dates as grounds for rejection. No humans existed outside Africa 250,000 years ago. Therefore, the Valsequillo evidence must be wrong regardless of scientific rigor.

The U.S. Geological Survey removed Steen-McIntyre from the project. They assigned new geologists to redate the Valsequillo deposits. The replacement team used different sampling strategies and alternative interpretations of the stratigraphic sequence. Their published results showed more acceptable ages, placing human occupation well within conventional timelines.

Steen-McIntyre obtained her original samples from storage and submitted them to independent laboratories for additional testing. The results confirmed her earlier work. The volcanic ash containing human artifacts was indeed 250,000 years old. The stratigraphic evidence supported human presence during the Middle Pleistocene.

Professional consequences followed quickly. Conference organizers declined her speaking proposal. Grant applications faced rejection without scientific review. Academic positions became unavailable. Steen-McIntyre's career effectively ended because she reported accurate scientific measurements.

The Valsequillo artifacts themselves presented compelling evidence for human presence. Bifacially worked stone points showed deliberate knapping techniques. Scrapers bore use-wear patterns from hide processing. Choppers displayed percussion marks from systematic tool making. The technology resembled early human industries known from Africa and Europe.

Independent archaeologists examined the artifact collections. Dr. Juan Armenta Camacho documented over 2,000 tools from securely dated geological contexts. The assemblage included sophisticated blade technology and complex reduction strategies. These were not random rocks broken by natural processes. They showed clear evidence of human manufacture.

Geological analysis supported the archaeological evidence—the volcanic ash layers formed during specific eruptions documented in regional volcanic records. Paleomagnetic analysis confirmed the orientation of Earth's magnetic field during deposition. Pollen samples revealed vegetation patterns consistent with Middle Pleistocene climates. Every independent line of evidence supported the antiquity of human occupation.

The wood fragments provided the most controversial evidence. Charcoal pieces embedded in the same ash layers as stone tools underwent radiocarbon analysis. The organic material had apparently reached the limits of carbon-14 dating, showing ages that were beyond the method's range. This evidence suggested the wood was far older than 50,000 years.

Critics argued that old carbon from coal deposits or ancient groundwater had contaminated the samples. Steen-McIntyre's team tested for these possibilities. They analyzed the chemical composition of the charcoal and compared it to local coal sources. The samples showed no evidence of contamination. The wood appeared to be genuine organic material from trees growing 250,000 years ago.

Additional wood fragments underwent amino acid racemization testing. This method measured the breakdown of protein structures over time. The results corroborated the geological ages. Protein degradation levels matched what would be expected for organic material 250,000 years old. Multiple independent dating methods pointed to the same conclusion.

The Valsequillo controversy revealed how scientific institutions respond to paradigm-threatening discoveries. Rather than investigating anomalous evidence, they often suppress it. Researchers who report inconvenient findings face professional punishment. The scientific method becomes subordinated to protecting established theories.

Steen-McIntyre's work demonstrated the reliability of geological dating methods compared to radiocarbon techniques. Volcanic minerals preserved accurate age information across hundreds of thousands of years. Stratigraphic relationships provided relative chronologies immune to chemical contamination. Geological evidence offered more reliable timelines than organic materials subject to carbon-14 uncertainties.

# Laboratory Sample Rejection Policies

Dr. Thomas Stafford opened his radiocarbon laboratory in 1980 with plans to revolutionize archaeological dating. His facility in Boulder, Colorado, used accelerator mass spectrometry to measure carbon-14 in tiny samples. The technology promised to date artifacts previously too small or precious for conventional analysis. Stafford expected to expand the chronological framework of American prehistory.

His first controversial case arrived in 1983. Archaeologists from the University of Wisconsin submitted bone samples from the Schaefer site. They suspected the mammoth remains were associated with human activity. Initial estimates suggested the bones might date to 14,000 years ago, pushing back evidence for early Americans.

Stafford's analysis produced a shock. The collagen samples yielded ages of 12,300 years, well within the conventional timeframe. The bone mineral, however, dated to 1,350 years. The same skeletal element had produced two ages separated by 11,000 years. Something was fundamentally wrong with the assumptions underlying radiocarbon dating.

The problem stemmed from differential contamination. Groundwater had dissolved and redeposited carbon throughout the bone structure. Bacteria had introduced modern carbon into ancient matrices. Chemical processes had selectively altered different bone components. Standard pretreatment methods failed to remove these contaminants.

Word spread quickly through the archaeological community. If bones could produce multiple contradictory ages, how could researchers trust any radiocarbon date? Stafford began developing new purification techniques to isolate original organic carbon from contamination. His methods revealed systematic problems with thousands of previously published dates.

Stafford's laboratory started receiving unusual requests. Archaeologists submitted samples with specific instructions about desired age ranges. They wanted dates that fit their interpretations of site chronologies. Some researchers explicitly asked for ages within acceptable parameters for publication or grant applications.

The pressure intensified when Stafford began dating samples from controversial sites. Pre-Clovis materials from Pennsylvania, Texas, and South Carolina consistently produced ages older than 15,000 years. These results supported human presence in the Americas long before the Bering Land Bridge supposedly opened for migration.\

Archaeological institutions responded predictably. They questioned Stafford's methodology despite his rigorous purification procedures. They suggested contamination had affected his results, without evidence. They proposed alternative interpretations of the geological contexts from which the samples came. They did everything except acknowledge the possibility that early Americans existed.

Stafford discovered that many laboratories routinely rejected samples that produced unacceptable ages. The rejection criteria were not based on scientific quality but on archaeological expectations. Samples yielding pre-Clovis dates underwent additional scrutiny unavailable to conventional ages. The system biased results toward confirming established models.

Dr. R.E. Taylor's laboratory at the University of California, Riverside, implemented formal policies limiting analysis of controversial samples. They required extensive documentation of stratigraphic context before accepting materials from pre-Clovis sites—no similar requirements applied to samples supporting orthodox chronologies. The double standard effectively prevented systematic investigation of early human evidence.

Commercial laboratories developed informal blacklists of researchers associated with controversial theories. Scientists studying pre-Clovis sites found their samples rejected without explanation. Alternative dating requests faced indefinite delays. Laboratories claimed technical problems prevented analysis, but these problems never affected conventional archaeological samples.

The financial incentives were clear. Laboratories depended on repeat customers from established archaeological programs. Universities, museums, and government agencies provided steady revenue streams for routine dating services. Researchers challenging orthodox theories represented tiny fractions of laboratory business. Alienating mainstream customers to support controversial work made no economic sense.

Dr. Beta Analytic in Miami became notorious for sample screening policies. They required preliminary information about expected ages before accepting materials for analysis. Samples with ages outside acceptable ranges underwent additional pretreatment that often destroyed the organic material. Researchers learned to provide misleading context information to ensure their samples received analysis.

Some laboratories developed code systems to identify controversial samples. Materials from pre-Clovis sites received special handling designed to produce older ages that could be dismissed as contaminated. These samples underwent aggressive chemical treatments that preferentially removed young carbon, artificially aging the results. The systematic bias supported predetermined conclusions about human chronology.

Stafford began documenting these practices in professional publications. His papers revealed how sample selection and laboratory policies systematically excluded evidence for early Americans. The peer review process rejected these studies, claiming they were beyond the scope of archaeological journals. The evidence for institutional bias never reached the broader scientific community.

Independent researchers started submitting blind samples to multiple laboratories. They collected material from the same contexts and distributed portions to different facilities without revealing the source. The results showed dramatic variation between laboratories analyzing identical samples. Some facilities consistently produced older ages, while others yielded systematically younger results.

The variation correlated with laboratory attitudes toward controversial archaeology. Facilities associated with orthodox institutions have produced generations that support conventional models. Independent laboratories or those sympathetic to alternative theories yielded older dates. The same carbon-14 atoms produced different ages depending on laboratory bias.

Quality control studies revealed additional problems. Laboratories analyzing international standards achieved consistent results on known-age materials. These same facilities showed dramatic disagreement when analyzing archaeological samples from controversial contexts. The technical capability existed for accurate dating, but institutional pressures influenced how that capability was applied.

*Ancient American Civilizations*

# Geographic Location Misreporting for Testing

Dr. Jeffrey Goodman faced a dilemma in 1975. His excavations at Flagstaff, Arizona, had produced human artifacts in geological deposits more than 100,000 years old. No radiocarbon laboratory would accept samples identified as coming from this controversial site. Goodman decided to misrepresent his sample locations to ensure testing would occur.

He submitted bone and charcoal fragments to multiple laboratories, describing them as coming from conventional archaeological sites in the Southwest. The false documentation placed the samples in contexts that would produce acceptable ages around 10,000 to 15,000 years. Laboratories processed the materials without question.

The results arrived six weeks later. Every sample had yielded infinite radiocarbon ages beyond the method's dating range. The organic materials contained no detectable carbon-14, suggesting ages exceeding 50,000 years. These results supported Goodman's field observations about the extreme antiquity of human occupation.

Goodman revealed the true sample locations in his published report. He explained how geographic misreporting had been necessary to obtain radiocarbon analysis. The confession created controversy throughout the archaeological community. Colleagues accused him of scientific fraud. Professional organizations considered sanctions for deceptive practices.

The incident exposed widespread geographic misreporting in American archaeology. Researchers routinely provided false location information to ensure controversial samples received laboratory analysis. The practice had become standard procedure for anyone investigating pre-Clovis sites or other challenging evidence.

Dr. Richard MacNeish encountered similar problems during his research in Mexico and Peru. His teams discovered human remains and artifacts in contexts suggesting great antiquity. American laboratories refused to analyze samples identified as coming from these controversial sites. MacNeish established relationships with European facilities that were more willing to process problematic materials.

European laboratories showed greater scientific objectivity regarding American prehistory. They had no institutional investments in specific models of human migration. Their results consistently supported greater antiquity for New World human presence than American institutions acknowledged. The geographic bias in laboratory policies became unmistakable.

MacNeish began systematically misreporting sample locations to domestic laboratories. He submitted Peruvian materials as coming from conventional sites in the American Southwest. Mexican samples were identified as originating from accepted archaeological contexts in other regions. This deception allowed comparison of results between biased and unbiased analytical facilities.

The comparative study revealed systematic age compression by American laboratories. Samples analyzed domestically with false geographic attribution consistently yielded younger ages than the same materials processed by European facilities. The age differences often exceeded several thousand years. American laboratories were systematically rejecting or altering results that contradicted orthodox chronologies.

Dr. Virginia Steen-McIntyre adopted similar strategies during her geological investigations. Her volcanic ash samples from Valsequillo required independent confirmation, but American laboratories refused analysis once they learned the site location. Steen-McIntyre sent duplicate samples to facilities in Europe and Asia, identifying them as coming from acceptable geological contexts.

International laboratories consistently confirmed her original age determinations. Volcanic minerals from Valsequillo were indeed 250,000 years old. The stratigraphic relationships supported human presence during the Middle Pleistocene. American laboratories had rejected accurate scientific data because it contradicted archaeological expectations.

Commercial dating services developed sophisticated screening procedures to identify misreported samples. They cross-referenced client addresses with known controversial sites. Researchers affiliated with alternative theories faced additional scrutiny regardless of sample documentation. The system effectively prevented systematic investigation of challenging archaeological evidence.

Some facilities required sworn affidavits regarding sample collection contexts. Researchers had to legally certify the accuracy of their location reports before laboratories would begin analysis. These requirements applied only to materials that potentially contradict orthodox theories. Conventional archaeological samples never faced similar documentation demands.

Dr. Dennis Stanford's Solutrean research encountered systematic laboratory discrimination. His evidence for Ice Age European contact with North America required extensive radiocarbon dating to establish chronological relationships. American laboratories consistently rejected his samples or imposed conditions that made analysis impossible.

Stanford developed a network of international collaborators who submitted his samples under their own names. European researchers provided legitimate geographic contexts for materials originally collected in North America. The subterfuge allowed systematic investigation of trans-Atlantic contact evidence during the Late Pleistocene.

Results from European laboratories consistently supported Stanford's theories. Stone tools from American sites showed ages and manufacturing techniques consistent with Solutrean origins. Genetic evidence from ancient human remains revealed European ancestry markers. The scientific evidence was compelling, but American institutions refused to acknowledge it.

The geographic bias extended beyond radiocarbon dating to other analytical methods. DNA laboratories showed greater willingness to analyze samples from conventional archaeological contexts. Materials from controversial sites faced additional scrutiny and often produced inconclusive results. The pattern suggested systematic discrimination based on theoretical implications rather than scientific merit.

Professional conferences began addressing the misreporting issue. Sessions on research ethics condemned deceptive practices without acknowledging the institutional bias that made deception necessary. The archaeological establishment blamed individual researchers rather than examining systemic problems with laboratory access and sample processing.

Some researchers attempted to formalize alternative analytical networks. They established independent dating facilities specifically designed to process controversial samples without theoretical bias. These initiatives faced funding challenges and professional opposition from established institutions unwilling to acknowledge competing interpretations of American prehistory.

# Statistical Anomalies in Same-Site Dating

Dr. C. Vance Haynes arrived at the Murray Springs site in Arizona in 1966, expecting to find clear evidence supporting the Clovis-first model of American prehistory. The Pleistocene deposits contained mammoth bones associated with distinctive fluted spear points. Standard radiocarbon analysis should have produced consistent ages around 11,000 years, confirming the orthodox timeline.

Instead, Haynes encountered statistical chaos. Bone samples from the same mammoth skeleton showed ages from 8,000 to 15,000 years. Charcoal fragments from one fire pit varied across 3,000 years when tested. Stone tools found close together seemed to be from different eras based on the organic materials found nearby.

The variation exceeded all reasonable expectations for measurement error. Standard statistical analysis required ages from the same context to cluster within narrow ranges reflecting analytical uncertainty. The Murray Springs dates showed no clustering at all. They formed random distributions across thousands of years with no apparent pattern.

Haynes suspected contamination had affected the samples. Groundwater might have introduced carbon from different time periods. Bacterial action could have altered organic chemistry. Root penetration might have mixed materials from various stratigraphic levels. He designed new collection procedures to minimize these sources of error.

Careful resampling produced identical results. Bones from the same articulated skeleton continued yielding wildly different ages. Charcoal pieces collected from the center of intact fire pits showed no statistical relationship to each other. The problem was not contamination but something more fundamental about radiocarbon dating assumptions.

Similar anomalies appeared at other Clovis sites across North America. The Blackwater Draw locality in New Mexico produced dates ranging from 9,000 to 14,000 years from the same stratigraphic level. Lehner Ranch in Arizona showed comparable scatter with no apparent explanation. Every major Clovis site revealed internal chronological contradictions when subjected to intensive dating.

Dr. Dennis Stanford's investigations at the Selby site in Colorado uncovered even more dramatic anomalies. His excavations revealed a sealed archaeological layer containing Folsom projectile points, distinctive artifacts supposedly dating to 10,000 years ago—Radiocarbon analysis of associated materials produced ages between 8,000 and 24,000 years with no statistical clustering.

The scatter could not be explained by contamination or measurement error. All samples came from the same sealed context with no evidence of mixing. The laboratory procedures were standard and had produced consistent results on materials from other sites. Certain archaeological contexts produced systematically unreliable radiocarbon ages.

Stanford began investigating whether natural processes could reset radiocarbon clocks in predictable ways. Certain soil chemistry conditions might alter carbon isotope ratios. Specific bacterial communities could selectively consume older or younger carbon. Unusual groundwater patterns might introduce carbon with altered isotopic signatures.

His research revealed complex interactions between organic materials and depositional environments. Bone collagen degraded at different rates depending on soil pH and mineral content. Charcoal could absorb carbon from surrounding sediments through slow chemical processes. Plant materials incorporated atmospheric carbon from various time periods during growth.

These processes created internal contradictions within individual samples. A single piece of charcoal might contain carbon from the tree's original growth plus contamination from groundwater, soil organic matter, and atmospheric absorption over thousands of years. Radiocarbon dating measured the average age of all carbon present, producing meaningless results.

Dr. R. E. Taylor's laboratory at UC Riverside began developing statistical methods to identify contaminated samples. His team analyzed patterns of age variation within archaeological sites to distinguish reliable dates from problematic results. The work revealed that most archaeological contexts showed some degree of internal chronological contradiction.

Taylor discovered that sites with good organic preservation typically produced the most consistent radiocarbon ages. Dry caves, frozen deposits, and waterlogged environments protected organic materials from post-depositional alteration. Open-air sites in temperate climates consistently yielded scattered and unreliable dating results.

The implications were staggering for American archaeology. Most evidence for human chronology came from open-air sites subject to the chemical processes that produced unreliable dates. Clovis sites, Archaic period deposits, and early agricultural contexts all showed statistical anomalies that called their dating into question.

Independent analysis revealed that site chronologies often depended on subjective selection of "acceptable" dates from larger populations of measurements. Archaeologists typically discarded results that seemed too old or too young, keeping only ages that fit their interpretations of cultural sequences. This practice created artificial consistency in published chronologies.

Dr. Paula Reimer's calibration research confirmed these statistical problems. Her team analyzed radiocarbon dates from archaeological sites worldwide, looking for patterns of internal consistency. American sites showed significantly more age scatter than European or Asian localities. The difference suggested systematic problems with either sample preservation or analytical procedures in New World archaeology.

The statistical anomalies were not randomly distributed. Sites yielding evidence for early human presence consistently showed greater age scatter than conventional archaeological localities. Pre-Clovis deposits typically produced dates ranging across 10,000 years

# Chapter 3: Caral - The City That Rewrote Civilization's Timeline

## Ruth Shady's Discovery in Peru's Supe Valley

Ruth Shady Solís walked across the barren landscape of Peru's Supe Valley in 1994. The desert stretched endlessly under the blazing sun. Most archaeologists avoided this region. They preferred the dramatic Inca ruins of Machu Picchu or the mysterious Nazca Lines. The Supe Valley looked empty. Worthless. A place where only hardy farmers scratched out a living from stubborn soil.

Shady saw something different. The hills scattered across the valley floor possessed unusual symmetry. Their slopes formed geometric patterns too regular for nature. Their positioning followed deliberate alignments pointing toward astronomical events. Local residents called them cerros - natural hills. They had been farming around these mounds for generations without realizing what lay buried beneath their feet.

The Peruvian archaeologist had spent years studying ancient settlements along the Pacific coast. She understood how river systems shaped early human habitation patterns. The Supe River carried rich sediments from the Andes mountains to the ocean. This created fertile soil in an otherwise arid region. Ancient peoples would have recognized this advantage. They would have established permanent settlements here.

Shady's initial survey revealed pottery fragments and stone tools scattered across the valley floor. Carbon dating placed these artifacts at 3500 BCE. This dating surprised even Shady herself. Such early dates suggested major cultural developments in Peru occurred simultaneously with the first Egyptian dynasties. Professional colleagues dismissed these findings. They argued the samples must be contaminated or the dating methods flawed.

The young researcher refused to abandon her investigation. She assembled a small team of archaeology students from the Universidad Nacional Mayor de San Marcos in Lima. Government funding remained scarce. International archaeological organizations showed no interest. Shady used her personal savings to purchase basic excavation equipment.

Her team worked without pay, motivated by scientific curiosity and Shady's infectious determination.

The first trenches revealed worked stone foundations beneath several mounds. The construction quality astounded the excavation team. Ancient builders had quarried massive granite blocks from distant mountains. They transported these stones across difficult terrain without wheeled vehicles or draft animals. The blocks fitted together with remarkable precision, creating walls that had endured nearly five millennia without mortar or metal fasteners.

As excavations expanded, the true scope of the site became clear. This was not a simple village or ceremonial center. Caral was an urban complex covering over 150 acres. Six large pyramid platforms dominated the city center. Smaller residential structures surrounded the ceremonial core. Sophisticated irrigation channels directed river water to agricultural terraces that still functioned after thousands of years.

The discovery attracted international attention by 1997. Carbon dating of organic materials from multiple locations consistently returned dates between 2600 and 2000 BCE. These results placed Caral among the world's oldest urban centers, contemporary with Egypt's Old Kingdom pyramids and Mesopotamia's earliest cities. The implications revolutionized the understanding of New World civilizations.

Shady's persistence had uncovered what would become known as the oldest city in the Americas. Her willingness to challenge established assumptions opened an entirely new chapter in human history. The barren hills of the Supe Valley held secrets that forced scholars to reconsider fundamental questions about the origins of civilization.

# 2600 BCE: Contemporary with Egyptian Pyramids

The morning sun crested the Andes mountains and struck Caral's Great Pyramid just as it had 4,600 years ago. This massive structure stood 60 feet high and covered nearly 5 acres at its base. Ancient architects had designed the monument to capture the first light of dawn on significant astronomical dates. The pyramid's stepped terraces created dramatic shadows that marked seasonal transitions with mathematical precision.

Egyptian pharaohs were building their eternal monuments at Giza during this same period. Djoser's Step Pyramid at Saqqara had recently risen from the desert sands. Imhotep's revolutionary architecture was transforming how humans conceived monumental construction. Half a world away, unknown architects in Peru were solving identical problems with equally sophisticated solutions.

The comparison between Caral and early Egyptian civilization reveals striking parallels. Both cultures developed complex social hierarchies centered on religious authority. Both invested enormous resources in monumental architecture designed to demonstrate cosmic connections. Both established trade networks that transported exotic materials across vast distances. Both developed mathematical and astronomical knowledge far beyond basic survival needs.

Egyptian pyramids served as tombs for divine pharaohs. The structures contained elaborate burial chambers, precious artifacts, and mystical texts guiding souls through the afterlife. Caral's pyramids served different purposes. No burials have been found within the structures. Instead, they functioned as platforms for public ceremonies and astronomical observations. The buildings celebrated life rather than death.

This fundamental difference reveals distinct approaches to spiritual understanding. Egyptian religion focused on individual immortality and divine kingship. Caral's culture emphasized community participation and cosmic harmony. Egyptian monuments proclaimed the power of individual rulers. Caral's architecture invited collective participation in seasonal rituals and agricultural ceremonies.

The construction techniques also differed significantly. Egyptian builders used massive limestone blocks quarried from nearby cliffs. They employed sophisticated ramps, levers, and pulleys to position stones weighing several tons each. The Great Pyramid contains over 2 million stone blocks fitted with incredible precision. Modern engineers still debate exactly how such accuracy was achieved.

Caral's builders chose a different approach. They constructed their pyramids using the shicra method - cotton or reed bags filled with stone rubble. These bags were stacked in interlocking patterns that created incredibly stable foundations. The technique provided natural earthquake resistance in Peru's seismically active region. Modern testing has confirmed that shicra construction can withstand ground acceleration exceeding most contemporary building codes.

The choice of materials reflected each civilization's environment and values. Egypt's endless limestone quarries made stone construction logical and economical. Peru's frequent earthquakes demanded flexible building methods that could absorb seismic energy without catastrophic collapse. Both cultures developed optimal solutions for their specific geographical challenges.

Agricultural systems also reveal sophisticated planning. Egyptian civilization depended entirely on Nile River floods that deposited fertile silt across the river valley. Farmers developed elaborate irrigation systems to distribute flood waters during the annual inundation. Crop cycles followed the river's natural rhythm with religious ceremonies marking each phase of agricultural development.

Caral's farmers faced different challenges. The Supe Valley received minimal rainfall. River flow varied dramatically between wet and dry seasons. Ancient engineers created sophisticated water management systems that captured and stored precious moisture. They built reservoirs, canals, and underground aqueducts that maintained agricultural productivity throughout the year.

Both civilizations invested in long-distance trade to acquire materials unavailable locally. Egyptian merchants traveled up the Nile River to obtain gold, ivory, and exotic woods from Nubia. They crossed the Red Sea to trade with communities in the Arabian and Indian Oceans. These commercial relationships brought wealth and foreign influences that enriched Egyptian culture.

Caral's trade networks reached from the Pacific Ocean to the high Andes mountains. Coastal communities provided marine resources, including fish, seaweed, and salt. Highland settlements contributed potatoes, quinoa, and precious stones. Amazon basin contacts supplied tropical products like coca leaves and colorful feathers. This extensive commerce created prosperity that supported monumental construction and artistic achievement.

The contemporary development of these distant civilizations suggests fundamental principles about human social evolution. Urban centers arise when agricultural surplus allows population concentration. Monumental architecture develops when societies can organize large-scale labor projects. Long-distance trade emerges when communities recognize mutual benefits from resource exchange. These patterns occurred independently across the world during the third millennium BCE.

*Ancient American Civilizations*

# Earthquake-Resistant Mesh Construction Techniques

The ground began to shake violently one afternoon in 2600 BCE. Caral's massive pyramids swayed like ships in a storm. Stone blocks weighing several tons shifted and ground against each other. Lesser buildings throughout the ancient city collapsed into rubble. When the earthquake ended, Caral's great monuments still stood. Their innovative construction methods had saved them from destruction.

Modern engineering analysis reveals why Caral's architecture survived Peru's devastating seismic activity. The ancient builders developed the shicra technique - a construction method using textile bags filled with stone rubble. These bags functioned like massive shock absorbers that distributed earthquake forces throughout the structure. The flexible connections between bag units prevented catastrophic failure during ground movement.

Archaeological investigation shows how this technique was implemented. Workers wove bags from cotton fibers or twisted reeds grown in the Supe Valley. Each bag measured approximately three feet in length and two feet in width. The bags were filled with carefully selected stone fragments, creating uniform building units weighing roughly 50 pounds each. This weight allowed individual workers to handle the components without mechanical assistance.

The bag construction process required sophisticated organization. Teams of workers prepared thousands of textile containers before major building projects began. Other teams quarried stone from nearby hills and broke the rock into appropriately sized fragments. The stone selection process was critical - pieces needed to be small enough to fit within the bags but large enough to create stable fill material.

Caral's architects arranged the filled bags in interlocking patterns that created incredibly strong foundations. Bottom layers used larger bags filled with heavier stone fragments. Upper layers employed smaller bags with lighter materials. This graduated approach distributed structural loads evenly throughout the pyramid base. The technique created monuments that were both massive and flexible.

The textile bag method provided multiple engineering advantages beyond earthquake resistance. The construction required no mortar or cement to bond individual components. Workers could disassemble and rebuild sections as needed during construction. Mistakes could be corrected without demolishing entire walls. The technique allowed rapid construction using readily available materials and simple hand tools.

Modern seismic testing has validated the ancient engineering principles. Engineers at Peru's Pontifical Catholic University constructed scale models of shicra walls and subjected them to simulated earthquake conditions. The test structures withstood ground acceleration levels that would destroy conventional stone masonry. The textile bag method outperformed many contemporary building techniques in seismic resistance.

The innovation required a deep understanding of local geological conditions. Caral lies near the intersection of two major tectonic plates. The Nazca Plate slides beneath the South American Plate, creating intense seismic activity along Peru's Pacific coast. Historical records document devastating earthquakes that have repeatedly destroyed Lima and other coastal cities. Ancient builders needed construction methods that could survive this hostile environment.

Evidence suggests Caral's architects learned from experience with earthquake damage. Early structures show experimental approaches to seismic resistance. Later buildings demonstrate refined techniques that incorporated lessons from structural failures. The learning process continued over several centuries as builders perfected their methods through trial and error.

The shicra technique influenced construction methods throughout ancient Peru. Archaeological sites from the same period show similar textile bag construction in other coastal valleys. The innovation spread inland to highland communities that adapted the technique for local materials and conditions. This widespread adoption demonstrates the method's practical effectiveness and cultural importance.

Chinese architects developed comparable earthquake-resistant techniques during the same historical period. Traditional Chinese buildings used flexible wooden joints that allowed structures to sway without collapsing during seismic events. The pagoda design incorporated multiple levels that could move independently. These solutions reflected similar engineering principles adapted to different materials and architectural traditions.

Japanese builders also evolved sophisticated earthquake-resistant methods. Traditional wooden temples used complex joint systems that absorbed seismic energy through controlled movement. The five-story pagoda at Horyuji Temple has survived over 1,300 years of earthquakes using these techniques. Modern Japanese architecture incorporates similar flexibility principles in contemporary skyscrapers.

The convergent development of earthquake-resistant construction across various cultures illustrates universal human responses to seismic hazards. Ancient builders worldwide understood that rigid structures failed during earthquakes. They independently devised flexible building techniques that could absorb and dissipate seismic energy. These innovations predates modern seismology by thousands of years.

Caral's shicra construction also delivered excellent thermal performance. The textile bags provided natural insulation that regulated temperature extremes. Interior spaces stayed cool during scorching desert days and retained warmth during cold nights. This climate control enhanced living conditions and decreased the need for fuel-consuming heating and cooling systems.

The technique required minimal environmental impact during construction. Workers used locally grown cotton and reeds rather than importing materials from distant regions. Stone quarrying took place near construction sites, reducing transportation needs. The construction process produced little waste since bags could be reused if buildings needed modification or expansion.

# Musical Instruments and Peaceful Society Evidence

The excavation team carefully brushed sand away from a small clay object buried beneath Caral's main pyramid. The artifact appeared to be a simple whistle, no larger than a child's fist. When team member Daniel Chu raised the ancient instrument to his lips and gently blew, a pure musical note echoed across the excavation site. After 4,600 years of silence, Caral was singing again.

This discovery marked the beginning of a remarkable revelation about ancient Peruvian society. Further excavations revealed dozens of musical instruments throughout the city. Bone flutes crafted from bird wings produced haunting melodies. Ceramic whistles shaped like animals created sounds that mimicked their natural calls. Large conch shells served as trumpets that could be heard for miles across the desert valley.

The instruments demonstrated a sophisticated understanding of acoustic principles. Flute makers had carefully calculated hole placement to produce specific musical scales. The spacing between finger holes followed mathematical relationships that created harmonious intervals. Different-sized flutes produced complementary tones that could be combined in ensemble performances.

Conch shell trumpets required advanced preparation techniques. Craftsmen removed the shell's pointed tip and created a precise mouthpiece opening. The internal chambers were modified to enhance resonance and volume. Some shells show evidence of repair work, suggesting these instruments were valued possessions maintained over long periods.

Archaeological context reveals how these instruments functioned in Caral society. Musical artifacts concentrate around ceremonial platforms and public gathering spaces. They appear with other ritual objects including decorated textiles, carved stone vessels, and exotic trade goods. The distribution pattern suggests music played essential roles in community ceremonies and religious observances.

The discovery process itself proved challenging. Many instruments were found in fragments scattered across different excavation levels. Patient conservation work was required to reconstruct complete objects from ceramic sherds and bone fragments. Each successful reconstruction added new understanding about Caral's musical traditions and technological capabilities.

Carbon dating placed the instruments between 2600 and 2000 BCE, making them among the world's oldest preserved musical artifacts. This timeline demonstrates that complex musical traditions developed alongside monumental architecture and urban planning. Caral's residents invested time and skill in creating beautiful sounds as well as impressive buildings.

The musical evidence gains significance when compared with other archaeological findings from Caral. Extensive excavations have revealed no weapons of any kind. No spear points, clubs, or defensive fortifications have been found anywhere in the city. This absence is

*Ancient American Civilizations*

remarkable considering the site's size and the wealth of artifacts recovered from other activity areas.

The lack of warfare evidence extends beyond individual weapons. Caral shows no signs of violent destruction. Buildings were abandoned rather than burned or demolished by enemies. Skeletal remains show no trauma from violent conflicts. The population appears to have departed peacefully when the city was eventually abandoned around 2000 BCE.

This peaceful character distinguishes Caral from many other early urban centers. Mesopotamian cities like Ur and Babylon surrounded themselves with massive defensive walls. Egyptian settlements relied on military protection from pharaonic armies. Early Chinese cities fortified themselves against constant warfare between competing kingdoms. Caral developed differently.

The absence of military infrastructure suggests alternative approaches to conflict resolution. Caral's leaders may have relied on diplomacy, trade relationships, and religious authority rather than military force. The extensive trade networks connecting the city to distant regions would have created mutual dependencies that discouraged violent confrontation.

Musical instruments may have played important roles in maintaining peace. Ceremonial performances could have reinforced social bonds and collective identity. Shared musical traditions would have created cultural unity that transcended individual differences. Religious ceremonies involving music may have provided mechanisms for resolving disputes without violence.

The acoustic properties of Caral's architecture support this interpretation. The pyramids and plazas were designed to amplify sound during public gatherings. Careful measurements show that speakers positioned on ceremonial platforms could be heard clearly throughout the surrounding residential areas. This acoustic design facilitated mass communication and community participation.

Evidence of musical education appears in the archaeological record. Small practice flutes show wear patterns suggesting extensive use by beginning musicians. Broken instruments were carefully repaired rather than discarded, indicating their value for learning and skill development. The community invested in passing musical knowledge to future generations.

The instruments themselves demonstrate remarkable artistic achievement. Ceramic whistles feature intricate sculptural details depicting birds, animals, and human figures. The craftwork combines functional acoustic design with beautiful visual aesthetics. These objects were clearly valued as artistic creations as well as musical tools.

Comparative studies reveal similar patterns in other peaceful ancient societies. The Indus Valley civilization showed minimal evidence of warfare despite controlling vast territories and resources. Their cities lacked defensive walls and military installations. Archaeological findings emphasize trade, craft production, and urban planning rather than military technology.

Modern ethnographic studies of indigenous Amazonian cultures provide additional context for understanding Caral's peaceful character. Many traditional societies in the region resolve conflicts through elaborate ceremonies involving music, dancing, and community dialogue. These cultural practices maintain social harmony without resorting to violence.

The musical instruments from Caral represent more than entertainment or artistic expression. They document a civilization that chose cooperation over conflict, harmony over warfare, and cultural development over military expansion. This alternative model of human social organization offers valuable insights for understanding the full spectrum of possibilities in early urban development.

# Pacific Coast to Andes Trade Networks

Manuel Vega held the small shell in his weathered palm and smiled. The excavation team had just uncovered this Spondylus shell from a ceremonial platform at Caral's center. The nearest source for this particular mollusk was the warm coastal waters of Ecuador, over 1,000 miles north of the Supe Valley. Someone had carried this precious object across mountains, deserts, and rivers to reach ancient Caral.

The discovery opened investigations into one of the ancient world's most extensive trade networks. Caral sat strategically positioned between Peru's Pacific coast and the high Andes mountains. The city controlled access to the Supe River valley, one of the few reliable water sources in this arid region. Ancient traders following this natural corridor had to pass through Caral's territory.

Archaeological evidence reveals the full scope of these commercial relationships. Exotic materials from distant regions appear throughout Caral's excavated areas. Obsidian from highland volcanic sources was crafted into sharp cutting tools. Colorful feathers from tropical birds adorned ceremonial costumes. Precious metals from mountain mines were worked into decorative objects. Each import represents successful long-distance expeditions across challenging terrain.

The trade system operated on principles of reciprocal exchange rather than monetary transactions. Coastal communities provided marine resources, including fish, salt, seaweed, and shells. Highland settlements contributed potatoes, quinoa, wool, and stone materials. Amazon basin groups supplied tropical products like coca leaves, medicinal plants, and exotic woods. Each region offered products unavailable elsewhere.

Cotton played a central role in Caral's commercial network. The Supe Valley's climate proved ideal for growing high-quality cotton fiber. Caral's residents developed advanced textile production techniques that created valuable trade goods. Archaeological excavations have recovered sophisticated looms, spinning tools, and textile fragments showing complex weaving patterns.

The cotton textiles served multiple functions beyond personal clothing. Large ceremonial textiles displayed intricate designs that may have recorded historical events or religious concepts. Smaller pieces functioned as containers, bags, and wrapping materials for other trade goods. The most elaborate textiles probably served as status symbols for wealthy traders and religious leaders.

Evidence suggests Caral's merchants traveled regularly to distant trading centers. Standardized weights and measures appear across multiple archaeological sites, indicating common commercial practices over vast territories. Similar ceramic styles and architectural features spread along trade routes, showing cultural exchange accompanying economic transactions.

The logistics of ancient trade required sophisticated organization. Expeditions needed to coordinate supplies, transportation, and security across journeys lasting weeks or months. Traders required detailed knowledge of routes, seasonal conditions, and local customs. The successful completion of these journeys demonstrates remarkable planning capabilities.

*Ancient American Civilizations*

Archaeological investigations at sites along trade routes reveal the infrastructure supporting this commerce. Way stations provided shelter, food, and security for traveling merchants. Specialized storage facilities preserved goods during transport across different climate zones. Road maintenance systems kept mountain passes and river crossings operational throughout the year.

The trade networks connected Caral to technological innovations developed in distant regions. Metallurgy techniques from highland areas reached coastal communities through commercial exchange. Agricultural crops spread to new environments along trade corridors. Construction methods and artistic styles diffused across vast territories through merchant contacts.

Religious and cultural exchange accompanied commercial transactions. Shared symbols appear in art and architecture across the trade network— similar ceremonial practices developed at distant sites connected by commerce. Marriage alliances between trading communities created lasting bonds that transcended simple economic relationships.

The scale of trade operations suggests dedicated merchant classes within Caral society. Specialized knowledge and capital investment were required to organize successful long-distance expeditions. Archaeological evidence shows differential access to imported goods, indicating social stratification based partly on commercial success.

Climate data reveals how environmental changes affected trade patterns. During favorable periods, routes remained open and commerce flourished. Drought conditions or severe weather could disrupt transportation and reduce trade volumes. Caral's ultimate abandonment around 2000 BCE may be linked to climate changes that disrupted the commercial networks supporting the city.

The archaeological record documents specific trade goods and their sources. Lapis lazuli from Chilean mines appears in jewelry and decorative objects. Tropical hardwoods from eastern forests were carved into ceremonial artifacts. Marine shells from both Pacific and Atlantic coasts show connections to communities across the entire South American continent.

Modern studies of indigenous Amazonian trade provide insights into how ancient networks may have operated. Contemporary groups maintain commercial relationships spanning hundreds of miles using traditional

*Ancient American Civilizations*

transportation methods. Seasonal trading expeditions still follow routes established by their ancestors. These patterns may preserve ancient practices dating back thousands of years.

The evidence from the Caral revolutionizes understanding of early South American civilization. Rather than isolated communities struggling for survival, the archaeological record reveals sophisticated societies connected by extensive trade networks. These commercial relationships supported urban development, technological innovation, and cultural exchange on a continental scale.

The success of Caral's trade networks depended on peaceful relationships between diverse communities. Military conflicts would have disrupted commerce and damaged the mutual trust required for long-distance trade. The city's peaceful character may have been essential for maintaining the commercial relationships that supported its prosperity.

The ultimate lesson from Caral's trade networks concerns human cooperation and ingenuity. Four and a half millennia ago, people overcame geographic barriers, cultural differences, and technological limitations to create commercial relationships spanning thousands of miles. Their achievement demonstrates the fundamental human drive to connect, exchange, and build together across any obstacle.

*Ancient American Civilizations*

# Chapter 4: El Mirador - The Maya Empire Time Forgot

## Guatemala's Hidden Jungle Metropolis

Dr. Richard Hansen pushed through tangled vines and thorny undergrowth in Guatemala's Petén jungle. The year was 1978. Local guides had brought him to what looked like natural hills covered in dense forest. Hansen carried surveying equipment and a deep suspicion. The hills seemed too regular, too symmetrical for nature's random hand.

Hansen climbed the largest mound. At the summit, he scraped away centuries of accumulated soil and leaf litter. His trowel struck limestone blocks. The guides had led him to buried pyramids.

Excavation began slowly. Hansen worked with a small team and limited funding. Each season brought new revelations. The mounds contained elaborate stone architecture. Carved facades showed intricate Maya artwork. Hieroglyphic inscriptions dated to centuries before famous Maya sites achieved prominence.

The jungle had swallowed an entire civilization. Local Maya communities possessed no oral traditions about the ruins. Modern archaeological surveys had missed the site completely. El Mirador had vanished so thoroughly from human memory that even its original name disappeared forever.

Hansen faced the same institutional skepticism as other researchers working on anomalous sites. Colleagues questioned his dates. Peer reviewers demanded additional evidence. Grant applications faced rejection. The Maya were supposed to be latecomers to urban civilization. Pre-Classic period settlements should be simple villages, not massive cities.

The evidence painted a different picture. El Mirador began its rise around 600 BCE. The city reached its zenith between 300 BCE and 100 CE. Construction continued for nearly seven centuries before the site's mysterious abandonment around 150 CE.

*Ancient American Civilizations*

This timeline places El Mirador's peak a whole millennium before Tikal, Palenque, and other celebrated Maya centres. The supposedly primitive Pre-Classic Maya had built urban complexes rivaling anything from later periods. They had achieved architectural sophistication that influenced Maya civilization for centuries to come.

Hansen's team mapped the site's true extent. El Mirador covered over 650 square kilometers. The urban core alone stretched across 38 square kilometers. Residential complexes, ceremonial plazas, and administrative buildings spread throughout the jungle. This was not a ceremonial center visited occasionally by scattered populations. El Mirador had been a genuine metropolis.

Population estimates reached between 100,000 and 200,000 inhabitants at the city's peak. Supporting such numbers required sophisticated agricultural systems, complex social organization, and extensive trade networks. The jungle city had functioned as the administrative heart of a far-flung empire.

Archaeological evidence revealed the scope of this ancient state. El Mirador controlled dozens of subsidiary settlements connected by elevated stone roadways. The empire stretched across modern-day Guatemala, Belize, and parts of Mexico. This political network predated any known Maya state formation by centuries.

Hansen's discoveries revolutionized the understanding of Maya origins. The civilization did not develop gradually from simple farming villages. El Mirador proved Maya urban culture had ancient roots stretching back over two millennia. The "collapse" of Classic Maya civilization looked less like societal failure and more like cyclical transformation.

The city's location deep in an impenetrable jungle explained its disappearance from historical consciousness. Spanish conquistadors never found El Mirador. Colonial chroniclers never recorded its existence. Even modern aircraft could not detect the ruins beneath the forest canopy. Only satellite imagery and LIDAR scanning finally revealed the site's full magnitude.

Hansen spent decades fighting for recognition and funding. Government bureaucrats showed little interest in ruins that tourists could not easily visit. International archaeological institutions preferred more accessible sites. El Mirador remained an academic orphan, studied by dedicated researchers working on shoestring budgets.

The jungle began reclaiming excavated areas faster than Hansen's small team could clear them. Roots penetrated the stone joints. Vines pulled apart carefully reconstructed walls. Each rainy season undid months of archaeological progress. El Mirador was disappearing again, returning to the green anonymity that had hidden it for over a thousand years.

Modern threats multiplied the challenges. Illegal logging operations pushed deeper into the Petén forests. Drug traffickers established clandestine airstrips near archaeological sites. Looters ransacked tombs and sculpture caches, selling artifacts to private collectors. El Mirador faced destruction from human greed after surviving natural forces for millennia.

Hansen became the site's passionate advocate. He lobbied government officials, courted international donors, and educated local communities about their archaeological heritage. His efforts bore fruit slowly. El Mirador gained protected status as part of Guatemala's Maya Biosphere Reserve. Tourism infrastructure began to develop to make the ruins more accessible.

The city began to reveal its secrets through meticulous excavation. Hansen's team uncovered massive temple complexes, elaborate royal tombs, and extensive urban districts. They found evidence of sophisticated water management systems, astronomical observation platforms, and craft production areas. El Mirador had been a fully functioning ancient metropolis.

# La Danta: Largest Pyramid in the Ancient Americas

The La Danta complex rises from El Mirador's heart like a mountain built by human hands. This massive construction dwarfs every other pyramid in the ancient Americas. Its builders moved over 2.8 million cubic meters of stone and fill to create a structure visible from space.

La Danta's true scale becomes apparent only through careful measurement. The pyramid reaches 72 meters above the surrounding plaza level. Its base covers 18 hectares. Total volume exceeds even Egypt's Great Pyramid of Khufu. The builders of El Mirador had achieved monumental architecture on a scale not matched elsewhere in the New World.

Construction required extraordinary organizational capabilities. Workers quarried limestone blocks from distant sources. Teams hauled massive stones through jungle terrain without wheeled transport or draft animals. Engineers planned the complex geometry needed to create stable slopes rising to such heights.

The pyramid did not grow through random addition over time. La Danta shows evidence of unified architectural planning. Its builders conceived the entire complex as an integrated whole. They calculated angles, measured distances, and coordinated construction phases across multiple generations of builders.

Three distinct pyramids combine to form La Danta's unified structure. The central pyramid rises highest, flanked by two smaller but still massive buildings. Enormous platforms connect all three structures into a single architectural statement. The effect creates an artificial mountain range dominating the jungle landscape.

Stone staircases climb La Danta's steep faces. These monumental steps allowed priests and rulers to ascend toward the sky in elaborate ceremonies. Each rise brought the climber closer to the realm of gods and ancestors. The physical act of ascending became spiritual transformation.

The pyramid's summit once supported elaborate temples and palaces. These wooden and stone structures provided venues for the most sacred rituals. Kings consulted with deities in chambers hundreds of feet above their subjects. The height separated rulers from common people both physically and symbolically.

Astronomical alignments governed La Danta's orientation. The structure's corners mark significant points in the solar calendar. Stairways frame sunrise and sunset positions during solstices and equinoxes. The pyramid functioned as a massive celestial calculator built from limestone blocks.

Hidden chambers riddle La Danta's interior. Archaeologists have discovered burial tombs, ritual caches, and structural voids within the pyramid. These spaces held sacred objects, royal remains, and ceremonial deposits placed during construction. The pyramid was not solid stone but a complex honeycomb of chambers and passages.

Construction techniques show remarkable engineering sophistication. Workers placed millions of tons of material without modern machinery.

They created stable slopes that have endured for over two millennia. The pyramid stands as testimony to ancient engineering capabilities that modern builders struggle to match.

Labor requirements for La Danta challenge assumptions about Pre-Classic Maya society. Moving 2.8 million cubic meters of material required thousands of workers laboring for decades. Feeding, housing, and organizing such massive workforces demanded complex administrative systems. El Mirador's rulers commanded resources rivaling any ancient civilization.

The pyramid's builders left no written records explaining their motivations. No surviving inscriptions describe the construction process. La Danta's purpose must be inferred from its form, alignment, and archaeological context. The monument speaks through stone rather than words.

Evidence suggests La Danta served multiple functions simultaneously. Religious ceremonies took place on its summit. Astronomical observations guided agricultural and ritual calendars. The structure's imposing presence demonstrated royal power to subjects and enemies alike. La Danta was temple, observatory, and symbol of political authority combined.

The pyramid's construction required sophisticated mathematical knowledge. Builders calculated precise angles to prevent collapse. They engineered drainage systems to channel rainwater safely. They understood principles of load distribution that prevented settling and structural failure. This technical expertise contradicts assumptions about "primitive" Pre-Classic Maya capabilities.

Stone for La Danta came from quarries many kilometers distant. Workers shaped blocks to precise specifications before transport. The logistics of moving such quantities of material through dense jungle terrain required careful planning and coordination. Supply chains extended across the entire El Mirador region.

Modern visitors ascending La Danta experience something approaching the original builders' intentions. The climb demands physical effort and stamina. Each level reached provides expanded views of the surrounding jungle. The summit offers perspectives impossible from ground level. The pyramid transforms the human relationship with landscape and sky.

# Sakbeob: Massive Stone Causeway Systems

White roads cut straight lines through the jungle darkness. Maya engineers built these elevated stone highways to connect El Mirador with distant settlements across their empire. The sakbeob stretched for dozens of kilometers in perfectly straight alignments, ignoring natural obstacles and terrain difficulties.

Construction began with precise surveying. Maya astronomers and engineers used celestial observations to establish true cardinal directions. They marked routes with wooden stakes and rope lines. The finished roads deviated less than one degree from their intended bearings across distances exceeding 30 kilometers.

Each sakbe rose above the surrounding swampy terrain on carefully constructed foundations. Workers hauled thousands of tons of limestone rubble to build elevated causeways that remained passable during rainy season flooding. The roads towered up to eight meters above ground level in low-lying areas.

Stone paving covered the roadway surfaces. Flat limestone slabs created smooth passages suitable for foot traffic and ceremonial processions. The roads measured between 10 and 30 meters in width, broad enough for large groups to travel together. Side walls contained the paved surfaces and prevented erosion during tropical downpours.

The Mirador-Calakmul sacbe represents the most ambitious road construction project in Pre-Classic Maya civilization. This massive highway connected El Mirador with its northern rival across 40 kilometers of difficult jungle terrain. The road required engineering solutions for crossing seasonal swamps, steep ridges, and dense forest.

Builders constructed this monumental highway without metal tools or wheeled transport. Workers shaped limestone blocks using stone hammers and wooden levers. They moved heavy materials through human labor alone. The roads stand as monuments to organized effort and technical ingenuity.

The sakbeob served multiple functions beyond simple transportation. Religious processions moved along the elevated highways during major festivals. Merchants carried trade goods between allied settlements.

Military forces used the roads for rapid deployment across the empire. Information traveled swiftly along these communication arteries.

Astronomical alignments governed sakbe orientations. Many roads point toward significant celestial events, such as solstice sunrises or Venus rising points. The highways doubled as massive astronomical instruments laid across the landscape. Maya priest-astronomers incorporated cosmic observations into road design.

Construction required massive labor investments. Building 40 kilometers of elevated highway needed thousands of workers laboring for decades. The roads consumed stone volumes approaching those used in pyramid construction. El Mirador's rulers commanded the resources and organization necessary for such ambitious projects.

The road system reveals El Mirador's political dominance over surrounding regions—secondary settlements connected to the capital through tributary causeways. The highway network imposed El Mirador's authority across the landscape. Roads became tools of imperial control as much as transportation infrastructure.

Modern archaeological surveys have traced sakbeob connections across hundreds of square kilometers. The network extended El Mirador's influence deep into modern Mexico, Belize, and Guatemala. This ancient highway system linked dozens of settlements into a unified political and economic entity.

Maintenance requirements for the Sakbeob demonstrate sustained administrative capabilities. Tropical rains eroded stone surfaces. Vegetation encroached on cleared rights-of-way. Keeping the roads functional required continuous labor and materials. The highway system could only survive with a strong central authority.

The roads fell into disrepair following El Mirador's abandonment around 150 CE. Jungle growth split stone paving. Fallen trees blocked passages. Seasonal flooding undermined foundations. Within centuries, the once-mighty highway system had vanished beneath secondary forest growth.

LIDAR surveys have recently revealed the full extent of El Mirador's road network. Laser scanning penetrates forest canopy to map stone causeways invisible to traditional aerial photography. These technological advances demonstrate Maya engineering achievements on scales previously unimaginable.

The sakbeob connected more than settlements. They linked astronomical observatories, ceremonial centers, and sacred landscape features into integrated networks. The roads created a unified cosmic geography spanning the Maya world. Travel along these highways carried spiritual as well as practical significance.

# 6th Century BCE to 1st Century CE Timeline

Construction at El Mirador began modestly around 600 BCE with small ceremonial platforms and residential areas. Early builders cleared forest patches for agriculture and settlement. They dug wells and constructed simple stone buildings. These pioneers established the foundation for future urban growth.

The initial phase lasted roughly two centuries. Population grew steadily as successful agriculture supported larger communities—trade connections developed with neighboring settlements. Local leaders accumulated wealth and authority. Social complexity increased as the community evolved from village to town.

Urban expansion accelerated dramatically around 400 BCE. Major construction projects began transforming El Mirador into a true city. Workers started building the massive platform that would support La Danta pyramid. Stone causeways connected the urban core with outlying residential areas. The settlement reached genuine urban scale and complexity.

The Middle Pre-Classic period (400-150 BCE) witnessed El Mirador's rise to regional dominance. The city established political control over surrounding settlements. Long-distance trade networks brought exotic goods from across Mesoamerica. Architectural projects reached unprecedented scales requiring massive labor investments.

The La Danta pyramid achieved its final form during this crucial period. Builders added successive layers to the massive structure over multiple generations. Each construction phase increased the monument's height and volume. The pyramid became a visible symbol of El Mirador's power and sophistication.

Religious architecture flourished alongside secular construction. Workers built elaborate temple complexes throughout the urban center. These sacred buildings housed ceremonies honoring Maya deities and ancestors. Religious festivals drew pilgrims from across the expanding Maya world.

The Late Pre-Classic period (150 BCE - 150 CE) marked El Mirador's golden age. The city reached maximum population and territorial extent. Architectural achievements peaked with the completion of major pyramid complexes. Artistic production achieved levels of sophistication matched by few ancient civilizations.

Writing systems developed during this period, though examples remain limited. Maya scribes carved hieroglyphic inscriptions on stone monuments and wooden lintels. These early texts recorded royal genealogies, astronomical calculations, and religious information. Literacy spread among elite classes throughout Maya society.

Astronomical knowledge reached remarkable sophistication. Maya priest-astronomers tracked planetary movements with precision exceeding many Old World civilizations. They calculated eclipse cycles, predicted Venus appearances, and correlated celestial events with earthly affairs. This scientific achievement influenced Maya culture for centuries.

Trade networks during El Mirador's peak extended across Mesoamerica. Merchants carried jade from the Guatemala highlands, obsidian from Mexican volcanic sources, and marine shells from both the Pacific and Atlantic coasts. These exotic materials reached El Mirador through complex exchange systems.

Political organization achieved unprecedented complexity. El Mirador's rulers governed territories spanning hundreds of kilometers. Administrative systems managed tribute collection, labor recruitment, and military affairs. Government structure prefigured political developments in later Maya states.

Population estimates for El Mirador's peak range from 100,000 to 200,000 inhabitants. Supporting such numbers required intensive agriculture, sophisticated food distribution, and complex social organization. The city functioned as a genuine urban center comparable to contemporary Old World cities.

Construction activity during the Late Pre-Classic period demonstrates remarkable engineering capabilities. Workers moved millions of tons of stone to build pyramids, causeways, and other monumental architecture.

*Ancient American Civilizations*

These achievements required mathematical knowledge, surveying techniques, and organizational skills approaching modern standards.

Decline began gradually around 100 CE. Construction activity decreased. The population started dispersing to smaller settlements. Trade networks contracted. The causes remain unclear, but environmental factors, political instability, or resource depletion may have contributed to El Mirador's gradual abandonment.

The final occupation period (100-150 CE) saw sporadic attempts to maintain El Mirador's urban functions. Rulers constructed smaller buildings using stones salvaged from earlier monuments. The population continued to decline as people migrated to other regions. The great city slowly returned to the jungle.

By 150 CE, major construction had ceased entirely. The last inhabitants abandoned El Mirador's ceremonial center. Secondary forest growth began reclaiming cleared areas. Within centuries, the once-mighty metropolis had vanished beneath the jungle canopy. Maya civilization continued elsewhere, but El Mirador's golden age had ended forever.

# Complete Cultural Memory Erasure

Something unprecedented happened to El Mirador after its abandonment around 150 CE. The city did not simply decline or transform into smaller settlements. It vanished completely from Maya cultural memory. Later Maya civilizations preserved no traditions about their greatest Pre-Classic achievement.

This erasure was so complete that when Spanish conquistadors arrived in the 16th century, they found no indigenous knowledge of El Mirador's existence. Maya informants described many ancient sites to colonial chroniclers. They preserved detailed oral traditions about Chichen Itza, Tikal, and other ceremonial centers. El Mirador received no mention in any colonial document.

The silence extends beyond Spanish records. Maya codices from the Post-Classic period contain no references to El Mirador. These bark-paper books preserved astronomical knowledge, historical chronicles, and religious traditions spanning centuries. El Mirador appears in none of them.

*Ancient American Civilizations*

Even the site's original name disappeared. "El Mirador" is a modern Spanish designation meaning "the lookout." The ancient Maya name for their greatest city has been lost forever. This represents cultural amnesia on a scale rarely documented in human history.

Archaeological evidence suggests deliberate abandonment rather than gradual decline. Workers carefully cached valuable objects before leaving. They sealed important tombs and buried sacred sculptures. The abandonment appears planned and coordinated rather than forced by external catastrophe.

The systematic nature of El Mirador's erasure suggests more than simple forgetfulness. Later Maya civilizations actively chose to forget their Pre-Classic heritage. This cultural amnesia may have served specific purposes in later political and religious developments.

New Maya kingdoms emerging during the Classic period (250-900 CE) needed to establish their own legitimacy. Acknowledging El Mirador's achievements might have undermined claims to political innovation and cultural superiority. Forgetting the past allowed Classic-period rulers to present themselves as civilization's founders.

Religious factors may have contributed to the erasure. El Mirador's gods and ceremonies might have conflicted with later theological developments. Maya's religious evolution may have necessitated the abandonment of earlier spiritual traditions. Cultural amnesia served religious transformation.

The scale of memory loss challenges conventional understanding of cultural continuity. Oral traditions typically preserve information about important events and places across many generations. El Mirador's complete disappearance from Maya consciousness suggests unusual circumstances surrounding its abandonment.

Environmental factors might explain the cultural forgetting. If ecological collapse forced El Mirador's abandonment, survivors may have chosen to forget the failed city. Cultural memory sometimes suppresses traumatic experiences. El Mirador's erasure could represent collective psychological coping.

The city's remote jungle location contributed to its disappearance from consciousness. Later, Maya centers developed in different regions with better agricultural potential or trade advantages. Physical separation from El Mirador made forgetting easier as populations moved elsewhere.

Linguistic changes during the Maya cultural transition might have accelerated memory loss. If Late Pre-Classic Maya spoke different languages from their Classic-period descendants, translation difficulties could have obscured historical traditions. Language evolution sometimes erases cultural memory.

Political fragmentation following El Mirador's collapse may have scattered the population groups that maintained historical knowledge. Elite families who preserved royal genealogies and historical traditions might have dispersed to different regions. Political continuity breaks often produce cultural amnesia.

The absence of Maya writing during El Mirador's peak contributed to memory loss. Without written records, historical information depended entirely on oral transmission. Oral traditions are more fragile than written sources and disappear more easily during cultural disruptions.

Modern rediscovery of El Mirador has restored the site to Maya consciousness. Contemporary Maya communities now take pride in their ancestors' achievements. Cultural memory can be reconstructed even after centuries of forgetting. El Mirador has returned to the Maya world through archaeological revelation.

The city's erasure and rediscovery offer lessons about cultural memory and historical consciousness. Human societies can forget their greatest achievements under specific circumstances. Archaeological investigation sometimes recovers lost heritage that oral traditions failed to preserve. El Mirador demonstrates both the fragility and resilience of cultural memory.

# Chapter 5: Teotihuacan - The City Without a Name

## Aztec Discovery: "Place Where Gods Are Born"

Moctezuma II stood at the edge of the ancient ruins in the year 1519. His royal procession had traveled north from Tenochtitlan to investigate reports of massive stone pyramids abandoned in the Mexican highlands. What the Aztec Emperor found defied every explanation his priests could offer.

Enormous pyramids rose from a valley floor like artificial mountains. Stone temples stretched along a perfectly straight avenue longer than any road in the Aztec Empire—residential compounds covered square miles of terrain. The construction quality exceeded anything Aztec engineers could achieve. Most troubling of all, no one remembered who had built this incredible city.

Moctezuma's advisors questioned local villagers living near the ruins. The farmers were unaware of the builders. Their ancestors had found the city already empty and overgrown. No oral traditions preserved the builders' names. No songs recalled their achievements. No legend explained their disappearance. The massive urban complex existed without identity or history.

The Aztec ruler walked the length of the central avenue. His footsteps echoed off stone walls that had stood silent for centuries. Elaborate murals decorated temple facades despite decades of exposure to wind and rain. Obsidian tools and pottery fragments littered plaza floors. Everything suggested recent abandonment, but the villagers insisted their grandfathers had found the city in identical condition.

Moctezuma named the mysterious metropolis Teotihuacan, meaning "the place where gods are born." The Aztecs believed only divine beings could have constructed something so magnificent and then vanished without a trace. They incorporated the ruins into their religious practices, conducting ceremonies among the abandoned temples. Aztec pilgrims journeyed from across the empire to walk the sacred avenue and offer prayers to unnamed deities.

The Spanish conquistador Hernán Cortés encountered Teotihuacan during his march toward the Aztec capital. His chroniclers described pyramids larger than European cathedrals arranged with mathematical precision along the central boulevard. They found no inhabitants, no defenders, no signs of recent occupation. The city stood empty except for Aztec priests maintaining shrines among the ruins.

Bernal Díaz del Castillo recorded his amazement at the architectural scale. The Pyramid of the Sun dominated the landscape like a man-made mountain. The Pyramid of the Moon anchored the northern end of the main avenue. Hundreds of smaller temples and residential structures filled the spaces between major monuments. The urban planning exceeded anything Spanish colonists had seen in the New World.

Archaeological investigations beginning in the 20th century revealed the true scope of Teotihuacan's achievement. Radiocarbon dating pushed the city's origins back to around 100 BCE. Construction continued for over six centuries. At its peak between 100-550 CE, Teotihuacan housed between 100,000 and 200,000 residents. This population density made it one of the world's largest cities during the early centuries of the Common Era.

The mystery of identity persisted through decades of excavation. Researchers found no royal tombs containing inscriptions. No stone monuments recorded dynastic histories. No codices preserved the builders' own accounts. The archaeological record contained abundant evidence of sophisticated urban civilization but revealed nothing about the people who created it.

# 100,000-200,000 Population at Peak

Dawn broke over the ancient metropolis around 400 CE. Smoke rose from thousands of cooking fires in residential compounds across the urban landscape. Merchants prepared their stalls in the Great Compound marketplace. Artisans opened workshops producing obsidian tools, ceramic vessels, and elaborate headdresses. Children played in courtyards surrounded by multi-story apartment buildings. Teotihuacan buzzed with activity rivaling any city in the contemporary world.

The population density staggered modern researchers when they began systematic mapping of the urban core. Apartment compounds lined every street—each residential complex housed multiple families in rooms arranged around central courtyards. Stone drainage systems carried waste water away from living areas. Sophisticated urban planning provided neighborhoods with markets, workshops, and smaller temples serving local populations.

Excavations in the La Ventilla district revealed the daily life of common residents. Families lived in single-room apartments within larger compounds. Each room contained sleeping areas, storage spaces, and small altars for household gods. Cooking took place in shared courtyards equipped with stone hearths and grinding platforms for preparing maize. Community areas provided space for social gatherings and religious ceremonies.

The Oztoyahualco compound demonstrated the housing arrangements of middle-class residents. This excavated complex contained 60 rooms arranged around seven courtyards. Approximately 100 people lived in the compound during its occupied period. Stone walls separated family apartments but allowed access to shared facilities. Elaborate murals decorated courtyard walls, depicting religious scenes and daily activities.

Teotihuacan's population came from across Mesoamerica. Chemical analysis of skeletal remains revealed residents with diverse geographic origins. People migrated from the Gulf Coast, the Maya regions, Oaxaca, and other distant areas to live in the great city. The urban population spoke multiple languages and practiced varied cultural traditions within the cosmopolitan environment.

The city's economic system supported this massive population through specialized production and long-distance trade. Workshops concentrated in specific neighborhoods produced goods for local consumption and export to distant markets. The obsidian industry alone employed thousands of craftsmen, turning volcanic glass into cutting tools, weapons, and decorative objects shipped across ancient Mexico.

Agricultural production in the surrounding valleys fed the urban population through intensive farming techniques. Teotihuacan engineers constructed irrigation systems channeling water from highland springs to terraced fields. Chinampas, or floating gardens, increased crop yields in marshy areas around nearby lakes. The agricultural surplus supported non-farming specialists living within the city.

Population estimates vary based on different calculation methods, but all studies confirm Teotihuacan's extraordinary demographic achievement. Conservative estimates place the peak population at 100,000 residents. More generous calculations suggest 200,000 people lived within the urban boundaries. Either figure made Teotihuacan larger than contemporary Rome and certainly the largest city in the ancient Americas.

The residential districts extended far beyond the ceremonial core. Apartment compounds continued for miles in every direction from the central pyramids. Suburban areas housed farmers, craftsmen, and merchants serving the urban economy. The total settled area covered over 20 square kilometers, making Teotihuacan one of the world's most extensive pre-industrial cities.

Managing this enormous population required sophisticated administrative systems. Standardized weights and measures facilitated commerce. Uniform architectural styles indicated centralized planning and construction oversight. The distribution of luxury goods suggests hierarchical social organization, though researchers have found no evidence of individual rulers or royal dynasties.

# Avenue of the Dead: 4-Kilometer Sacred Boulevard

The great avenue stretched before morning visitors like a stone river flowing between pyramid shores. Pilgrims from distant regions began their ceremonial walk at dawn, starting from the Ciudadela complex in the south. Their barefoot steps echoed off limestone pavement as they moved northward toward the Pyramid of the Moon. The journey covered 4.2 kilometers of sacred space designed to transform human consciousness through architectural experience.

Construction crews had worked for generations to create this magnificent processional way. They excavated millions of cubic meters of earth to establish the avenue's foundations. They quarried limestone blocks from distant hillsides and transported them to the construction site. They laid each stone with precision, creating a perfectly straight roadway wider than any boulevard in ancient Mexico.

The avenue's alignment followed astronomical principles rather than geographic convenience. Teotihuacan's architects oriented the central axis 15.5 degrees east of true north. This precise angle aligned the avenue with key dates in the agricultural calendar, particularly the solar zenith passages occurring in May and August. When the sun reached its highest point overhead, it cast no shadows along the avenue's length.

Major temple complexes lined both sides of the sacred roadway. The Temple of the Feathered Serpent dominated the southern section, its facades decorated with carved stone serpents and jaguars. Smaller pyramid platforms punctuated the avenue's middle sections, each designed for specific ceremonial functions. Residential complexes for priests and high-ranking officials occupied the areas between religious structures.

Processions along the avenue followed ritual calendars marking important agricultural and religious celebrations. Thousands of participants would gather at the southern entrance before dawn. They carried offerings of jade, obsidian, shells, and precious textiles to deposit at various shrine locations. The procession moved slowly northward, stopping at designated platforms for prayers, music, and ceremonial dances.

The Pyramid of the Sun commanded the avenue's eastern horizon. This massive structure rose 65 meters above the surrounding plaza, making it visible from every point along the processional route. Pilgrims could see their ultimate destination from the moment they began walking. The pyramid's bulk grew larger with each step northward, creating dramatic visual effects as the procession advanced.

Archaeological excavations revealed the sophisticated engineering beneath the avenue's surface. Stone-lined drainage channels carried rainwater away from the ceremonial space. Underground storage chambers held offerings and ritual equipment used during major celebrations. Access tunnels allowed priests to appear suddenly in the middle of processions, emerging from hidden openings in the pavement.

The avenue's width accommodated enormous crowds during peak ceremonial periods. The roadway measured 40 meters across at its widest points, providing space for thousands of simultaneous participants. Side plazas expanded the available area when major festivals drew pilgrims from across Mesoamerica. The urban planning demonstrated a sophisticated understanding of crowd management and ceremonial logistics.

Sacred geometry governed the avenue's proportions and the spacing of major monuments along its length. The distance between pyramid platforms followed mathematical ratios based on astronomical cycles. The width of plaza areas corresponded to the heights of adjacent temple structures. Every architectural element contributed to an integrated design that linked earth and sky through the built environment.

Merchants established temporary markets along the avenue during major religious festivals. Vendors sold food, crafts, and religious items to visiting pilgrims. These commercial activities helped support Teotihuacan's economy and provided resources for maintaining the ceremonial complex. The avenue functioned simultaneously as a sacred space and an economic opportunity.

Modern visitors walking the avenue experience the same dramatic effects that ancient pilgrims encountered. The pyramid monuments grow larger with each step northward. The urban landscape unfolds in carefully planned sequences of views and vistas. The architectural experience builds tension and anticipation, culminating in arrival at the Pyramid of the Moon plaza at the avenue's northern terminus.

# Orion Constellation Alignment with Pyramids

Mexican archaeoastronomer Jesús Galindo made a discovery in 1963 that fundamentally changed our understanding of Teotihuacan's cosmic significance. Standing atop the Pyramid of the Sun during the spring equinox, Galindo observed that the pyramid's orientation precisely matched the position of Orion's Belt as it appeared on the horizon during Teotihuacan's construction period. This alignment was no coincidence.

The builders of Teotihuacan had created a terrestrial mirror of celestial patterns. The three main pyramids along the Avenue of the Dead corresponded exactly to the three bright stars of Orion's Belt - Alnitak, Alnilam, and Mintaka. The Pyramid of the Sun represented Alnitak, the eastern star—a smaller pyramid structure aligned with Alnilam in the center. The Pyramid of the Moon corresponded to Mintaka, the western star.

Hugh Harleston Jr., an American engineer, conducted detailed measurements of the pyramid complex during the 1970s. His calculations revealed that the relative positions and sizes of the Teotihuacan pyramids matched the brightness and locations of the Orion stars with remarkable precision. The architectural plan preserved the constellation's configuration in permanent stone form.

The construction of this astronomical alignment required extraordinary technical knowledge and planning capabilities. The architects needed accurate observations of stellar positions over multiple years. They calculated proper pyramid sizes and placement to maintain proportional relationships. They oriented the entire urban plan to preserve the celestial correspondence across the massive scale of the city.

The Pyramid of the Sun served as the primary anchor point for the astronomical design. Its base dimensions measured 220 meters on each side, making it larger than the Great Pyramid of Giza. The structure rose to 65 meters in height, providing an artificial horizon point visible from great distances. Every measurement followed precise mathematical ratios corresponding to Orion's position in ancient skies.

Teotihuacan's builders incorporated multiple layers of astronomical knowledge into their urban design. The city's main axis aligned with the Pleiades star cluster during its heliacal rising around 100 CE. Secondary structures tracked the movements of Venus, Mars, and other celestial bodies significant to Mesoamerican calendars. The entire urban landscape functioned as a three-dimensional astronomical instrument.

The Orion correlation extended beyond simple stellar mapping. Ancient Mexican cultures associated Orion with creation myths and seasonal agricultural cycles. The constellation's appearance in pre-dawn skies marked the beginning of the rainy season, essential for crop growth. The stars' movement across the night sky provided a natural calendar for timing religious ceremonies and agricultural activities.

Archaeological evidence supports the astronomical interpretation of Teotihuacan's design. Excavations have revealed numerous artifacts related to celestial observation, including mirror discs, crystal spheres, and carved stone calendars. Priestly residences contained rooms with sight lines aligned to specific stellar rising and setting points. The city's inhabitants clearly possessed sophisticated astronomical knowledge.

The precision of the Orion alignment suggests Teotihuacan's architects inherited astronomical traditions from earlier Mesoamerican cultures. The Olmec civilization had created celestial alignments in its ceremonial centers centuries before Teotihuacan's construction. This knowledge passed through generations of priest-astronomers who preserved and refined their understanding of cosmic cycles.

Modern archaeoastronomy has confirmed additional stellar alignments throughout the Teotihuacan complex. The Temple of the Feathered Serpent incorporates angles corresponding to the Pleiades cluster position. Smaller pyramid structures track the rising points of bright stars like Aldebaran and Regulus. The entire urban plan reflects comprehensive astronomical knowledge rivaling any ancient civilization.

Computer simulations recreating ancient skies over Teotihuacan have verified the mathematical precision of the pyramid alignments. The stellar correlations remain accurate across the centuries of the city's occupation, from approximately 100-600 CE. This consistency demonstrates that Teotihuacan's builders understood long-term astronomical cycles and incorporated this knowledge into permanent architectural form.

# Underground Mercury-Lined Tunnel Systems

Sergio Gómez descended into absolute darkness on an October morning in 2003. The Mexican archaeologist had discovered a hidden entrance beneath the Temple of the Feathered Serpent, sealed for over a thousand years by ancient priests. His headlamp illuminated stone steps leading deep into the earth.

What he found in the depths below would challenge every assumption about Teotihuacan's mysterious builders.

The tunnel stretched 103 meters underground, running directly beneath the pyramid's center. Stone walls rose to form a vaulted ceiling high enough for walking. The passages had been deliberately sealed with tons of rock, clay, and sand. Whoever closed these tunnels intended they would never be opened again.

Gómez's team worked for over a decade to excavate the underground complex. They removed thousands of cubic meters of fill material placed by the original builders. Each layer revealed new artifacts: jade ornaments, obsidian blades, carved wooden objects, and strange metallic spheres of unknown purpose. The tunnel contained the richest archaeological deposit ever discovered at Teotihuacan.

The most astonishing discovery lay deeper in the tunnel system. The walls and ceiling were covered with pyrite and mica powder, creating reflective surfaces that shimmered in artificial light. When Gómez's team illuminated the tunnel with torches, the mineral coating created the illusion of walking through a starlit cavern. The effect was magical and otherworldly.

Hundreds of metallic spheres covered the tunnel floor. Each sphere measured between 4 and 12 centimeters in diameter. Chemical analysis revealed they were made of jarosite, a golden-colored iron sulfate mineral. The spheres had been carefully crafted, not naturally formed. Their purpose remained a mystery to modern archaeologists.

Ground-penetrating radar surveys revealed additional tunnel systems beneath other major pyramids at Teotihuacan. The Pyramid of the Sun appeared to have a natural cave at its center, possibly incorporated into the structure during construction. The Pyramid of the Moon showed evidence of multiple chambers and passageways. Teotihuacan's builders had created an underground world as sophisticated as their surface architecture.

The most shocking discovery came from chemical analysis of residues found throughout the tunnel system. Soil samples contained high concentrations of liquid mercury, a toxic heavy metal rarely seen in ancient American contexts. The mercury appeared to have been intentionally placed throughout the underground chambers, creating pools of the silvery liquid metal.

Mercury held special significance in ancient Mesoamerican religion and science. The Maya associated liquid mercury with the underworld and used it in ritual contexts. The Aztecs called mercury "water of the gods" and believed it possessed supernatural properties. Teotihuacan's builders may have used mercury to create sacred spaces connecting the physical and spiritual worlds.

The underground chambers indicated intentional flooding with mercury. Stone basins held residues of the liquid metal. Drainage channels transported mercury throughout the tunnel system. The builders had created underground rivers of quicksilver flowing beneath their pyramid temples. This marked the largest recorded use of mercury in the ancient Americas.

Modern toxicology studies have revealed the dangerous effects of mercury exposure on human health. The metal damages the nervous system and can cause hallucinations, tremors, and altered states of consciousness. Ancient priests entering the mercury-filled tunnels may have experienced profound psychological effects they interpreted as divine visions or communication with gods.

The tunnel construction required sophisticated engineering knowledge. The builders excavated solid rock to create the underground chambers. They waterproofed the walls to prevent flooding from groundwater. They designed ventilation systems to make the spaces habitable for human occupancy. The underground architecture rivaled the complexity of surface construction.

Archaeological evidence suggests the tunnels served multiple functions. Some chambers contained astronomical observation equipment for tracking celestial movements. Others housed ritual objects and offerings to underworld deities. The mercury-lined passages may have been used for priest initiation ceremonies involving altered states of consciousness.

Carbon-14 dating placed the tunnel construction between 100-200 CE, during Teotihuacan's early development period. The underground chambers were sealed around 250 CE and remained closed until Gómez's discovery. The builders invested enormous resources in creating elaborate spaces they intended to use for only 150 years before permanent closure.

The discovery of mercury-lined tunnels adds another layer to Teotihuacan's mystery. The builders possessed knowledge of chemistry, metallurgy, and human psychology that conventional archaeology struggles to explain. They created underground environments designed to produce specific mental and spiritual effects. The tunnels represent a level of sophistication that challenges our understanding of ancient American capabilities.

Ongoing excavations continue to reveal new chambers and passages beneath Teotihuacan's pyramids. Each discovery provides additional evidence of the builders' extraordinary technical knowledge and spiritual practices. The underground world of Teotihuacan may hold keys to understanding the identity and ultimate fate of this lost civilization.

# Chapter 6: Cahokia - North America's Lost Metropolis

## Mississippi River Valley's 40,000-Person City

Dr. Melvin Fowler stepped out of his truck on a humid Illinois morning. It was in 1961. Before him stretched acres of farmland dotted with mysterious earthen mounds. Local farmers had been plowing around these hills for generations. Most assumed they were natural formations left by glacial activity. Fowler suspected something far more significant.

The largest mound rose nearly 100 feet above the surrounding prairie. Its flat top and terraced sides suggested human construction on a massive scale. Fowler began his survey work with a small team and limited funding from Southern Illinois University. What they discovered over the following decades would rewrite North American prehistory.

The mounds were not random hills. They formed part of a carefully planned urban center covering over 4,000 acres. This ancient city housed between 15,000 and 40,000 people at its peak around 1100 CE. The population density exceeded medieval London. The urban planning rivaled contemporary cities anywhere in the world.

Cahokia had grown from a small settlement into North America's first true metropolis over several centuries. The transformation began around 900 CE when local communities started converging on this strategic location. The site offered access to major rivers, fertile floodplains, and abundant natural resources. More importantly, it became a spiritual center drawing pilgrims from across the continent.

Archaeological evidence reveals the city's sophisticated organization. Residential districts surrounded the central ceremonial core. Craft specialists worked in designated neighborhoods. Elite families occupied houses atop smaller mounds, overlooking commoner dwellings in the valleys below. Storage facilities held surplus food for redistribution during lean seasons. The entire complex functioned as an integrated urban system.

The city's growth required unprecedented coordination. Thousands of workers moved millions of cubic feet of soil to construct the monumental earthworks. They quarried clay from specific locations to ensure structural stability. They layered different soil types to prevent erosion and settlement. The engineering knowledge required for such projects necessitated a sophisticated mathematical understanding and a centralized planning authority.

Cahokia's influence extended far beyond the immediate region. Satellite communities adopted the city's architectural styles, pottery designs, and ceremonial practices. Trade goods from Cahokia workshops reached settlements hundreds of miles away. The city became the hub of a cultural network spanning much of eastern North America.

The urban center reached its zenith during the Mississippian period, roughly 1050 to 1200 CE. The population peaked around 1100 CE when the city covered an area larger than medieval Paris. Construction projects during this era created the massive earthworks that still dominate the landscape today.

French explorers traveling down the Mississippi River in the 17th century found the area virtually empty. Native American groups lived in the region but showed no knowledge of the ancient city's builders. The mounds had become overgrown with forest. The great plazas had returned to prairie grassland. An entire civilization had vanished, leaving only earthen monuments to mark their passing.

# Monks Mound: Largest North American Earthwork

The morning sun cast long shadows across Monks Mound as Fowler's team began their systematic survey. The structure dwarfed everything around it. Its base covered 14 acres. Its height reached 100 feet. The volume of earth contained in the mound exceeded the Great Pyramid of Giza.

French monks had given the mound its name after establishing a monastery nearby in the early 1800s. They had no idea they were building beside North America's largest prehistoric structure. The mound's true significance became clear only after decades of archaeological investigation.

Careful excavation revealed the mound's construction history. Builders had created it in stages over several centuries. Each phase required moving thousands of tons of earth in baskets carried on human backs.

The builders selected specific clay types for different layers. They included organic materials to bind the soil. They engineered drainage systems to prevent water damage.

The final structure contained over 22 million cubic feet of carefully placed earth. Construction crews had shaped it into four terraces rising like giant steps toward the flat summit. Ramps and stairways provided access between levels. The entire project demonstrated engineering skills rivaling any ancient civilization.

The mound's summit once supported a massive wooden building. Archaeological evidence suggests this structure served as the residence for Cahokia's paramount chief. The building's dimensions exceeded 100 feet in length. Its elevated position provided commanding views across the entire urban complex and surrounding countryside.

Carbon dating of wood samples from various construction phases revealed the mound's building chronology. Work began around 950 CE with the first modest earthwork. Successive generations expanded and heightened the structure. The final construction phase occurred around 1200 CE when builders added the highest terrace and summit building.

The construction process required unprecedented social organization. Thousands of workers needed coordination, feeding, and supervision. Raw materials had to be located, transported, and stockpiled. Specialized craftsmen created tools and supervised technical aspects of the work. The entire project could only succeed under strong centralized authority.

Religious beliefs motivated the massive construction effort. The mound's orientation aligned with cardinal directions and astronomical events. Its height lifted the paramount chief closer to the celestial realm. Its visibility from throughout the urban area reinforced the ruler's sacred authority. The structure functioned as both residence and cosmic symbol.

Modern visitors climbing to the mound's summit can appreciate the scale of the achievement. The view encompasses miles of surrounding landscape. The geometric precision of the terrace construction becomes apparent from this elevated perspective. The enormous labor investment required becomes undeniable when experienced firsthand.

# Woodhenge: Circular Astronomical Observatory

Patrick Munson discovered the first wooden post holes in 1961 during routine excavation west of Monks Mound. The dark stains in the soil seemed unremarkable at first glance. Munson's careful mapping revealed their true significance. The posts had been arranged in precise circles with specific astronomical alignments.

The discovery revolutionized the understanding of Cahokian astronomical knowledge. The wooden posts had functioned as observation markers for tracking solar and lunar cycles. The builders had possessed a sophisticated understanding of celestial mechanics. They had encoded this knowledge in permanent architectural form.

Excavation revealed evidence for multiple Woodhenge circles constructed over several centuries—the earliest dates to around 950 CE. Subsequent generations rebuilt and expanded the observatory. Each version contained between 24 and 72 posts arranged in perfect circles. The largest circle measured 476 feet in diameter.

The posts themselves had long since decayed, but their placement patterns survived in the archaeological record. Computer analysis of post positions revealed precise alignments with sunrise and sunset positions throughout the year. Key markers corresponded to solstices, equinoxes, and other significant astronomical events.

The most sophisticated circle, designated Woodhenge III, contained 48 posts with remarkable precision. The builders had positioned key markers to frame the sunrise on summer and winter solstices as viewed from the center. Other posts marked the rising points for equinoxes and cross-quarter days. The entire system functioned as a giant solar calendar.

The construction required advanced mathematical knowledge. The builders had calculated exact compass bearings for each post position. They had surveyed the circle's center point and radius with remarkable accuracy. They had understood concepts of geometry that European mathematics would not formalize for centuries.

The observatory served multiple functions in Cahokian society. Priests used it to predict seasonal changes crucial for agricultural timing. They scheduled religious ceremonies to coincide with astronomical events.

*Ancient American Civilizations*

They demonstrated their sacred knowledge through public observations of celestial phenomena.

The Woodhenge circles connected Cahokian spiritual beliefs with natural cycles. The builders viewed the cosmos as an integrated system of earthly and celestial forces. Their observatory enabled them to actively participate in cosmic rhythms, rather than merely observing them passively. The structure embodied their understanding of humanity's place in the universal order.

Archaeological evidence suggests the observatory remained in use for over 300 years. Successive generations maintained the wooden posts and rebuilt structures as needed. The long period of continuous use demonstrates the lasting importance of astronomical observation in Cahokian culture.

# Continental Trade Network Evidence

Warren Wittry uncovered the first exotic artifacts in 1954 during excavations in Cahokia's residential areas. Copper beads from Lake Superior mines lay beside marine shells from the Gulf of Mexico. Obsidian blades from western mountains rested near flint tools from Arkansas quarries. The diversity of materials pointed to trade networks spanning the entire continent.

The discovery launched decades of research into Cahokian commerce. Each artifact told part of a larger story about economic relationships reaching from the Atlantic to the Rocky Mountains. The scale and sophistication of these trade connections rivaled anything in the contemporary world.

Mica sheets from the North Carolina mountains had been worked into ceremonial ornaments by Cahokian craftsmen. The thin, reflective material required careful handling during transport across hundreds of miles. Its presence in burial goods demonstrated the high value placed on rare materials obtained through long-distance exchange.

Galena crystals from northwestern Illinois mines provided raw material for specialized crafts. Cahokian workers shaped the lead ore into beads, ornaments, and ceremonial objects. Chemical analysis of finished products revealed the specific quarry sources. The mining and transport operations required organized labor and sophisticated logistics.

Shark teeth from the Atlantic and Gulf coasts appeared in Cahokian tool assemblages and ornamental contexts. Their presence proved contact with coastal peoples through either direct expeditions or extended trade chains. The teeth served both functional and symbolic purposes in Cahokian culture.

Stone tools manufactured from Arkansas novaculite demonstrated access to the finest chert sources in eastern North America. The high-quality stone has extremely sharp edges, ideal for cutting and carving. Cahokian craftsmen created elaborate ceremonial blades from this premium material.

Catlinite pipes carved from Minnesota red stone appeared in elite burial contexts. The distinctive red pipestone could only be obtained from specific quarries in the upper Midwest. Its use in sacred smoking ceremonies connected Cahokian religious practices with distant spiritual traditions.

The trade networks operated through both direct expeditions and intermediate exchange partners. Archaeological evidence suggests Cahokian traders traveled to distant resource areas. They established relationships with local groups controlling access to desired materials. They created trading posts at strategic locations along major river routes.

Cahokian products moved outward along the same trade routes that brought exotic materials to the city. Distinctive pottery styles, copper ornaments, and specialized tools manufactured in Cahokia appeared at sites across the Southeast and Midwest. The city functioned as both consumer and producer in the continental exchange system.

The trade relationships required diplomatic skills and cultural knowledge. Cahokian traders needed to understand diverse customs, languages, and social protocols. They served as cultural ambassadors as well as commercial agents. Their activities spread Cahokian influence far beyond the city's physical boundaries.

# 14th Century Mysterious Abandonment

George Holley noticed the change during his 1950s excavations in Cahokia's residential areas. House foundations from the city's peak period showed signs of careful maintenance and regular rebuilding. Later structures appeared hastily constructed and quickly abandoned. The archaeological evidence pointed to a gradual decline followed by a sudden evacuation.

The abandonment process began around 1200 CE when population growth slowed and then reversed. Construction projects became smaller and less frequent. Some residential areas showed signs of partial abandonment as families moved elsewhere. The great urban center that had dominated North American prehistory began its slow collapse.

Multiple factors contributed to Cahokia's decline. Climate change has led to cooler temperatures and shorter growing seasons. The Medieval Warm Period, which had supported large-scale agriculture, gave way to conditions that stressed food production. Crop failures and resource shortages undermined the city's ability to support its massive population.

Environmental degradation compounded the climate problems. Centuries of intensive occupation had depleted local resources. Deforestation removed trees needed for construction and fuel. Soil erosion reduced agricultural productivity in the surrounding floodplains. The city had grown beyond its environmental carrying capacity.

Social and political tensions likely intensified as resources became increasingly scarce. Competition between elite factions may have weakened central authority. Tributary communities may have withdrawn their support as the city's power declined. The complex social system that had created Cahokia's greatness became a liability during hard times.

The final abandonment occurred surprisingly quickly. Archaeological evidence suggests most residents left within a few decades around 1300 CE. They took portable possessions but left behind massive earthworks and substantial buildings. The evacuation appears to have been organized rather than panicked.

Where did the Cahokians go? Some probably joined related communities along the Mississippi River system. Others may have migrated westward onto the Great Plains. Still others could have moved eastward into the Ohio River valley. The dispersal of Cahokian cultural traditions scattered them across much of North America.

Native American groups living in the region when Europeans arrived showed no knowledge of the ancient city. Tribal traditions contained no memories of the great metropolis or its builders. The Illinois, Missouri, and other local tribes treated the mounds as mysterious landmarks left by unknown ancestors.

French explorers in the 17th century found the area sparsely populated. Jacques Marquette and Louis Jolliet paddled past the ruins in 1673 without recognizing their significance. Later, French settlers established farms and villages among the ancient earthworks. They had no idea they were living beside North America's greatest prehistoric achievement.

The abandonment left one of archaeology's greatest mysteries. How could a city that had dominated a continent for centuries disappear so completely from human memory? The answer probably lies in the dispersal pattern of the refugees. Scattered among many different communities, the Cahokians gradually lost their distinct identity. Their urban traditions gave way to the village-based cultures that Europeans later encountered.

Modern Cahokia preserves only a fraction of the original site. Urban development has destroyed dozens of mounds and residential areas— interstate highways cut through the ancient plazas. Industrial facilities occupy former ceremonial grounds. The surviving earthworks provide glimpses of a vanished world that once rivaled any city on earth.

The story of Cahokia challenges assumptions about North American prehistory. Native peoples had created complex urban civilizations long before European contact. They had developed sophisticated technologies, far-reaching trade networks, and monumental architecture. Their achievements rivaled contemporaneous civilizations anywhere in the world. The evidence lies preserved in Illinois soil, waiting for those willing to see past longstanding prejudices about the ancient Americas.

# Chapter 7: Desert Dwellers - The Anasazi Achievement

## Four Corners Region Cliff Dwellings

The morning sun struck the sandstone cliff face at Mesa Verde, Colorado. Dr. Richard Wetherill guided his horse along the narrow canyon rim in December 1888. His cattle had wandered into this remote corner of the high desert. What Wetherill discovered in the shadows beneath the overhanging rock changed American archaeology forever.

A complete city hung suspended in the cliff face. Stone walls rose three and four stories high, tucked perfectly into the natural alcove. Circular towers anchored the corners. Rectangular rooms stretched across the protected space. Storage chambers filled with ancient corn kernels sat undisturbed. Clay pots rested on stone shelves exactly where their makers had placed them centuries earlier.

Wetherill called it Cliff Palace. The name captured his amazement at finding sophisticated urban architecture in one of North America's most challenging environments. The structure contained 150 rooms and 23 ceremonial chambers. More than 100 people had once lived in this single cliff dwelling. The builders had solved problems of water collection, food storage, defense, and comfort in a landscape where survival challenged even modern visitors.

The Four Corners region spans the junction of Colorado, Utah, Arizona, and New Mexico. High mesas rise from desert floors. Deep canyons cut through layered sandstone. Annual rainfall barely reaches ten inches. Summer temperatures soar above 100 degrees. Winter winds howl through the canyons, dropping temperatures below zero. Most modern cities could not survive here without a constant supply from outside sources.

Ancient peoples thrived in this environment for over 700 years. They built hundreds of cliff dwellings across the region. Each location demonstrated careful selection based on solar exposure, wind protection, water access, and defensive advantages. The builders understood their environment with precision that came from generations of observation and adaptation.

*Ancient American Civilizations*

Construction required immense planning and coordination. Builders carried every stone, timber, and handful of mortar up cliff faces or down from mesa tops. They shaped sandstone blocks using harder stone hammers. They fitted each piece into walls that have withstood centuries of freeze-thaw cycles, flash floods, and high desert winds. No mechanical lifting devices helped them position roof beams 30 feet above the canyon floors.

The architectural solutions revealed a deep understanding of desert survival. South-facing alcoves captured winter sunlight for warmth. Overhanging cliffs provided shade during scorching summers. Natural rock formations channeled precious rainwater into storage areas. Underground springs emerged from cliff bases, providing reliable water sources even during drought years.

Cliff dwellings are connected through hidden pathways carved into rock faces. Hand and toe holds allowed movement between levels without exposing residents to enemies or weather. Some routes required rope climbing skills that matched modern rock-climbing techniques. Children learned these pathways from infancy, developing the balance and strength necessary for three-dimensional village life.

Defense considerations shaped every design choice. Single entrances could be blocked with wooden barriers or stone slabs. Elevated positions provided clear views of approaching threats. Storage rooms built into the deepest recesses of alcoves protected food supplies from raiders. Guard posts positioned at strategic points allowed communication between settlements through smoke signals and reflected sunlight.

# Mesa Verde: Multi-Story Desert Architecture

Balcony House showcased the ultimate achievement in cliff dwelling engineering. The structure rose 600 feet above the canyon floor, accessible only through a tunnel barely wide enough for one person. Visitors today must climb 32-foot ladders and crawl through tight passages to reach the main rooms. Ancient residents navigated these obstacles daily, carrying water, food, and children.

The builders maximized every square foot of available space. Ground floor rooms served multiple functions - food preparation during the day, sleeping quarters at night. Second stories provided additional living space and storage. Third levels housed specialized workshops for pottery making, weaving, and tool manufacture. Roof areas became courtyards where daily life unfolded under open sky.

Construction techniques adapted local materials with extraordinary skill. Builders selected sandstone blocks for their weather resistance and workability. They mixed mortar from local clay, water, and organic binding agents. Wooden beams came from pine and fir trees growing on distant mesa tops. Every material had to be transported by human power alone.

Wall construction followed precise patterns developed through generations of experience. Large foundation stones provided stability on uneven cliff surfaces. Smaller blocks filled gaps and created level courses. Mortar sealed joints against wind and rain. The walls tapered slightly as they rose, distributing weight and improving earthquake resistance. Interior surfaces received smooth plaster made from fine clay and organic additives.

Room sizes were determined by function and available space—living quarters measured 6 by 8 feet on average, sufficient for family sleeping and storage. Granaries built into the driest locations stretched 12 to 15 feet long, holding enough corn to sustain families through the winter months. Kivas, the ceremonial chambers, followed standard circular patterns regardless of available space, demonstrating the spiritual importance of these structures.

Ventilation systems solved the challenge of smoke removal in enclosed spaces. Fireplaces built into corners directed smoke toward natural chimneys formed by cliff cracks. Deliberately placed gaps between roof beams allowed hot air to escape upward. Fresh air entered through doorways and windows positioned to create cross-ventilation. These systems prevented carbon monoxide poisoning in tightly sealed winter quarters.

Water management required constant attention and ingenious solutions. Natural seeps provided reliable sources even during drought periods. Builders carved channels to direct water flow into storage basins. Clay-lined reservoirs held rainwater collected from rock surfaces during brief but intense desert storms. Some dwellings featured interior wells dug down to underground springs.

*Ancient American Civilizations*

# Hovenweep: Precision Stone Tower Construction

Thirty miles west of Mesa Verde, another architectural wonder rose from the high desert. Hovenweep's towers dominated the landscape with geometric precision that seemed to defy the organic curves of desert sandstone. These structures reached heights of 20 feet or more, built entirely from carefully fitted stone blocks without mortar or internal support frames.

Castle Rock, the most impressive tower, stood like a medieval fortress transported to the American Southwest. The circular structure measured 15 feet in diameter at its base and rose in perfectly vertical walls. Small windows pierced the stonework at regular intervals, providing interior light and defensive positions. A single doorway, elevated 6 feet above ground level, controlled all access to the interior.

The construction of these towers challenged every assumption about ancient building capabilities. Builders had no pulleys, cranes, or mechanical lifting devices. They raised multi-ton stone blocks to heights of 20 feet using only human strength, wooden levers, and earthen ramps. Each stone required precise shaping to fit perfectly with its neighbors. Gaps between blocks measured less than an inch, creating walls so stable they have survived 700 years of high desert weather.

The engineering principles behind tower construction revealed a sophisticated understanding of structural mechanics. The circular bases distributed weight evenly, preventing foundation settling in sandy soil. Walls tapered slightly inward as they rose, creating inherent stability that improved with height. Interior cross-walls provided additional support and created separate chambers for different functions.

Square Tower House demonstrated a different approach to the same engineering challenges. The rectangular structure rose from a natural sandstone ledge, incorporating the living rock into its foundation. Builders extended walls upward from this solid base, creating a structure that seemed to grow naturally from the cliff face. The design merged human architecture with natural geology so seamlessly that determining where rock ended and construction began required careful examination.

Holly Tower introduced another architectural innovation - the keyhole doorway. The entrance began as a standard rectangular opening at ground level, then expanded into a T-shape that allowed passage for people

*Ancient American Civilizations*

carrying large loads. This design solved practical problems of moving pottery, baskets, and food supplies into elevated storage areas. The distinctive shape became a trademark of Hovenweep construction techniques.

Interior spaces within the towers served specialized functions. Ground floors typically housed storage areas for corn, beans, and other preserved foods. Upper levels provided living quarters with fireplaces, sleeping areas, and work spaces. The highest chambers functioned as observation posts, offering panoramic views across miles of desert landscape. Guards stationed in these positions could spot approaching visitors or enemies hours before they reached the settlement.

Window placement followed careful calculations based on solar angles and seasonal changes. South-facing openings captured winter sunlight for interior warming. North-facing windows provided cool air circulation during summer heat. East and west exposures allowed sunrise and sunset observations, important for agricultural and ceremonial timing. The precision of these alignments suggested builders possessed detailed knowledge of astronomical cycles.

# Advanced Water Management Systems

Water controlled life and death in the high desert. Annual precipitation averaged less than 12 inches per year, arriving in brief intense storms during summer monsoons and winter snows. Ancient builders developed complex systems to capture, store, and distribute every precious drop. These engineering achievements rivaled Roman aqueducts in sophistication and exceeded them in efficiency.

Check dams built across seasonal drainage channels created the foundation of the entire system. Builders constructed stone barriers 3 to 4 feet high across natural water courses. During flash floods, these dams slowed water flow and trapped sediment behind them. Over time, fertile soil accumulated in these artificial terraces, creating agricultural plots where crops could survive on retained moisture long after surface water disappeared.

The dam construction required precise understanding of desert hydrology. Builders selected sites where bedrock lay close to the surface, preventing water from seeping away underground. They positioned barriers to withstand flood forces that could move boulders weighing several tons. Stone placement followed engineering principles that distributed hydraulic pressure evenly across the structure. Most of these dams continue to function perfectly after seven centuries of use.

Terraced fields stretched for miles below the check dams, transforming natural canyons into productive agricultural landscapes. Each terrace measured 50 to 100 feet long and 20 to 30 feet wide, sized to match available water flow and family labor capacity. Stone retaining walls held soil in place during severe storms. Carefully graded surfaces directed water movement between levels, ensuring every terrace received adequate moisture.

Crop selection matched water availability with remarkable precision. Corn varieties adapted to desert conditions could survive on minimal rainfall supplemented by runoff from surrounding cliffs. Beans planted between corn rows added nitrogen to the soil and provided protein in the human diet. Squash vines spread across terrace surfaces, their broad leaves reducing evaporation and providing additional food sources. This agricultural triad supported substantial populations in an environment that challenges modern farming techniques.

Reservoir systems captured and stored water from natural rock surfaces. Mesa tops functioned as enormous watershed areas, channeling rainfall into carefully constructed collection basins. Builders carved channels through solid sandstone to direct water flow over distances of several hundred yards. Clay linings sealed storage areas against evaporation and seepage. These reservoirs could hold thousands of gallons, sustaining communities through extended drought periods.

Spring development represented the most sophisticated water management achievement. Builders located underground water sources by observing vegetation patterns, seasonal moisture changes, and natural seepage areas. They excavated carefully designed tunnels to tap these springs without disturbing the natural flow patterns. Stone-lined channels carried water from sources to consumption areas, sometimes requiring construction across steep canyon walls and around natural obstacles.

Domestic water systems brought spring water directly into cliff dwellings through ingenious distribution networks. Builders carved channels into cliff faces, creating gravity-fed systems that delivered water to interior courtyards and storage areas. Some houses featured stone-lined basins that functioned as household reservoirs, holding several days' water supply for cooking, drinking, and limited washing. Overflow systems prevented waste during periods of abundant flow.

# 1270 CE: Coordinated Regional Departure

The year 1270 marked the beginning of one of archaeology's greatest mysteries. Across the Four Corners region, thousands of people began abandoning cliff dwellings and mesa-top villages they had occupied for generations. The departure was not sudden panic or military retreat. Evidence suggests a planned, coordinated evacuation that unfolded over several decades.

Tree-ring studies revealed the environmental conditions that triggered the decision. A severe drought began around 1276 and persisted for 23 years. This was not the first drought the region had experienced, but it proved more severe and longer-lasting than previous dry periods. Stream flows dropped to minimal levels. Springs that had flowed for centuries went dry. Agricultural yields fell below subsistence levels even in the most productive areas.

The response demonstrated remarkable social organization and forward planning. Communities did not wait for starvation to force hasty evacuations. Archaeological evidence shows systematic removal of valuable items, careful sealing of storage areas, and deliberate abandonment of structures too large or fragile to transport. People took pottery, tools, and personal possessions but left behind grinding stones, large storage jars, and architectural elements that could be recreated at new locations.

Population movements followed established trade routes and kinship networks rather than random migration patterns. Groups traveled south toward the Rio Grande valley and the Little Colorado River basin, areas with more reliable water sources and established agricultural communities. The migrations were not desperate refugee movements but organized relocations that maintained family and clan relationships across hundreds of miles.

Archaeological evidence at destination sites confirms the successful integration of Four Corners populations into existing communities. New architectural styles emerged, combining cliff dwelling techniques with local building traditions. Pottery designs merged Four Corners geometric patterns with southern artistic motifs. Agricultural practices improved as refugees introduced advanced water management techniques to their new homes.

The abandoned cliff dwellings preserve evidence of the departure process. Storage rooms contain pottery vessels deliberately broken to prevent use by others, a practice that demonstrated respect for abandoned homes and discouraged casual reoccupation. Wooden roof beams show careful removal rather than hurried destruction. Personal items left behind were placed in protected locations, suggesting their owners expected to return someday.

Some cliff dwellings showed signs of ritual closure ceremonies. Sacred objects were buried in special locations within kivas and residential areas. Fires were lit in ceremonial chambers and allowed to burn completely, leaving deposits of ritual ashes mixed with rare materials brought from distant locations. These practices transformed abandoned structures into memorial sites honoring ancestral connections to the land.

The decision to leave demonstrated a profound understanding of environmental limits and sustainable resource use. Rather than depleting remaining water sources and destroying agricultural lands through overuse, communities chose voluntary relocation that preserved the Four Corners region for future generations. This decision required cultural values that placed long-term environmental health above short-term settlement preferences.

Modern Pueblo peoples, descendants of the cliff dwellers, maintain oral traditions that describe the departure as a necessary spiritual journey rather than forced abandonment. According to these traditions, each place has its proper time of human occupation. When that time ends, people must move on to allow the land to rest and regenerate. The Four Corners departure was not failure but fulfillment of ancient obligations to maintain balance between human needs and natural systems.

The empty cliff dwellings stand today as monuments to human achievement and environmental wisdom. The builders solved extraordinary engineering challenges in one of North America's most demanding environments. They created architectural masterpieces that continue to inspire modern designers and builders. Most importantly, they demonstrated that advanced civilizations can make difficult decisions to preserve their environment for future generations.

Their departure was not the end of their story but its transformation into legend. The skills, knowledge, and cultural values they developed in the Four Corners region spread throughout the Southwest, enriching dozens of communities that continue to honor their cliff-dwelling ancestors. The empty towers and silent rooms remind us that sometimes the greatest achievement lies not in conquering an environment but in knowing when to step away and let it heal.

# Chapter 8: Chaco Canyon - Reading the Cosmic Clock

## Sun Dagger: Solstice and Equinox Marker

Anna Sofaer climbed the steep sandstone face of Fajada Butte on a blazing June morning in 1977. The New Mexico sun beat down mercilessly on the high desert plateau. Sofaer, an artist and amateur archaeologist, had noticed unusual rock formations near the summit during previous visits to Chaco Canyon. Three massive stone slabs leaned against the cliff face at peculiar angles. Behind them, carved into the rock wall, a spiral petroglyph caught her attention.

The spiral measured eighteen inches across. Its carefully carved groove spiraled inward from the outer edge to a central point. Local Pueblo peoples had created similar designs for centuries, but this carving seemed different. Its placement behind the stone slabs suggested deliberate planning. Sofaer suspected the arrangement had astronomical significance.

On June 21st, the summer solstice, she positioned herself behind the stone slabs at precisely noon. A thin shaft of sunlight pierced through the gap between two of the massive rocks. The beam struck the spiral carving with mathematical precision. The light formed a perfect dagger of illumination that bisected the spiral exactly through its center. The beam measured less than two inches wide and six inches long. It lasted for eighteen minutes before the sun's movement shifted the light away from the target.

Sofaer returned to Fajada Butte throughout the year to document the light patterns. During the winter solstice on December 21st, two parallel shafts of light appeared. They framed the spiral's outer edges with extraordinary accuracy. The twin daggers of illumination bracketed the carving like celestial parentheses marking the sun's southernmost journey.

The spring and autumn equinoxes produced another configuration entirely. On March 20th and September 22nd, a single light beam cut through the spiral at an angle, kissing the spiral's edge with perfect timing. The ancient creators had designed a natural solar calendar with precision rivaling modern instruments.

Sofaer's documentation revealed the sophistication behind this astronomical device. The three stone slabs weighed several tons each. Their current positions could not have occurred naturally. Human hands had moved and adjusted these massive rocks to create specific shadow patterns. The spiral carving itself showed careful planning. Its size, depth, and orientation aligned perfectly with the seasonal light displays.

The discovery sparked intense interest from professional astronomers. Dr. Robert Preston from the U.S. Naval Observatory traveled to Chaco Canyon to verify Sofaer's observations. His measurements confirmed her findings. The Sun Dagger marked solar events with an accuracy of plus or minus one day across the entire year. This precision exceeded the capabilities of most ancient calendars worldwide.

Further investigation revealed additional complexities. The stone arrangement also tracked lunar cycles with remarkable accuracy. During the 18.6-year major lunar standstill, when the moon reaches its maximum northern and southern positions, additional light patterns appeared on the spiral. These lunar markers occurred so rarely that their discovery suggested generations of continuous observation and refinement.

The Sun Dagger functioned as more than a calendar. It served as a cosmic computer, calculating the intersection of solar and lunar cycles over decades. The ancient astronomers of Chaco Canyon had created a three-dimensional instrument that could predict eclipses, plan agricultural activities, and coordinate religious ceremonies with celestial events.

Local Navajo guides had known about the site for generations. They called it "the place where the sun talks to the stone." Their oral traditions described ancient peoples who "read the sky like a book" and "built houses that listened to the stars." These stories, dismissed by early archaeologists as folklore, proved to contain accurate descriptions of astronomical practices.

The site's vulnerability became apparent in the 1980s. Tourist traffic began destabilizing the delicate stone arrangements. Vibrations from hiking boots and camera equipment threatened the precise alignments developed over centuries. The National Park Service restricted access to protect the monument, but natural erosion continued threatening the stone slabs.

By 1989, one of the three key stones had shifted slightly due to natural weathering. The Sun Dagger's light patterns became less precise. The ancient astronomical device, which had functioned for over a thousand years, began losing its accuracy. Modern attempts to restore the original alignments faced ethical dilemmas about interfering with natural processes.

The Sun Dagger stands as a testament to the astronomical expertise of Chaco Canyon's builders. They understood solar mechanics with precision that modern science respects. They created permanent instruments that would function for centuries without maintenance. They encoded complex mathematical relationships into stone arrangements that continue teaching us about their sophisticated worldview.

# 18.6-Year Lunar Cycle Architectural Alignments

Dr. Michael Zeilik arrived at Chaco Canyon in 1982 with a mission to map every architectural alignment in the ancient complex. An astronomer at the University of New Mexico, Zeilik brought specialized equipment to measure building orientations with precision unavailable to earlier researchers. His surveys would reveal astronomical knowledge of breathtaking sophistication.

The major lunar standstill occurs every 18.6 years when the moon reaches its extreme northern and southern positions on the horizon. This cycle results from complex gravitational interactions between Earth, moon, and sun. Modern astronomy requires years of careful observation to document the full cycle. Ancient peoples who tracked this phenomenon possessed extraordinary patience and mathematical ability.

Zeilik's first target was Casa Rinconada, Chaco Canyon's largest circular ceremonial structure. The great kiva measured 63 feet in diameter and featured carefully placed openings around its perimeter. Previous archaeologists had noted that the main doorway faced north, unusual for Ancestral Puebloan architecture. Most kiva entrances oriented toward the southeast.

Setting up his theodolite at the center of Casa Rinconada, Zeilik measured the azimuth of each architectural feature. The northern entrance aligned precisely with the major lunar standstill's northernmost moonrise position. The measurement matched astronomical predictions within half a degree. This accuracy could not result from coincidence.

Further measurements revealed additional lunar alignments throughout the structure. Wall niches, interior features, and secondary openings are all related to specific lunar positions during the 18.6-year cycle. The builders had created a three-dimensional lunar observatory disguised as a ceremonial building.

Pueblo Bonito, Chaco Canyon's most famous great house, yielded even more startling discoveries. The building's peculiar D-shaped plan had puzzled archaeologists since its discovery in the 1890s. Zeilik's measurements revealed the structure's true purpose. The building functioned as a massive lunar calendar encoded in stone.

The room blocks of Pueblo Bonito aligned with different phases of the major lunar standstill. The building's central wall, which divided the structure into northern and southern sections, pointed directly toward the moon's maximum southern position during standstill events. Individual room clusters marked intermediate positions in the lunar cycle.

Construction details supported the astronomical interpretation. Doorways, windows, and interior walls throughout Pueblo Bonito incorporated lunar alignments. Room 33, situated at a pivotal point in the structure, featured a window that framed the standstill moonrise with perfect accuracy. The opening measured exactly the right size to accommodate the moon's apparent diameter during these events.

Hungo Pavi, another major great house, displayed similar lunar connections. The building's main axis aligned with the major standstill's extreme positions. Room arrangements followed patterns based on lunar mathematics. Even minor architectural details reflected astronomical considerations.

The complexity of these alignments suggested professional astronomical knowledge. Tracking the major lunar standstill requires nearly two decades of continuous observation. The cycle's subtle variations demand mathematical sophistication to predict accurately. The Chacoan builders possessed both the patience and expertise necessary for such long-term projects.

Modern Pueblo peoples confirmed the astronomical interpretations. Hopi elders described traditional knowledge about lunar cycles and their relationship to agricultural timing. Rio Grande Pueblo communities maintained ceremonial calendars based on lunar observations spanning multiple generations. These contemporary practices reflected ancient traditions preserved across centuries.

The 18.6-year cycle influenced construction scheduling at Chaco Canyon. Major building projects began and ended to coincide with standstill events. Tree-ring dating of wooden beams revealed that construction phases aligned with the lunar calendar. The builders timed their most ambitious projects to ceremonial moments when earth and sky achieved perfect harmony.

Archaeological evidence supported the astronomical theories. Specialized artifacts found in great houses included carved stone discs, painted ceramics, and turquoise ornaments decorated with lunar symbols. These objects suggested a professional priesthood dedicated to astronomical observation and calendar maintenance.

The lunar alignments extended beyond individual buildings to encompass the entire Chaco Canyon complex. Roads, water management systems, and ceremonial features all incorporated astronomical orientations. The ancient planners had created a landscape-scale observatory where human activities synchronized with celestial cycles.

Climate data from tree rings indicated that major construction periods coincided with favorable weather patterns during lunar standstill years. The builders may have recognized correlations between astronomical cycles and environmental conditions. Their timing of construction projects reflected both celestial knowledge and practical weather prediction.

# Great Houses: Hundreds of Rooms in Astronomical Order

Pueblo Bonito rose from the canyon floor like a massive stone crescentn, its 650 rooms arranged in perfect geometric harmony. Neil Judd led the first systematic excavation of this architectural marvel in 1921, but he could never have imagined the cosmic blueprint hidden within its walls. Each room block, every doorway, and all interior features followed patterns dictated by the movements of sun, moon, and stars.

The building's construction spanned nearly three centuries, from 850 to 1150 CE. Each generation of builders added new room blocks according to the same astronomical principles. The result was a four-story structure that functioned as both a residential complex and a celestial observatory.

*Ancient American Civilizations*

Over 800 people could live comfortably within its walls during peak occupation periods.

The great house's D-shaped floor plan reflected sophisticated geometric knowledge. The curved back wall traced a perfect arc based on astronomical calculations. The straight front wall aligned with the summer solstice sunrise. The building's central axis pointed directly toward the moon's southernmost position during major standstill events. These orientations were no accident.

Room arrangements followed patterns based on solar geometry. The northern room blocks contained exactly 29 ground-floor chambers, matching the average lunar month. The southern section held 28 rooms, corresponding to the sidereal lunar month. Mathematically trained architects had encoded calendar systems directly into the building's layout.

Interior features reinforced the astronomical themes. Room 33, positioned at the building's exact center, contained a circular fire hearth aligned with the cardinal directions. Four wooden posts supported the roof at positions marking the solstices and equinoxes. The room functioned as a three-dimensional calendar where priests could track seasonal changes through shadow patterns cast by the posts.

Upper-story rooms provided elevated platforms for astronomical observation. Windows in these chambers framed specific celestial events with precision. The famous corner window in the building's southwestern section captured the winter solstice sunrise. Other openings marked equinoxes, lunar standstills, and the rising positions of bright stars used for navigation.

Chetro Ketl, Chaco Canyon's second-largest great house, demonstrated similar astronomical sophistication. The building contained over 500 rooms arranged in a rectangular plan oriented to cardinal directions. Construction began around 1020 CE and continued for over a century. Each building phase incorporated additional astronomical features.

The great kiva at Chetro Ketl measured 62 feet in diameter and featured unique architectural elements. Six massive stone pillars supported the roof at positions corresponding to the six lunar months between standstill events. The pillars' arrangement created sight lines toward different lunar positions throughout the 18.6-year cycle.

Pueblo del Arroyo displayed the most complex astronomical arrangements of any Chaco great house. Built between 1075 and 1110 CE, the structure incorporated alignments to solar, lunar, and stellar events simultaneously. The building's tri-wall structure created multiple observation platforms for tracking different celestial cycles.

The construction process itself reflected astronomical timing. Tree-ring analysis of wooden beams revealed that major building campaigns began during specific lunar phases. Ground-breaking ceremonies occurred at winter solstice. Room dedication rituals took place during equinoxes. The builders synchronized their construction schedule with the cosmic calendar they were creating.

Specialized rooms within the great houses served specific astronomical functions. Corner rooms with no internal access contained stone platforms for instrument storage. Chambers with unusual ventilation systems may have housed fire altars used for nighttime observations. Rooms with precisely positioned wall openings framed celestial events too subtle for casual observation.

The great houses communicated with each other through architectural alignments. Sight lines between buildings created an integrated observation network spanning the entire canyon. Signals could be passed between structures during important astronomical events. The entire complex functioned as a distributed observatory with multiple interconnected observation posts.

Population estimates based on room counts and archaeological evidence suggest that Chaco Canyon housed between 2,000 and 5,000 people during its peak period. This concentration of residents provided the workforce necessary for continuous astronomical observation and data recording. Professional astronomer-priests could dedicate their lives to celestial studies.

The great houses also served economic functions related to their astronomical purpose. Accurate calendar systems enabled precise agricultural timing. Traders could schedule long-distance expeditions to arrive at destinations during optimal weather conditions. Religious ceremonies could be coordinated across vast distances through shared astronomical knowledge.

Artifact distributions within the great houses reflected their astronomical functions. Rooms associated with celestial observation contained specialized tools: carved stone discs for measuring angles, polished obsidian mirrors for reflecting sunlight, and ceramic vessels painted with astronomical symbols. These objects suggest professional astronomical equipment.

# Straight Roads: 30-Foot-Wide Ceremonial Pathways

The road stretched arrow-straight across the high desert, ignoring every natural obstacle in its path. Where hills blocked the way, ancient engineers cut through solid rock. Where arroyos interrupted the route, they built stone causeways. Nothing deflected this pathway from its predetermined course toward the horizon.

Thomas Lyons first spotted the roads from an airplane in 1971. As a remote sensing specialist for the National Park Service, Lyons was conducting aerial photography surveys of Chaco Canyon when he noticed unusual linear features extending far beyond the ancient ruins. The markings appeared too straight and purposeful to be natural formations.

Ground reconnaissance confirmed Lyons' suspicions. These were indeed roads, but unlike any transportation network built by ancient peoples anywhere in the world. The pathways averaged 30 feet in width, far broader than necessary for foot traffic. They maintained precise orientations across distances exceeding 50 miles. Their construction required engineering skills that historians had never attributed to Ancestral Puebloan cultures.

The Great North Road became the most intensively studied of these mysterious pathways. Beginning at Pueblo Bonito's front entrance, the road ran due north for 50 miles through some of New Mexico's most challenging terrain. It climbed mesa walls, crossed deep canyons, and maintained its bearing with compass-like accuracy. The destination remained unclear, as the road seemed to end abruptly in the middle of the desert.

Construction techniques varied according to local conditions. In soft soil areas, builders excavated roadbeds 2 to 4 feet deep. They lined the excavations with carefully selected stones and filled them with smaller rocks and gravel. The resulting surface could support heavy foot traffic for centuries without maintenance.

*Ancient American Civilizations*

Rocky terrain required different approaches. Ancient engineers carved roadways directly into sandstone bedrock using stone tools. They removed thousands of tons of rock to create passages through natural barriers. The precision of this rock cutting exceeded anything expected from a culture supposedly lacking metal tools.

Aerial surveys revealed the full extent of the road network. Over 400 miles of constructed roadways connected Chaco Canyon to distant communities throughout the Four Corners region. Some roads led to major population centers like Aztec Ruins and Salmon Ruins. Others terminated at isolated shrines or seemingly empty locations in the wilderness.

The roads' orientations followed astronomical principles rather than practical transportation needs. Many pathways pointed directly toward solstice and equinox positions on the horizon. Others aligned with the rising and setting positions of bright stars used for navigation. The road network functioned as a giant compass rose centered on Chaco Canyon.

Archaeological evidence along the roadways provided clues about their use. Pottery sherds, stone tools, and food remains suggested regular foot traffic over extended periods. However, the artifact densities were much lower than expected for major transportation corridors. The roads served purposes beyond simple travel between communities.

Modern Pueblo peoples offered insights into the roads' significance. Hopi elders described traditional concepts of "straight paths" that connected sacred sites across long distances. These spiritual highways required ritual purification before travel. Religious pilgrimages followed predetermined routes between important ceremonial locations.

The construction process itself carried ceremonial significance. Oral traditions described community gatherings where hundreds of people worked together on road projects. These construction events combined practical labor with religious observance. The completed pathways created permanent connections between communities and sacred landscapes.

Stairways carved into cliff faces provided access between different elevation levels along the roads. These stone steps were cut with precision that amazed early archaeologists. Some stairway systems contained over 100 individual steps carved directly into vertical rock

*Ancient American Civilizations*

faces. Hand and toe holds assisted travelers navigating the steepest sections.

Signal stations positioned along the roads enabled long-distance communication. Stone platforms built at elevated locations provided clear sight lines between distant points. During important events, fire signals could relay messages across the entire network within hours. This communication system coordinated activities across a region larger than many European kingdoms.

Roadside shrines marked essential points along the major pathways. These small stone structures contained offerings left by travelers: pottery vessels, turquoise beads, carved shell ornaments, and prayer sticks. The shrines provided rest stops where pilgrims could make spiritual preparations before continuing their journeys.

Tree-ring dating of wooden posts found along roadways indicated that construction occurred in coordinated phases during the 11th century. Major building campaigns coincided with astronomical events, particularly lunar standstills. The roads were not built randomly but according to ceremonial calendars based on celestial cycles.

Modern attempts to walk the ancient roads revealed their remarkable engineering. Despite centuries of erosion and neglect, the roadbeds remained clearly visible across much of their length. The original construction had been so substantial that the pathways survived a millennium of desert weather with minimal deterioration.

# Acoustic Engineering in Sacred Structures

The sound began as a whisper and grew into something magnificent. Dr. David Lubman stood at the base of the great stairway leading to El Castillo pyramid at Chichen Itza, 800 miles southeast of Chaco Canyon. When he clapped his hands once, the stone steps above him returned a haunting echo that sounded like the call of a quetzal bird. Maya engineers had designed their pyramid as a giant musical instrument.

This discovery sent Lubman on a quest to document acoustic phenomena at ancient American sites. His background in architectural acoustics, combined with sophisticated audio recording equipment, revealed that many prehistoric structures incorporated deliberate sound engineering.

Chaco Canyon would prove to contain some of the most advanced acoustic designs ever created.

Casa Rinconada, the great kiva at Chaco Canyon, demonstrated acoustic properties that defied explanation. The circular chamber measured 63 feet in diameter with stone walls rising 14 feet above the floor. When Lubman and his team conducted sound tests inside the structure, they discovered something remarkable. A person speaking in a normal voice at the chamber's center could be heard clearly by listeners anywhere along the perimeter walls.

The acoustic enhancement resulted from carefully calculated proportions. The kiva's diameter-to-height ratio created natural amplification for human voices. Sound waves reflected off the curved walls and concentrated at specific listening positions. The architects had designed a public address system using only stone and mathematical knowledge.

Further tests revealed additional acoustic features. Certain positions on the kiva floor produced distinctive echo effects. Footsteps at these locations generated sounds resembling thunder, rainfall, or animal calls. Priests conducting ceremonies could create audio effects that enhanced the spiritual atmosphere of religious gatherings.

Pueblo Bonito contained multiple rooms with specialized acoustic properties. Room 33, the building's central chamber, functioned as an echo chamber where whispered conversations could be heard throughout the structure. The room's dimensions and wall treatments created acoustic conditions that allowed private communications between distant parts of the building.

Upper-story rooms in Pueblo Bonito served as acoustic observation posts. Chambers positioned directly above the plaza could monitor conversations and activities occurring far below. The buildings' architects had created surveillance systems that enabled discreet monitoring of public gatherings and private meetings.

The acoustic engineering extended to outdoor spaces as well. Plaza areas between major structures were shaped to enhance sound projection. Natural rock formations were modified to create reflection surfaces that carried human voices across long distances. Public announcements made from elevated platforms could reach audiences scattered throughout the canyon.

Specialized artifacts found at Chaco sites supported the acoustic interpretations. Wooden flutes, bone whistles, and shell trumpets demonstrated the residents' interest in musical instruments. Ceramic vessels designed for specific tonal qualities served as resonators during ceremonial performances. The material culture reflected a society that valued acoustic refinement.

Modern Pueblo communities provided a cultural context for understanding Chaco's acoustic features. Traditional ceremonies incorporated complex soundscapes combining human voices, musical instruments, and natural acoustics. Ritual performances in contemporary kivas still demonstrated sophisticated understanding of architectural acoustics principles.

The acoustic properties of Chaco structures influenced their ceremonial use. Rooms with exceptional sound enhancement hosted important religious gatherings. Chambers with echo effects were reserved for specific types of spiritual practices. The buildings' architects had matched acoustic properties to ceremonial functions with remarkable precision.

Maintenance of acoustic properties required ongoing attention to architectural details. Wall surfaces needed periodic refinishing to preserve optimal reflection characteristics. Interior features required careful positioning to maintain sound enhancement effects. The residents understood that acoustic performance depended on meticulous building maintenance.

Digital audio analysis revealed the sophisticated mathematics behind Chaco's acoustic design. Room dimensions followed proportional relationships based on harmonic ratios. Wall curvatures incorporated geometric principles that optimized sound reflection patterns. The ancient architects had applied acoustic engineering principles that modern designers struggle to match.

The acoustic features also served practical communication needs. Signal systems based on distinctive sound patterns enabled long-distance messaging between structures. Acoustic warning systems could alert residents to approaching dangers or important events. The sound engineering enhanced both ceremonial and administrative functions.

Environmental factors influenced the effectiveness of Chaco's acoustic systems. Sound transmission varied with temperature, humidity, and wind conditions. The ancient residents developed operational procedures that maximized acoustic performance under different weather conditions. Their understanding of environmental acoustics exceeded that of most contemporary sound engineers.

Archaeological evidence suggested that acoustic specialists lived at Chaco Canyon during its occupation period. Specialized tool kits for fine-tuning architectural features indicated professional knowledge of sound engineering. The concentration of acoustic expertise at one location reflects the site's importance as a regional center for advanced technical knowledge.

# Chapter 9: Amazon Architects - The Forest Cities

## LIDAR Discoveries: 450+ Geometric Earthworks

Dr. Alceu Ranzi pressed his face against the small airplane window as it banked over the Brazilian rainforest in 1999. Below him, the endless green canopy stretched to every horizon. Then something caught his eye. Geometric shapes appeared in a recently deforested area. Perfect circles and squares cut into the red earth. Lines too straight to be natural. Patterns too precise to be coincidental.

Ranzi had spent decades studying the Amazon basin. He knew every theory about its ancient inhabitants. Small hunter-gatherer bands. Scattered fishing villages. Simple societies living lightly on the land. The shapes below suggested something entirely different. These were the marks of organized communities. Large populations. Sophisticated planning.

The pilot circled lower. More geometric forms came into view. Octagons connected by perfectly straight roads. Rectangular enclosures surrounding circular plazas. Canal systems linking distant sites. The precision rivaled ancient Roman engineering. The scale exceeded anything European colonists had ever described.

Ranzi began photographing everything he could see. His camera captured dozens of earthworks in a single flight. Each formation showed deliberate design. Each location revealed careful site selection. Communities had not randomly chosen these places. They had planned entire landscapes according to principles modern archaeologists barely understood.

The discovery launched twenty-five years of intensive research. International teams equipped with cutting-edge technology descended on the Amazon. LIDAR sensors mounted on aircraft could penetrate the jungle canopy and map ground features with centimeter precision. Satellite imagery revealed patterns invisible from ground level. Ground-penetrating radar exposed buried structures beneath forest floors.

Results exceeded every expectation. Over 450 geometric earthworks appeared across the Amazon basin. Some measured over 350 meters in diameter. Others formed complex networks spanning dozens of square kilometers. The sites concentrated in western Brazil, eastern Peru, and northern Bolivia. They followed river systems and occupied elevated terraces safe from seasonal flooding.

Each earthwork required enormous labor investment. Workers had moved millions of cubic meters of soil using only wooden tools and human muscle. They carved ditches up to 4 meters deep and 10 meters wide. They built earthen walls rising 3 meters above ground level. Construction projects involved hundreds of people working for decades.

The geometric precision amazed archaeologists. Circles achieved near-perfect roundness. Squares maintained exact right angles. Connecting roads ran in straight lines for kilometers regardless of topography. Builders had possessed sophisticated surveying techniques and mathematical knowledge. They understood geometry, astronomy, and landscape engineering at levels comparable to ancient civilizations anywhere in the world.

Dating evidence placed most constructions between 1000 and 1500 CE. Some sites showed evidence of much earlier occupation. Pottery fragments and charcoal samples suggested human presence stretching back over 2000 years. These were not recent developments. Amazonian societies had been creating monumental earthworks for millennia.

The earthworks served multiple purposes. Some functioned as ceremonial centers with central plazas surrounded by earthen walls. Others appeared defensive with complex ditch and rampart systems— many combined residential, ceremonial, and agricultural functions in integrated urban complexes. Archaeological excavations revealed post holes from massive wooden structures, elaborate burial sites, and sophisticated drainage systems.

Dr. Michael Heckenberger spent years mapping earthwork distributions across the southern Amazon. His research revealed intentional spacing between sites. Communities maintained territories of specific sizes. Travel routes connected distant settlements. The organization suggested regional governance systems and coordinated resource management on scales previously unimaginable for Amazonian societies.

The environmental impact was equally surprising. Earthwork construction had required extensive forest clearing. Soil analysis showed evidence of controlled burning and selective tree removal. Agricultural terraces surrounded many sites. Raised fields improved drainage and prevented erosion. Ancient engineers had modified entire watersheds to support dense populations.

Modern indigenous communities preserve oral traditions describing these ancient builders. Stories speak of powerful ancestors who could move earth with supernatural abilities. Elders describe times when the forest was filled with cities and roads. Archaeological evidence supports these memories. The Amazon was never an untouched wilderness. It was a managed landscape shaped by human engineering for thousands of years.

# Llanos de Moxos: Raised Agricultural Field Systems

The flooding came every year like clockwork. Dr. Clark Erickson watched from his helicopter as the Beni River overflowed its banks across the Llanos de Moxos in Bolivia. Water spread across hundreds of square kilometers of grassland. The seasonal inundation turned solid ground into temporary lakes. Fish swam where cattle had grazed weeks earlier.

Most archaeologists saw this landscape as unsuitable for ancient agriculture. Annual floods made permanent settlement impossible. Saturated soils prevented crop cultivation. The region could only support small populations of hunter-gatherers who followed the water cycle between higher and lower ground.

Erickson saw something different. His aerial photographs revealed subtle patterns across the flooded plains. Long ridges rose slightly above the water level. Straight lines connected distant elevated areas. Geometric shapes appeared in the grassland like crop circles drawn by ancient hands. The patterns were too regular to be natural. They showed evidence of massive human modification.

Excavation revealed the truth. Ancient engineers had transformed the Llanos de Moxos into the world's largest wetland agricultural system. They built thousands of raised fields across 6000 square kilometers of seasonally flooded savanna. Individual fields measured up to 200 meters long and 3 meters high. Canals between fields provided drainage during wet seasons and irrigation during dry periods.

Construction began over 2000 years ago. Workers used wooden tools and woven baskets to move enormous quantities of soil. They built fields in carefully planned networks with standardized dimensions and orientations. Canal systems connected individual farms into integrated watershed management projects. The scale rivaled public works programs in ancient Egypt or Mesopotamia.

The engineering solved fundamental environmental challenges. Raised fields provided well-drained planting surfaces during flood seasons. Canal water moderated temperature extremes and extended growing seasons. Aquatic plants and fish in canals supplied additional food sources. Organic matter from canal cleaning fertilized field soils. The system created productive agriculture in environments that defeated modern farmers.

Agricultural output supported dense populations. Ceramic evidence and settlement mounds indicate thousands of people lived across the Llanos de Moxos. Villages occupied elevated locations connected by elevated causeways that remained passable during floods. Trade networks linked agricultural communities with populations in surrounding highlands and lowlands.

The raised field technology spread throughout the Amazonian river systems. Similar agricultural earthworks appeared in Colombia, Venezuela, Guyana, and Suriname. Each region adapted the basic principles to local environmental conditions. Highland communities built terraces on mountain slopes. Lowland groups created drainage systems in wetland areas. River communities developed flood control projects along major waterways.

Dr. William Denevan calculated that raised field agriculture could have supported over one million people across the Amazon basin. His population estimates challenged every previous assessment of pre-Columbian Amazonian societies. The river systems had been home to complex civilizations with sophisticated technologies and dense urban populations.

Spanish colonial documents provide glimpses of these agricultural societies. Early explorers described vast cultivated landscapes along major rivers. They reported large settlements with impressive architecture and complex social organization. Francisco de Orellana's 1542 expedition documented continuous towns for hundreds of kilometers along the Amazon River.

Disease and disruption destroyed these agricultural civilizations within decades of European contact. Smallpox and other epidemics killed up to

*Ancient American Civilizations*

90% of indigenous populations. Survivors abandoned raised field systems and retreated to smaller settlements in remote areas. Forest gradually reclaimed agricultural landscapes. Rivers that had supported hundreds of thousands of people appeared nearly empty to later explorers.

The raised fields provide crucial insights into sustainable agriculture. Modern attempts to recreate ancient techniques have produced remarkable results. Experimental raised fields yield three times more crops than conventional agriculture in the same environments. They require no external fertilizers or pesticides. They improve soil quality over time rather than depleting it.

Climate change makes these ancient technologies increasingly relevant. Rising sea levels threaten coastal agriculture worldwide. Changing precipitation patterns challenge conventional farming methods. Raised field principles offer solutions for food production in marginal environments. Ancient Amazonian engineers developed techniques modern agriculture desperately needs to learn.

# Terra Preta: Human-Made Super-Fertile Soil

Wim Sombroek knelt and scooped up a handful of black soil from the Amazon forest floor. The earth felt different from typical rainforest dirt. It was richer, darker, and more crumbly. Chemical analysis would soon reveal its extraordinary composition. This soil contained three times more organic carbon than the surrounding areas. Phosphorus levels exceeded anything found in natural Amazonian soils. The black earth was not natural. Humans had created it.

Sombroek had discovered terra preta de índio - the black earth of the Indians. These soil deposits appeared at archaeological sites throughout the Amazon basin. They covered areas ranging from small garden plots to expanses of several square kilometers. Wherever terra preta occurred, ancient settlements had flourished. The correlation was perfect and undeniable.

Local farmers had known about black earth for generations. They preferred terra preta areas for planting crops. Corn, beans, and manioc grew larger and faster in black soil. Harvests were more abundant and reliable. Even after centuries of cultivation, terra preta remained more fertile than virgin forest soils. The earth seemed to regenerate itself.

Scientific investigation revealed the secret. Ancient Amazonian peoples had systematically created fertile soil through controlled composting and soil amendment. They mixed charcoal, ash, food waste, human waste, fish bones, and organic matter into carefully managed deposits. Microorganisms broke down organic materials and fixed nutrients in stable forms. The process created permanently fertile growing medium.

Charcoal was the crucial ingredient. Ancient peoples produced biochar through controlled burning of organic materials in low-oxygen environments. The resulting carbon was nearly pure and highly stable. It provided structure for soil organisms and prevented nutrient leaching. Terra preta contained up to 70 times more charcoal than natural soils.

Dr. Johannes Lehmann spent decades studying the Terra Preta formation. His research revealed a sophisticated understanding of soil chemistry among ancient Amazonian peoples. They knew exactly which materials to combine and in what proportions. They understood how different organic inputs affected soil properties. They managed composting processes to maximize nutrient retention and minimize harmful compounds.

The soil creation process required generations to complete. Families added organic matter to the same locations year after year. Children continued projects started by their grandparents. Communities invested decades in building soil capital for future generations. The approach required long-term thinking and collective commitment rarely seen in agricultural societies.

Terra preta supported much denser populations than previously thought possible in Amazonian environments. Natural rainforest soils are notoriously poor. Heavy rainfall leaches nutrients from surface layers. Tropical heat rapidly decomposes organic matter. Most plant nutrients are locked up in living vegetation rather than available in soil. Agricultural communities typically required large territories to support small populations.

Black earth changed these calculations completely. Terra preta plots produced abundant harvests year after year without declining fertility. Single sites could support hundreds of people indefinitely. Population density in terra preta areas reached levels comparable to intensive agricultural regions in other parts of the world. The Amazon had been home to complex urban civilizations.

*Ancient American Civilizations*

Archaeological evidence supports these population estimates. Terra preta sites contain deep deposits of pottery fragments, stone tools, and other cultural materials. Artifact density indicates continuous occupation for centuries or millennia. Settlement patterns show village hierarchies and regional integration typical of complex societies. The largest sites cover dozens of hectares and contain monumental earthworks.

Spanish colonial documents describe dense populations along Amazonian rivers. Early explorers reported continuous settlements for hundreds of kilometers. They described complex societies with social stratification, specialized crafts, and regional trade networks. These accounts seemed exaggerated until terra preta research confirmed their accuracy.

Modern agriculture is desperately trying to recreate the properties of terra preta. Biochar production has become a significant research focus. Scientists are experimenting with different organic inputs and management techniques. Some attempts have shown promising results. Others have failed to achieve terra preta's remarkable stability and fertility.

The challenge lies in understanding the complete system. Terra preta was not simply charcoal mixed with organic matter. It was the product of specific cultural practices, environmental conditions, and biological processes that modern science has not fully decoded. Ancient Amazonian peoples possessed knowledge about soil management that took centuries to develop and perfect.

Dr. Bruno Glaser's research team has identified over 3000 Terra Preta sites across the Amazon basin. New discoveries continue at a rapid pace. Each site provides additional insights into ancient soil management techniques. The research reveals the Amazon as a landscape shaped by human engineering rather than pristine wilderness.

Terra preta offers hope for sustainable agriculture in tropical environments. Conventional farming quickly depletes rainforest soils and requires constant external inputs. Terra preta principles could enable productive agriculture while building soil fertility over time. Ancient Amazonian innovations may provide solutions to modern food security challenges.

*Ancient American Civilizations*

# Kuikugu: Urban Complex with Defensive Earthworks

Dr. Michael Heckenberger wiped sweat from his forehead as he climbed the earthen rampart surrounding Kuikugu. The defensive wall rose 4 meters above the forest floor and stretched in a perfect circle around the ancient settlement. Construction had required moving thousands of tons of soil using only wooden tools and human labor. The engineering rivaled fortifications anywhere in the ancient world.

Kuikugu lay hidden in the Upper Xingu basin of central Brazil. Dense jungle canopy concealed the site from aerial observation. Only ground exploration could reveal its remarkable architecture. Heckenberger spent fifteen years mapping the complex with indigenous guides who preserved oral traditions about their ancestors' achievements.

The settlement covered over 20 square kilometers with a complex internal organization. Central plazas served as focal points for residential clusters. Raised roads connected different neighborhoods and extended for kilometers into surrounding forest. Defensive ditches and ramparts protected the entire urban area. The planning showed a sophisticated understanding of urban design and military engineering.

Construction began around 1200 CE during a period of population growth and social complexity in the Upper Xingu region. Multiple communities cooperated in building projects that required coordinated labor from hundreds of workers. Leadership hierarchies organized construction activities and managed resource distribution. The scale indicated centralized political authority over regional populations.

Kuikugu was not unique. Heckenberger's research revealed nineteen similar settlements across the Upper Xingu basin. Each site showed evidence of monumental earthworks, defensive systems, and urban planning. The settlements formed an integrated network connected by elevated roads and waterway management systems. Total population may have reached 50,000 people in a region previously thought to support only scattered hunter-gatherer bands.

The defensive earthworks suggest regional conflict and warfare. Communities invested enormous resources in fortification systems that served no purpose except military protection. Settlement locations emphasized defensive advantages. Many sites occupied elevated positions with commanding views of surrounding territory. Strategic placement indicated organized military competition between different groups.

Archaeological evidence reveals sophisticated military technology. Excavations uncovered large quantities of projectile points, including specialized war arrows different from hunting points. Skeletal remains show evidence of violent death and battlefield injuries. Trophy taking and ritual display of enemy remains indicated warrior cultures with complex military ideologies.

The urban organization impressed professional city planners. Streets followed geometric patterns with standardized widths and orientations. Residential areas showed evidence of social stratification with elite compounds near central plazas and common housing in peripheral zones. Public architecture included ceremonial buildings, community storage facilities, and specialized craft workshops.

Water management systems controlled seasonal flooding and provided reliable water supplies. Engineers diverted natural streams through artificial channels. They built reservoirs to store water during dry seasons. Drainage systems prevented flooding in residential areas. The hydraulic engineering required a detailed understanding of local hydrology and long-term environmental planning.

Agricultural systems supported the large urban population. Raised field complexes surrounded settlements and extended along river valleys. Forest gardens provided tree crops and supplementary foods. Fish weirs and dams increased aquatic protein production. The integrated agricultural systems could support population densities of 1000 people per square kilometer.

Trade networks connected Kuikugu with distant regions. Exotic materials found at the site included marine shells from the Atlantic coast, volcanic glass from the Andes, and specialized stones from highland quarries. Trade goods moved along river systems and overland routes maintained by regional political alliances. The economic integration indicates sophisticated commercial systems.

Spanish colonial documents provide limited information about Upper Xingu societies. Early explorers reported large settlements and complex chiefdoms along major rivers. But European diseases arrived before detailed ethnographic observation could occur. Indigenous populations collapsed within decades of first contact. Survivors abandoned urban centers and adopted simplified lifestyles focused on demographic survival.

Modern Kuikugu descendants preserve oral traditions about their ancestors' achievements. Stories describe powerful chiefs who commanded large armies and built impressive monuments. Genealogies trace descent from ancient rulers who established the political foundations of contemporary indigenous communities. Ceremonial practices maintain connections to ancestral urban centers.

The Kuikugu discoveries transformed the understanding of ancient Amazonian societies. Previous archaeological models had assumed the region could only support small, dispersed populations. The earthwork complexes revealed urban civilizations with monumental architecture, complex political systems, and sophisticated technologies. The Amazon had been home to states and empires comparable to those found elsewhere in the ancient world.

Contemporary indigenous communities use Kuikugu research to support land rights claims and cultural revitalization efforts. Archaeological evidence documents indigenous peoples' long-term occupation and sophisticated management of Amazonian landscapes. The research validates traditional knowledge and counters stereotypes about indigenous capabilities and environmental relationships.

# Pre-Contact Million-Person Forest Populations

Antonio de Herrera never expected to see what stretched before him along the Amazon River in 1542. Village after village lined both banks for hundreds of kilometers. Smoke rose from countless cooking fires. Canoes filled the river like a maritime highway. The Spanish chronicler estimated populations in the hundreds of thousands. His reports seemed impossible to later generations, who found only scattered settlements in the same areas.

Herrera traveled with Francisco de Orellana's expedition down the Amazon River. The Spanish explorers were the first Europeans to navigate the entire river system. Their accounts describe continuous settlements from the Andes to the Atlantic. They reported large towns with impressive architecture, complex social organization, and sophisticated agricultural systems. Indigenous populations appeared to number in the millions.

Later explorers found a very different Amazon. River banks that had supported dense populations appeared nearly empty. Large settlements had vanished. Agricultural systems lay abandoned. The few remaining indigenous communities seemed to represent simple hunter-gatherer societies with limited technological capabilities. European observers concluded that earlier accounts had been greatly exaggerated.

Modern research reveals the truth behind this demographic collapse. Disease epidemics introduced by European contact killed up to 90% of indigenous populations within a century. Smallpox, measles, and other infections spread faster than European explorers themselves. Communities collapsed before most could be observed or documented. The Amazon that later Europeans encountered was a post-apocalyptic landscape.

Dr. William Denevan pioneered research into pre-contact Amazonian populations. His analysis of early colonial documents, archaeological evidence, and environmental data suggested indigenous populations far exceeding previous estimates. The Amazon basin may have supported over 6 million people before European contact. Population densities along major rivers rivaled those of contemporary European agricultural regions.

The demographic estimates depend on understanding ancient Amazonian agricultural systems. Conventional models assumed slash-and-burn farming could only support scattered populations. Terra preta research revealed intensive agriculture capable of supporting dense urban settlements. Raised field systems provided reliable food production in seasonally flooded environments. Forest management techniques increased wild food availability.

Archaeological site distributions support high population estimates. Systematic surveys find indigenous settlements every few kilometers along major rivers. Site densities indicate continuous occupation with little unused territory. Artifact concentrations suggest individual settlements housed hundreds or thousands of people. The archaeological record points to millions of inhabitants across the Amazon basin.

Environmental evidence confirms large-scale human impact on Amazonian landscapes. Pollen analysis shows extensive forest clearing for agriculture beginning over 2000 years ago. Soil chemistry indicates widespread burning and cultivation. Species distributions reflect human selection and management over centuries. The Amazon was not a pristine wilderness but an anthropogenic landscape shaped by indigenous engineering.

Genetic studies of Amazonian tree species reveal human influence on forest composition. Food plants show evidence of artificial selection and dispersal by human communities. Valuable species occur at higher frequencies near archaeological sites. Forest diversity patterns reflect indigenous management practices rather than natural processes. Humans had been actively managing Amazonian ecosystems for millennia.

Modern indigenous communities preserve ecological knowledge developed over thousands of years. They maintain a sophisticated understanding of plant properties, animal behavior, and environmental cycles. Traditional management practices enhance the biodiversity and productivity of forest ecosystems. Indigenous territories show higher conservation success than government-protected areas.

The population collapse had catastrophic environmental consequences. Agricultural systems collapsed as communities died or fled. Forest gardens returned to wilderness. Raised field systems flooded and disappeared. Species maintained by human cultivation became extinct or rare. The Amazon that Europeans came to see as "natural" was actually a degraded landscape recovering from demographic catastrophe.

Climate change research reveals the global impact of Amazonian depopulation. Reforestation following the indigenous population's collapse removed significant amounts of carbon dioxide from the atmosphere. The cooling effect may have contributed to the Little Ice Age that affected global climate during the 16th and 17th centuries. Amazonian demographic collapse influenced worldwide environmental conditions.

Contemporary environmental debates often ignore indigenous history in the Amazon. Conservation policies treat the region as wilderness requiring protection from human impact. Indigenous communities face restrictions on traditional land use practices. Archaeological research reveals these policies misunderstand both historical ecology and indigenous capabilities.

Dr. Charles Clement's research documents over 11,000 years of indigenous landscape management in the Amazon. Forest composition, soil fertility, and species diversity all reflect human influence. Indigenous communities created and maintained the ecosystems that conservationists seek to protect. Effective environmental management requires incorporating indigenous knowledge and recognizing indigenous rights.

The million-person population estimates challenge fundamental assumptions about human-environment relationships in tropical forests. Conventional models assumed rainforest environments could only support small hunter-gatherer populations. Amazonian research reveals sophisticated urban civilizations that enhanced rather than degraded forest ecosystems. Indigenous societies achieved sustainable development on scales modern governments struggle to accomplish.

Genetic studies of contemporary indigenous populations preserve traces of ancient demographic patterns. DNA analysis reveals founder effects and population bottlenecks consistent with massive die-offs during the colonial period. Modern communities represent survivors of much larger ancestral populations. Their cultural traditions maintain fragments of knowledge systems that once supported millions of people.

The Amazonian demographic catastrophe ranks among history's greatest tragedies. Entire civilizations vanished within decades of European contact. Knowledge systems developed over millennia disappeared forever. Environmental management practices that sustained millions of people were lost. The scale of destruction exceeded anything caused by wars or natural disasters.

Recovery remains incomplete five centuries later. Indigenous populations continue to face pressures from development, disease, and cultural disruption. Traditional knowledge systems struggle to survive in rapidly changing environments. Archaeological sites face destruction from logging, mining, and agricultural expansion. The Amazon's indigenous heritage requires urgent protection and support.

Understanding pre-contact Amazonian populations changes perspectives on indigenous capabilities and environmental relationships. These were not simple societies living lightly on the land. They were complex civilizations that created sustainable abundance through sophisticated ecological management. Their achievements offer crucial insights for addressing contemporary environmental challenges and supporting indigenous rights and knowledge systems.

*Ancient American Civilizations*

# Chapter 10: El Dorado - The City That Never Was, Yet Always Existed

## Lake Guatavita: Original Golden Man Ceremony

The canoe glided across Lake Guatavita's mirror-still surface in the pre-dawn darkness. Four priests paddled the sacred vessel toward the center of the circular lake, high in Colombia's eastern mountains. Their passenger sat motionless, his naked body covered entirely in gold dust mixed with tree resin. The ritual had begun before sunrise, as tradition demanded.

The Muisca cacique, their supreme leader, carried offerings in woven baskets beside him, including gold figurines crafted by master artisans. Emeralds were mined from sacred caves, and ceramic vessels painted with geometric patterns were passed down through generations. These treasures would soon vanish forever beneath the dark waters.

Spanish conquistadors first heard whispers of this ceremony in 1537. They called it El Dorado - the gilded one. Indigenous peoples spoke of a man covered in gold who made offerings to the lake's spirit. The Spaniards listened with fevered attention. Gold meant wealth beyond imagination. Wealth meant power. Power meant survival in the brutal world of colonial conquest.

Captain Gonzalo Jiménez de Quesada led the first expedition into Muisca territory. His men had already pillaged countless villages across the Caribbean coast. They murdered chiefs who refused to reveal treasure locations. They tortured prisoners until gold appeared. The reports of El Dorado promised riches that would surpass even their bloodiest victories.

The reality disappointed them. The ceremony occurred only during the investiture of a new cacique, perhaps once in a generation. The gold dust washed off in the lake water. The offerings sank beyond recovery. No golden city crowned the mountaintops. No streets paved with precious metal gleamed in the highland sun.

Antonio de Sepúlveda attempted to drain Lake Guatavita in 1580. His workers cut a notch in the rim, allowing thousands of gallons to escape. The water level dropped enough to reveal muddy shorelines littered with gold and emerald offerings. Sepúlveda recovered enough treasure to fund his expedition and provide substantial profits for Spanish colonial authorities.

The drainage attempt revealed the ceremony's true magnitude. Generations of caciques had made offerings at this sacred site. The lake bottom held thousands of artifacts spanning centuries of Muisca religious practice. Each piece reflected sophisticated metallurgy and artistic achievement. The Spanish saw only raw material to be melted down for shipment to Europe.

Alexander von Humboldt visited the lake in 1801 during his scientific expedition through South America. Local residents still remembered stories about the golden man ceremony. They described how the new cacique would fast for days before his investiture. His body was prepared with sticky tree sap. Gold dust was blown through tubes until he gleamed like a living statue.

The ceremony itself carried profound spiritual significance. The Muisca believed their ancestors had given them dominion over the land in exchange for regular offerings. The cacique's transformation into a golden being symbolized his connection to divine power. His submersion in the lake represented death and rebirth. The treasures he cast into the water fed the spirits who controlled rain, fertility, and abundance.

Hartwell Moseley successfully drained much of Lake Guatavita in 1965 using modern pumping equipment. His team recovered over 4,000 individual artifacts from the exposed lake bed. Gold figurines showed remarkable artistic sophistication. Tiny birds with spread wings. Human figures in ceremonial poses. Complex geometric patterns that matched astronomical observations.

The recovered artifacts now reside in Bogotá's Gold Museum. Visitors can examine the craftsmanship that Spanish colonizers reduced to mere bullion. Each piece tells stories about Muisca religious beliefs, social organization, and technical skills. The golden cacique raft, discovered by farmers in a cave near Lake Guatavita in 1969, recreates the original ceremony in miniature detail.

The lake itself holds deeper significance than the treasure it once concealed. Colombian geologists have determined its origin as a meteorite impact crater formed millions of years ago. The perfectly circular shape attracted Muisca attention long before they developed the golden cacique ceremony. Natural hot springs around the rim provided evidence of supernatural forces dwelling beneath the surface.

Modern environmental analysis reveals why the Muisca considered Lake Guatavita sacred. The water contains unusually high mineral concentrations that support unique plant and animal species. Rare algae create color shifts across the surface depending on seasonal conditions. Fish populations follow migration patterns that correlate with astronomical events the Muisca incorporated into their calendar system.

The ceremony continued in secret even after Spanish colonization. Indigenous communities adapted their religious practices to avoid persecution. They substituted copper for gold when precious metals became too dangerous to possess. The lake remained a pilgrimage destination for people who remembered the old ways.

Lake Guatavita spawned the legend of El Dorado, but the legend grew far beyond its origins. Spanish dreams of golden cities attracted expeditions across the entire South American continent. Each failure led to wilder speculation about riches waiting deeper in the jungle, higher in the mountains, further beyond the next river bend.

# Percy Fawcett: 1925 Disappearance Seeking "Z"

Colonel Percy Harrison Fawcett studied his maps by candlelight in the Brazilian frontier town of Cuiabá. Rain drummed against the window of his hotel room. The year was 1925. His final expedition into the Amazon would begin at dawn.

Fawcett had spent two decades exploring South America's most dangerous regions. The Royal Geographical Society had commissioned him to map the borders between Brazil, Bolivia, and Peru. He had survived disease, hostile encounters, and geographical obstacles that claimed other explorers' lives. His reports described a continent far more complex than European maps suggested.

The Brazilian interior held secrets that conventional archaeology refused to acknowledge. Fawcett had discovered pottery shards in areas supposedly uninhabited since prehistoric times. The stone arrangements are too regular to be natural formations. Earthworks visible from high ridges that suggested ancient engineering projects. Indigenous peoples spoke of ruined cities hidden in the forest depths.

*Ancient American Civilizations*

His obsession began with a manuscript he studied at the National Library of Rio de Janeiro. Portuguese colonial authorities had commissioned the document in 1753. It described a lost city discovered by bandeirantes - fortune seekers who penetrated Brazil's interior searching for gold and slaves. The manuscript provided detailed descriptions of massive stone construction, hieroglyphic inscriptions, and architectural features that implied advanced civilization.

The bandeirantes had followed river systems deep into Mato Grosso territory. They found a city abandoned but intact. Stone buildings rose multiple stories above paved plazas. Carved figures decorated doorways and wall surfaces. Water systems channeled streams through the urban center. The construction rivaled anything the Portuguese had seen in Europe or Asia.

Fawcett named this lost city "Z" in his correspondence with geographical societies and potential expedition sponsors. He believed Z represented remnants of Atlantis or a similar advanced civilization that had existed in South America thousands of years ago. His theories attracted ridicule from academic archaeologists, but they also generated enough interest to fund multiple expeditions.

His first attempt to locate Z occurred in 1920. The expedition included his son Jack and photographer Raleigh Rimell. They followed the Xingu River system into regions no white men had previously explored. Hostile indigenous groups forced them to retreat after several months without finding the lost city. Fawcett returned convinced he had been searching in the wrong area.

Fawcett refined his theories based on indigenous oral traditions. Multiple tribes described ancient peoples who had built stone cities before disappearing. The stories shared common elements across different linguistic groups. Advanced builders had arrived from the east. They possessed knowledge of astronomy and agriculture. They constructed monuments aligned with celestial events. Their departure had been sudden and complete.

Brazilian government officials warned Fawcett about the dangers of his planned 1925 expedition. Recent conflicts with indigenous groups have made the Mato Grosso region highly hazardous to outsiders. The rainy season would begin soon, making travel nearly impossible. Supplies would run out before the expedition could establish reliable food sources.

*Ancient American Civilizations*

Fawcett dismissed these concerns. His previous experiences had taught him survival skills that other explorers lacked. He could navigate using astronomical observations. He understood how to obtain food and medicine from forest resources. Most importantly, he had developed relationships with indigenous communities who could provide guidance and protection.

The final expedition departed Cuiabá on April 20, 1925. Fawcett traveled with his eldest son, Jack, and Jack's friend Raleigh Rimell, both recent graduates of English universities eager for adventure. They carried minimal supplies to increase mobility. Their route would take them northeast toward the headwaters of the Tapajós River system.

Fawcett's last known communication reached the outside world on May 29, 1925. He wrote to his wife Nina from an indigenous village called Dead Horse Camp. The letter expressed optimism about their progress and mentioned friendly contact with local inhabitants. Fawcett believed they were approaching the region where Z would be found.

The three men vanished completely after leaving Dead Horse Camp. No confirmed sighting, artifact, or remains ever surfaced despite dozens of search expeditions over subsequent decades. The Brazilian government sent military patrols to investigate. Fellow explorers risked their lives attempting rescue operations. Anthropologists questioned indigenous communities across the entire region.

Rumors proliferated about Fawcett's fate. Some claimed he had been killed by hostile tribes defending their territory. Others suggested he had survived and established himself as a chief among indigenous peoples. The most romantic theories proposed that he had actually found Z and chosen to remain there rather than return to civilization.

Recent archaeological discoveries suggest Fawcett may have been searching in exactly the right location. Satellite imagery and ground-penetrating radar have revealed extensive earthworks throughout the upper Xingu basin. These geometric formations include circular plazas, rectangular compounds, and connecting roadways that span hundreds of square kilometers.

The earthworks show clear evidence of sophisticated urban planning. Different areas served residential, ceremonial, and agricultural functions. Population estimates based on structural remains suggest these sites supported thousands of inhabitants. Carbon dating places the major

*Ancient American Civilizations*

construction phase between 1200 and 1600 CE, precisely the time period Fawcett had theorized for his lost civilization.

Indigenous oral histories support Fawcett's theories about advanced ancient builders. The Kuikuro people describe their ancestors as skilled engineers who transformed the forest landscape through deliberate cultivation and construction projects. They speak of ancient chiefs who possessed astronomical knowledge and directed massive public works that required coordinated labor from multiple communities.

Modern researchers have documented over 20 major archaeological sites in the region where Fawcett disappeared. These discoveries vindicate his belief that the Amazon basin had supported complex civilizations. The cities he sought did exist. They were hidden not by jungle growth, but by European assumptions about indigenous capabilities.

Fawcett's disappearance became more famous than his discoveries. Adventure writers created fictional accounts of his expeditions. Hollywood produced movies based on his life. His story overshadowed the archaeological insights that had motivated his explorations. The man who sought to prove ancient American achievements became remembered primarily for his mysterious fate.

The tragedy of Fawcett's disappearance lies not in the loss of three lives but in the loss of opportunity. His theories about Amazonian civilizations were decades ahead of academic archaeology. Had he survived to document his discoveries, our understanding of ancient America might have advanced by generations. Instead, his insights died with him in the forest he loved.

# Forest Canopy Hiding Geometric Urban Patterns

Dr. Clark Erickson climbed the observation tower overlooking Bolivia's Llanos de Moxos region. Dawn light filtered through morning mist rising from flooded grasslands below. He adjusted his binoculars and studied the landscape patterns that had puzzled researchers since aerial photography first revealed them in the 1960s.

Geometric shapes stretched to the horizon in every direction. Perfect circles, straight lines, rectangular compounds, and curved earthworks created a vast archaeological complex spanning thousands of square kilometers. These formations were not natural. Human hands had shaped this landscape through centuries of deliberate engineering.

The Llanos de Moxos flood completely during the rainy season. For six months each year, water covers the grasslands to depths of several meters. Early Spanish explorers described the region as empty swampland unsuitable for permanent settlement. Archaeological evidence tells a different story.

Indigenous peoples had transformed this challenging environment into one of the world's most productive agricultural systems. They built raised fields connected by canal networks that channeled floodwaters into controlled irrigation systems. Fish populations thrived in the artificial waterways. Crops grew year-round on elevated plots that remained above flood levels.

The scale of construction defies conventional assumptions about pre-Columbian American societies. Individual raised field systems cover areas larger than major European cities. The earthworks required moving millions of tons of soil using only human labor and simple tools. The engineering knowledge necessary for such projects implies a sophisticated understanding of hydraulics, soil science, and regional climate patterns.

Erickson's research team used ground-penetrating radar to map subsurface structures beneath the visible earthworks. They discovered that the geometric patterns extended much deeper than surface observations suggested. Buried canals, elevated platforms, and artificial mounds created three-dimensional landscapes that maximized both agricultural productivity and flood control.

The raised field systems supported population densities comparable to modern intensive agriculture. Conservative estimates suggest the Llanos de Moxos region supported over 100,000 inhabitants at its peak development. These people were not scattered hunter-gatherers. They lived in permanent settlements connected by engineered transportation networks that functioned during both flood and dry seasons.

Archaeological evidence reveals a social organization capable of coordinating massive public works projects. Different earthwork complexes show consistent design principles and construction techniques across hundreds of kilometers. This standardization required communication systems, specialized labor forces, and centralized planning authorities that could direct resources toward long-term regional development goals.

The forest islands scattered throughout the flooded grasslands contain additional surprises. These elevated areas remained dry during flood season and supported different types of construction. Residential platforms, ceremonial mounds, and defensive earthworks created vertical settlement patterns that maximized available land use. Tree species found on these islands include many that were deliberately planted for food, medicine, and construction materials.

Ceramic analysis reveals sophisticated pottery traditions associated with the raised field cultures. Vessel forms include storage jars capable of holding hundreds of liters, specialized cooking pots designed for particular food types, and ceremonial pieces decorated with complex geometric and zoomorphic motifs. The artistic styles show influences from both Amazonian and Andean cultural traditions.

The abandonment of the Llanos de Moxos earthwork systems remains mysterious. Carbon dating suggests the major construction phase occurred between 500 and 1400 CE. Spanish colonial documents from the 1500s describe the region as sparsely inhabited by nomadic groups. Something had caused the collapse of a civilization that had flourished for nearly a millennium.

Disease epidemics brought by European contact provide the most likely explanation for the abandonment. Indigenous American populations had no immunity to smallpox, measles, and other Old World diseases. Mortality rates often exceeded 90 percent in affected communities. The Llanos de Moxos agricultural systems required constant maintenance that became impossible with drastically reduced populations.

The geometric earthworks gradually became invisible to outside observers. Seasonal flooding concealed the raised fields beneath water and vegetation. Forest growth obscured the connecting causeways and residential platforms. By the time scientific archaeology began investigating the Amazon basin, these achievements had been forgotten by everyone except local indigenous communities.

Modern satellite imagery revolutionized archaeological investigation of forested regions. High-resolution photographs revealed geometric patterns invisible from ground level. Computer analysis enhanced subtle variations in vegetation color and density that indicated buried structures.

*Ancient American Civilizations*

Geographic Information Systems allowed researchers to map extensive site complexes that had been hidden for centuries.

The application of LIDAR technology to Amazonian archaeology produced even more dramatic discoveries. Light Detection and Ranging systems can penetrate forest canopy and create precise topographic maps of ground surface features. These surveys revealed that geometric earthworks extend throughout the Amazon basin in much greater densities than anyone had imagined.

Recent LIDAR surveys of the Brazilian Amazon have documented over 450 major earthwork sites. These geometric formations include circular enclosures, rectangular compounds, connecting roadways, and defensive ditches arranged in complex patterns across the landscape. Individual sites range from several hectares to massive complexes covering hundreds of square kilometers.

The earthwork sites show clear evidence of urban planning principles. Residential areas occupy elevated locations with good drainage and defensive advantages. Ceremonial complexes feature circular plazas surrounded by earthen mounds and platforms. Agricultural zones include raised fields, water management systems, and storage facilities. Transportation networks connect different functional areas through engineered causeways that remain passable year-round.

Population estimates for the earthwork cultures suggest millions of people lived in the Amazon basin before European contact. These inhabitants modified forest composition through selective cultivation of valuable plant species. They managed animal populations through controlled hunting and the protection of breeding areas. They created artificial landscapes that integrated human settlement with ecosystem management.

The ecological engineering practiced by Amazonian cultures produced forest environments more biodiverse than natural succession would have created. Archaeological sites today support unusual concentrations of fruit trees, medicinal plants, and other useful species. Soil enrichment through terra preta formation created permanently fertile areas that continue to produce exceptional crop yields centuries after abandonment.

European colonial authorities completely misunderstood these achievements. They classified the Amazon as pristine wilderness because they could not recognize indigenous modifications to forest ecosystems.

*Ancient American Civilizations*

Their maps showed empty spaces where complex civilizations had actually flourished. Their policies assumed vacant lands available for colonization where sophisticated societies had managed resources sustainably for centuries.

# Ecological Engineering vs. Stone Architecture

Michael Heckenberger pushed through dense undergrowth following a barely visible path through the Brazilian Amazon. His Kuikuro guide pointed toward subtle changes in forest composition that revealed ancient human modification. Certain tree species appeared in arrangements too regular for natural growth patterns. Soil color variations indicated buried cultural deposits.

Heckenberger had spent decades documenting indigenous engineering achievements that conventional archaeology overlooked. European training taught him to search for stone monuments, metal artifacts, and permanent structures. The Amazon required different recognition skills. Here, civilizations built with earth, water, and living plants.

The Kuikuro people inhabit the upper Xingu River region, where their ancestors created one of South America's most sophisticated urban complexes. Archaeological evidence suggests continuous occupation spanning over 1,000 years. The contemporary community retains traditional knowledge of ancient engineering techniques that modern science is only beginning to grasp.

Their settlement patterns reflect principles of ecological integration that European cities never achieved. Villages occupy strategic locations that provide access to diverse environmental zones. Forest management creates mosaic landscapes where different areas serve specialized functions. Fish weirs, turtle nesting beaches, and managed groves provide reliable resource bases that support permanent populations.

The ancient Kuikuro built roads connecting multiple settlements across hundreds of square kilometers. These causeways required moving thousands of tons of earth to create elevated surfaces that remained passable during flood seasons. Bridge construction spanned major waterways using techniques that left minimal archaeological traces. The transportation network enabled trade, communication, and coordinated defense across the entire region.

Residential areas followed urban planning principles that maximized both privacy and community interaction. Houses surrounded circular plazas that served as centers for ceremonial activities, craft production, and social gatherings. Elevated platforms provided foundations that remained dry during seasonal flooding. Underground storage pits preserved food supplies and valuable materials.

The Kuikuro agricultural system transformed forest environments into productive landscapes that supported much higher population densities than hunting and gathering could sustain. They created forest gardens where useful species were concentrated in convenient locations. Controlled burning is used to manage forest succession and encourage particular plant communities. Fish farming in artificial ponds supplemented wild-caught protein sources.

Archaeological investigation reveals the accurate scale of these modifications. Ground-penetrating radar detects buried earthworks that extend far beyond visible surface features. Soil analysis reveals layers of terra preta formation that indicate intensive occupation and waste management. Pollen studies document changes in forest composition that reflect human selection pressures.

The earthworks surrounding Kuikuro settlements include defensive ditches, elevated platforms, and artificial lakes that served both practical and ceremonial functions. These constructions required a sophisticated understanding of hydrology, soil mechanics, and regional climate patterns. The engineering knowledge necessary for such projects was developed through generations of accumulated experience.

European observers consistently underestimated these achievements because they conflicted with assumptions about technological progress. Stone construction seemed more "advanced" than earthwork engineering. Permanent structures appeared more "civilized" than adaptive architecture. Metal tools suggested greater sophistication than organic technology.

These biases prevented recognition of ecological engineering as a legitimate form of technological achievement. Amazonian cultures developed solutions to environmental challenges that were often more sustainable than European alternatives. Their cities integrated with forest ecosystems rather than replacing them. Their agriculture enhanced biodiversity rather than reducing it.

The contrast becomes stark when comparing Amazonian settlements with European colonial towns. Spanish and Portuguese colonists clear-cut forests to create agricultural land. They imported European crop varieties that required constant inputs of labor and fertilizer. They built stone structures using construction techniques poorly adapted to tropical conditions.

Indigenous settlements worked with existing ecological processes rather than against them. Forest management created useful plant communities that required minimal maintenance. Agricultural techniques enriched soils through waste recycling and controlled burning. Architecture used materials and designs appropriate for local climate conditions.

The population crash following European contact destroyed most evidence of these achievements. Epidemic diseases killed an estimated 90 percent of indigenous inhabitants within a century of first contact. Surviving populations often abandoned their traditional settlements to escape slavery and forced conversion. Forest growth quickly concealed abandoned earthworks and agricultural systems.

Spanish colonial documents sometimes mention impressive indigenous settlements, but these accounts were usually dismissed as exaggerations. European colonial authorities had political incentives to minimize indigenous achievements. Acknowledging sophisticated American civilizations would have complicated legal justifications for territorial conquest and resource extraction.

Modern archaeological investigation reveals the true magnitude of pre-Columbian Amazonian civilizations. Satellite imagery detects geometric earthworks across millions of square kilometers. Ground-truthing confirms that these patterns represent intentional landscape modifications rather than natural formations. Population estimates based on settlement patterns suggest the Amazon basin supported between 8 and 12 million inhabitants before European contact.

The terra preta soils created by Amazonian cultures represent one of humanity's greatest agricultural innovations. These artificially enriched soils remain dramatically more fertile than surrounding natural soils centuries after abandonment. Modern attempts to replicate terra preta formation have achieved limited success despite access to advanced scientific knowledge and industrial technology.

Contemporary environmental challenges make Amazonian ecological engineering increasingly relevant to modern sustainability discussions. Climate change, biodiversity loss, and soil degradation require solutions that work with natural processes rather than against them. Indigenous knowledge systems offer proven approaches to these problems that Western science is beginning to appreciate.

The Kuikuro and other surviving Amazonian cultures maintain traditional ecological knowledge that developed over millennia of sustainable resource management. Their practices demonstrate how human populations can enhance rather than degrade forest ecosystems. Their settlements demonstrate how cities can be integrated with, rather than isolated from, their environmental contexts.

Recent collaborative research between indigenous communities and academic archaeologists has revolutionized understanding of Amazonian civilizations. Traditional knowledge guides archaeologists toward significant sites and helps interpret material remains. Scientific techniques provide precise dating and detailed analysis that complement oral historical traditions.

# European Misunderstanding of Forest Cities

Captain Francisco Orellana squinted through morning mist rising from the Amazon River. The year was 1542. His small fleet of makeshift boats had been traveling downstream for months, searching for a route back to Spanish settlements on South America's Pacific coast. What he saw ahead challenged everything Europeans believed about the interior of the New World.

Smoke columns rose from numerous fires along both riverbanks. Cleared areas showed geometric patterns that suggested deliberate planning. Canoes moved purposefully between landing sites that appeared to serve substantial inland populations. The river that Spanish maps labeled as empty wilderness clearly supported dense human settlement.

Orellana's expedition chronicler, Gaspar de Carvajal, recorded detailed observations of Amazonian settlements that his contemporaries found impossible to believe. He described cities extending inland beyond the horizon. Ceramic vessels large enough to hold an entire pig. Roadways wide enough for ten men walking abreast. Population centers that appeared to house thousands of inhabitants.

The Dominican friar wrote about encountering "very large settlements and very pretty country and very fruitful land" throughout their journey. He estimated seeing over 200 villages during their descent of the river system. Many settlements featured "very pretty country houses" and evidence of sophisticated agriculture. The indigenous inhabitants demonstrated advanced pottery, textiles, and metalworking skills.

Spanish colonial authorities received these reports with skepticism. Other expeditions into the Amazon basin had found only scattered groups of indigenous peoples living in temporary shelters. The interior appeared to be a sparsely inhabited wilderness unsuitable for European colonization. Carvajal's descriptions seemed exaggerated or fabricated.

The disconnect between Orellana's observations and later Spanish experiences reflected the demographic catastrophe that followed first European contact. Disease epidemics spread faster than exploration parties could travel. Indigenous populations along major river systems suffered mortality rates exceeding 90 percent within decades of initial contact. Entire cities disappeared before Spanish colonists could document their existence.

Subsequent European explorers found exactly what they expected - empty forest with minimal human presence. The abandoned settlements had been reclaimed by vegetation growth. Surviving indigenous groups had retreated to interior locations away from river routes used by European expeditions. The demographic collapse had made Carvajal's earlier observations appear fictional.

European colonial maps gradually erased evidence of Amazonian civilizations. Cartographers removed settlement symbols from areas where later expeditions found no inhabitants. Rivers lost their indigenous names and received European designations. Vast regions became labeled as unexplored wilderness available for future colonization projects.

The myth of empty Amazonia served important political functions for European colonial governments. International law required that colonial claims be based on effective occupation or indigenous permission. Empty lands could be claimed through discovery and settlement. Acknowledging substantial indigenous populations would have complicated territorial disputes between Spain and Portugal.

Scientific racism provided intellectual justification for dismissing indigenous achievements. European scholars argued that tropical climates prevented the development of advanced civilizations. They claimed that indigenous Americans lacked the intellectual capacity for sophisticated urban planning. These theories made archaeological evidence of Amazonian cities seem inherently implausible.

Alexander von Humboldt's early 19th-century explorations began to challenge assumptions about Amazonian emptiness. The Prussian naturalist documented extensive earthworks in the Llanos de Moxos region of Bolivia. He found evidence of sophisticated hydraulic engineering and agricultural systems. His observations suggested that substantial populations had once inhabited areas that appeared uninhabited.

Humboldt's reports attracted limited attention from the European scientific community. His botanical and geological discoveries received extensive publication and discussion. His archaeological observations were largely ignored or dismissed as speculative. The scientific establishment was not ready to acknowledge advanced indigenous civilizations in tropical South America.

The rubber boom of the late 19th century brought renewed European attention to Amazonian river systems. Commercial expeditions penetrated previously unexplored regions in search of valuable tree species. Their reports occasionally mentioned archaeological remains that suggested former human presence in areas that appeared to be pristine forest.

These commercial explorers lacked scientific training to document or interpret archaeological evidence properly. They were interested in economic resources rather than indigenous history. Their reports provided tantalizing hints about ancient settlements without the detailed observations necessary for serious archaeological investigation.

Early 20th-century ethnographers began systematic studies of surviving Amazonian indigenous communities. They documented complex social organizations, sophisticated ecological knowledge, and oral traditions that described more populous ancient times. These studies suggested that contemporary small-scale societies might be remnants of formerly larger civilizations.

The ethnographic research revealed indigenous knowledge systems that had been developed over generations. Traditional agriculture involved managing hundreds of plant species in complex forest garden systems.

Astronomical knowledge guided seasonal activities with mathematical precision. Social institutions coordinated resource sharing across extended kinship networks spanning vast territories.

Such sophisticated knowledge systems implied substantial populations and long-term cultural continuity. Small nomadic groups could not have developed or maintained such complex traditions. The evidence suggested that contemporary indigenous societies had been severely disrupted by historical events rather than representing their traditional social organization.

Archaeological investigation of the Amazon basin accelerated during the mid-20th century as improved transportation made previously inaccessible regions available for scientific study. Researchers began finding material evidence that supported indigenous oral traditions about ancient cities and complex societies.

Betty Meggers and Clifford Evans conducted influential archaeological surveys during the 1950s and 1960s. They documented extensive ceramic traditions and settlement patterns that indicated much higher population densities in prehistoric times. Their work provided scientific confirmation for hypotheses about Amazonian civilizations that had previously been dismissed as speculation.

The environmental limitations model developed by Meggers argued that Amazonian soils were too poor to support dense agricultural populations. This theory suggested that indigenous societies had always been limited to small-scale hunting and gathering adaptations. Archaeological evidence of larger settlements was explained as temporary aggregations or external influences from more advanced Andean cultures.

This model dominated Amazonian archaeology for several decades and continued to minimize indigenous achievements. It provided scientific justification for assumptions about tropical limitations that supported colonial-era dismissals of indigenous capabilities. The theory prevented recognition of archaeological evidence that contradicted its basic premises.

Recent archaeological research has thoroughly discredited the environmental limitations model. Discoveries of extensive earthwork complexes, terra preta soil formation, and sophisticated agricultural systems demonstrate that Amazonian environments could support

*Ancient American Civilizations*

substantial sedentary populations. The limitations were political and epidemiological rather than environmental.

Modern population estimates suggest the Amazon basin supported between 8 and 12 million inhabitants before European contact. These populations were organized into complex chiefdoms and confederations that managed resources across vast territories. Their settlements included permanent towns with thousands of inhabitants connected by engineered transportation networks.

The recognition of Amazonian civilizations represents one of archaeology's most dramatic paradigm shifts. Regions previously dismissed as pristine wilderness are now understood to be cultural landscapes shaped by millennia of human management. Indigenous societies previously characterized as simple hunter-gatherers are now recognized as sophisticated ecological engineers.

This transformation in scientific understanding highlights how cultural biases can prevent recognition of archaeological evidence. European assumptions about civilization, technology, and environmental adaptation created blind spots that persisted for centuries. Only when these assumptions were explicitly challenged could the evidence of Amazonian achievements be adequately evaluated.

The story of European misunderstanding illustrates broader patterns in the historical encounter between indigenous American civilizations and European colonial societies. Archaeological evidence of sophisticated indigenous achievements was consistently dismissed, minimized, or ignored because it contradicted European assumptions about cultural superiority and territorial rights.

Modern collaborative research between indigenous communities and academic archaeologists offers models for more accurate and respectful investigation of ancient American civilizations. Traditional knowledge guides archaeologists toward significant discoveries and provides interpretive frameworks that complement scientific analysis. This partnership approach produces a more complete understanding than either indigenous knowledge or Western science could achieve independently.

The Amazon basin represents one of humanity's greatest experiments in sustainable civilization. Indigenous societies developed technologies and social institutions that supported millions of people for over a millennium without causing environmental degradation. Their achievements offer crucial insights for addressing contemporary global challenges related to climate change, biodiversity conservation, and sustainable development.

Recognition of Amazonian civilizations also provides important context for understanding other ancient American achievements. The geometric earthworks, sophisticated agriculture, and ecological engineering documented in the Amazon basin demonstrate indigenous capabilities that were expressed differently in other regions. Stone architecture in the Andes and Maya lowlands represents one approach to monumental construction, but earth and forest architecture in Amazonia represents an equally sophisticated alternative.

The European misunderstanding of forest cities ultimately prevented appreciation of one of humanity's most remarkable civilizational achievements. Amazonian societies developed sustainable relationships with their environments that modern industrial civilization has not been able to replicate. Their knowledge systems offer proven solutions to environmental challenges that become more urgent with each passing year.

# Chapter 11: Sacred Waters - Maya Cities Beneath the Waves

## Cenotes: Portals to Xibalba Underworld

The rope cut into Miguel's hands as he descended into darkness. Forty feet below the jungle floor, his headlamp beam pierced black water that had remained untouched for centuries. The cenote opened like a cathedral around him. Limestone walls rose in perfect circles, carved by countless years of underground rivers eating through the Yucatan bedrock.

Miguel was not the first person to enter this sacred pool. Maya priests had walked these same stone ledges over a thousand years ago. They carried offerings of jade, gold, and copal incense into the depths. They believed the cenotes connected the earthly realm with Xibalba, the Maya underworld where gods dwelled and souls journeyed after death.

The Maya knew every cenote in their territory. They mapped underground river systems that stretched for hundreds of miles. They understood the seasonal water cycles that filled and emptied these natural wells. Most importantly, they recognized the spiritual power contained within these portals between worlds.

Each cenote received careful attention from Maya engineers and priests. Stone platforms extended over the water's edge. Carved steps led down to ceremonial bathing areas. Channels directed rainwater into the sacred pools during the wet season. The Maya transformed natural geological features into architectural spaces for communion with the divine.

Dr. Guillermo de Anda rappelled into Cenote Sagrado at Chichen Itza in 2019. His underwater archaeology team had spent months preparing for this dive. The cenote held legendary status among researchers. Spanish chronicles described vast offerings of gold and precious objects thrown into its depths during the height of Maya civilization.

De Anda's team found more than treasure. Human skulls rested on underwater ledges exactly where Maya priests had placed them centuries ago. Ceramic incense burners sat upright on stone platforms sixty feet below the surface. Jade masks stared through crystal-clear water with expressions unchanged by time.

The discoveries revealed sophisticated underwater ritual practices. Maya priests had constructed permanent altars beneath the water line. They installed stone sculptures in underwater caves accessible only to trained divers. They created ceremonial spaces where spiritual activities took place in complete darkness, surrounded by the eternal stillness of underground pools.

Carbon dating of organic materials found in cenotes confirmed their use across many centuries. The Maya returned to the same sacred waters generation after generation. They maintained underwater shrines through political upheavals, climate changes, and social transformations. The cenotes provided continuity in a changing world.

Children learned about cenotes from their parents and grandparents. Maya oral traditions passed down detailed knowledge about which pools connected to specific gods, which times of year required particular ceremonies, and which objects should be offered to ensure divine favor. This information never appeared in stone inscriptions or bark paper books. It lived in memory and practice.

The deepest cenotes reached over 300 feet into the earth. Maya divers descended these incredible depths without modern equipment. They held their breath for minutes at a time. They navigated pitch-black underwater passages using only their knowledge of cave systems learned through years of training.

Archaeological evidence shows Maya divers could reach depths that challenge even modern technical divers. Artifacts recovered from extreme depths show no signs of having fallen accidentally. They were placed deliberately in specific locations by people who knew exactly where they were going in the underwater darkness.

The cenotes connected Maya cities in ways that went beyond practical water supply. Underground rivers linked sacred pools across hundreds of miles. Maya pilgrims could travel from one holy site to another by following submerged passageways. They moved between communities through an underground network invisible from the surface.

This hidden transportation system allowed Maya priests and nobles to disappear completely from public view. They could vanish into cenotes near one city and surface days later at distant ceremonial centers. The underground world provided a parallel realm where spiritual and political activities took place away from ordinary observation.

*Ancient American Civilizations*

Maya creation mythology placed the origin of humanity in underwater caves. According to their sacred books, the gods shaped the first humans from maize dough in caverns beneath the earth. The cenotes were not merely sources of water. They were birthplaces where divine forces had brought their ancestors into existence.

# Sac Actun: Longest Flooded Cave System

Roberto Rojo pushed through the narrow passage connecting two underwater chambers. His dive light illuminated limestone formations that had grown undisturbed for thousands of years. Behind him, three other cave divers followed the guide rope deeper into the Sac Actun system.

The team was mapping what would become officially recognized as the world's longest underwater cave network—more than 215 miles of surveyed passages wound beneath the Yucatan Peninsula. The system connected dozens of cenotes across an area larger than many countries.

Maya knowledge of this underground world exceeded anything modern science had documented. Archaeological evidence showed they had explored cave systems that researchers are still discovering today. Stone tools and ceramic vessels appear in passages so remote that reaching them requires hours of technical diving through dangerous restrictions.

The Maya left deliberate markers throughout the cave system. Broken pottery sherds point toward passages leading to other cenotes. Stone cairns mark underwater junctions where multiple tunnels intersect. These navigation aids suggest systematic exploration and mapping of the underground realm over many generations.

Dr. Dominique Rissolo led the first scientific expedition to document Maya artifacts in the deepest reaches of Sac Actun. His team found evidence of human activity in chambers located miles from any known entrance. Charcoal deposits showed where Maya explorers had burned torches in air-filled caverns. Soot stains on limestone walls traced ancient pathways through the darkness.

The complexity of Maya cave exploration impressed modern technical divers. Reaching some artifact locations required swimming through multiple sumps, navigating tight restrictions, and following underground rivers for thousands of meters. The Maya accomplished these journeys without wetsuits, dive lights, or breathing apparatus.

Ancient Maya texts describe underground journeys that lasted several days. Hero twins in Maya mythology traveled through cave systems on their way to confront the lords of Xibalba. These stories may preserve actual knowledge about multi-day cave expeditions that took Maya explorers far from their home communities.

Archaeological evidence supports the possibility of extended underground journeys. Food remains and temporary campsites appear in deep cave chambers. Water storage vessels suggest that Maya cave explorers carried supplies for lengthy expeditions. They understood the physical demands of navigating complex underground systems.

The Sac Actun caves contain evidence of large-scale ceremonial activities. Underwater chambers hold multiple altars, extensive pottery deposits, and human remains from numerous individuals. These were not isolated ritual offerings. They document systematic religious practices that brought many people into the deepest parts of the cave system.

Researchers found carved stone monuments in underwater chambers accessible only through technical diving. The monuments show clear evidence of having been carved in place rather than transported from the surface. Maya artisans worked in complete darkness, creating sacred objects in the heart of the underworld.

The cave system preserves a complete record of Maya religious practices across many centuries. Different chambers contain artifacts from various time periods. The Maya continued using the same underwater ceremonial spaces through cultural transitions, political changes, and environmental challenges. The caves provided stability when surface conditions became uncertain.

Modern hydrological studies confirmed that the Sac Actun system functions as a single connected watershed. Underground rivers carry water from cenotes in the interior to coastal springs near the Caribbean Sea. The Maya understood this connectivity and used it for both practical and spiritual purposes.

Water levels in cenotes across the peninsula rise and fall together as a single system. Maya observations of these patterns allowed them to predict seasonal changes and plan agricultural activities accordingly.

They possessed detailed knowledge of underground hydrology that modern scientists are still working to understand fully.

The Maya integrated their understanding of cave systems into their urban planning. Major ceremonial centers were built at locations where multiple underground rivers converged. Surface architecture followed patterns determined by hidden underground features. The visible cities were built according to the invisible geography of the underworld.

# Chichen Itza: El Castillo Built Over Sacred Waters

Ground-penetrating radar pulses penetrated the limestone beneath El Castillo pyramid. Dr. René Chávez Segura watched his computer screen as data revealed what Maya builders had known for over a thousand years. Directly beneath the pyramid's center lay a massive cenote, filled with water that had remained hidden since the monument's construction.

The discovery explained why the Maya chose this specific location for their most important pyramid. They were building over the exact spot where the surface world connected with the underworld. El Castillo was not simply placed on convenient ground. It was positioned as a cosmic axis linking heaven, earth, and the realm of the ancestors.

The construction of the pyramid required extraordinary engineering to span the underground void. Maya architects designed the monument's foundation to distribute weight around the edges of the cenote rather than directly over the water. They created a stable platform above an underground cathedral without disturbing the sacred pool below.

The builders incorporated the cenote into the pyramid's spiritual function. Four stairways descended from the summit to ground level, pointing toward the cardinal directions. The northern stairway aligned precisely with the hidden cenote beneath the structure. Worshippers climbing toward the temple unconsciously followed the path toward the underground portal.

Maya priests were aware of the concealed cenote throughout Chichen Itza's occupation. Sacred ceremonies at the pyramid acknowledged the underground water through prayers, offerings, and ritual activities. The pyramid and cenote functioned as a unified sacred complex with visible and invisible components.

*Ancient American Civilizations*

Recent investigations revealed additional underwater features surrounding the hidden cenote. Side passages connect the central pool to other water-filled chambers beneath the ceremonial plaza. The entire architectural complex sits above an interconnected system of sacred pools and underground passages.

The Maya designed surface drainage to interact with the underground water system. Rainwater collected from pyramid terraces and plaza surfaces flowed into channels that led toward the hidden cenote. Surface water and underground water mixed in sacred union beneath the monument.

Dr. James Brady's explorations of similar pyramid-cenote combinations at other Maya sites revealed a consistent pattern. Major ceremonial centers were built over significant underground features. The Maya possessed detailed knowledge of subsurface geology that influenced their architectural decisions across the entire region.

The relationship between El Castillo and its hidden cenote explains the pyramid's acoustic properties. Sound waves from ceremonies at the pyramid's base create specific echo patterns that interact with the underground chambers. The Maya designed the structure to produce supernatural sound effects that reinforced beliefs about communication with the underworld.

Clap your hands at the base of El Castillo's northern stairway. The echo that returns sounds like the call of the quetzal bird, sacred to the feathered serpent god Kukulkan. This acoustic phenomenon results from precise calculations about the pyramid's proportions and the underground spaces beneath it.

The Maya timed construction activities to avoid disturbing the sacred waters. Archaeological evidence suggests they built the pyramid during dry seasons when cenote water levels dropped to their lowest points. They knew seasonal fluctuations and planned accordingly to maintain the spiritual integrity of the underground realm.

Surface ceremonies at El Castillo connected directly to underwater rituals in the concealed cenote. Priests conducted parallel activities above and below ground during important calendar dates. The pyramid served as a ceremonial platform for activities that extended into the underwater world beneath it.

The hidden cenote explains why Chichen Itza remained important to Maya communities long after its political power declined. The sacred waters beneath El Castillo continued to attract pilgrims and religious practitioners through the colonial period and into modern times. The spiritual significance of the location transcended political changes.

Maya descendants living near Chichen Itza preserved knowledge about the underground waters through oral traditions. Local families knew about the cenote beneath El Castillo generations before archaeological instruments confirmed its existence. Traditional knowledge maintained accurate information that formal archaeology took decades to rediscover.

# Underwater Stone Altars and Ceremonial Items

The jade mask stared through forty feet of crystal-clear water. Dr. Pilar Luna descended toward the artifact that had rested on its underwater altar for over eight centuries. Her breathing apparatus sent bubbles spiraling toward the distant cenote opening far above. Around her, the limestone chamber held dozens of ceremonial objects placed deliberately by Maya priests who had made similar descents using only their ability to hold their breath.

Luna's underwater archaeology team documented over 200 individual artifacts scattered across the cenote floor. Each object occupied a specific position that suggested careful placement rather than random disposal. Stone incense burners sat upright on natural ledges. Ceramic vessels rested in niches carved into the cenote walls. Gold bells hung from limestone formations where Maya divers had attached them using organic cordage that had long since dissolved.

The artifacts revealed sophisticated underwater construction techniques. Maya craftsmen had modified the natural cenote environment to create ceremonial spaces beneath the water surface. They carved recesses into limestone walls to hold specific objects. They constructed stone platforms at precise depths to serve as underwater altars. They installed permanent fixtures that transformed natural caves into underwater temples.

Carbon dating of organic materials associated with the artifacts provided precise dates for underwater ceremonial activities. The cenote received religious attention from 600 CE through the Spanish conquest and beyond. Maya priests maintained underwater shrines for over nine centuries, returning repeatedly to the same sacred locations generation after generation.

The variety of materials found in underwater contexts demonstrated extensive trade networks connecting Maya communities with distant regions. Pacific coast shells appeared alongside jade from the Guatemala highlands and gold from Colombia. Maya underwater offerings incorporated precious materials from across Mesoamerica and beyond.

Ceramic analysis revealed that underwater pottery came from multiple Maya cities across different time periods. The cenote served as a regional pilgrimage destination rather than a local religious site. People traveled hundreds of miles to make offerings in these particular sacred waters. The underwater shrines attracted worshippers from throughout the Maya world.

Stone altars explicitly built for underwater use showed evidence of continuous ritual activity. Residue analysis detected traces of copal incense, cacao, blood, and other ceremonial substances on altar surfaces. Maya priests conducted complete religious ceremonies in the underwater environment, not merely dropping objects from the surface.

The positioning of artifacts followed consistent patterns that suggested standardized ritual protocols. Incense burners appeared at specific depths related to Maya calendar calculations. Jade objects were positioned at specific compass orientations within the cenote chambers. The underwater placement of ceremonial items followed precise religious rules rather than random distribution.

Human remains associated with underwater altars provided evidence for different types of sacrificial practices. Some individuals appeared to have drowned during ritual activities. Others showed evidence of having been killed above ground before their bodies were placed in underwater tombs. The cenotes served multiple functions in Maya death rituals.

Dr. Luis Alberto Martos's analysis of bone chemistry from underwater human remains revealed information about Maya diet and social status. Individuals sacrificed in cenotes came from elite social classes based on their bone isotope signatures. These were not random victims but carefully chosen people whose deaths carried special spiritual significance.

The preservation conditions in cenotes maintained organic materials that rarely survive in other archaeological contexts. Wooden objects, textile fragments, and plant remains provided detailed information about Maya material culture. The underwater environment created time capsules that preserved complete ceremonial assemblages.

Ongoing excavations continue to reveal the scale of Maya underwater religious activities. New cenote explorations regularly produce additional artifacts and underwater architectural features. The Maya created an entire hidden world of ceremonial spaces beneath the Yucatan Peninsula that researchers are still discovering and documenting.

Modern Maya communities maintain traditional knowledge about specific cenotes and their associated ceremonial practices. Local families continue to make offerings at sacred pools, following practices passed down through generations. The underwater temples remain active religious sites after more than a thousand years of continuous use.

# Hoyo Negro: 12,000-Year-Old Human Remains

Alberto Nava kicked his fins against the limestone wall and descended deeper into the flooded cavern. His dive lights illuminated a chamber the size of a cathedral. At 130 feet below the surface, the cave floor came into view. Scattered across the sediment lay bones that would revolutionize our understanding of the first Americans.

The skeleton belonged to a teenage girl who had fallen into the cave over 12,000 years ago. When she died, Hoyo Negro was a dry cavern accessible through surface openings. Rising sea levels at the end of the Ice Age had flooded the chamber, creating perfect preservation conditions that maintained her remains through twelve millennia.

Dr. James Chatters led the international team that analyzed the skeleton, which they named Naia, after the Greek water nymphs. Her bones provided the oldest intact human remains ever found in the Americas. More importantly, her DNA connected her directly to modern Native American populations, proving genetic continuity across thousands of years.

The discovery resolved a long-standing puzzle about early American populations. Previous skeletal remains from the Paleoindian period showed physical features that differed from modern Native Americans.

Critics had used these differences to question indigenous peoples' connections to the earliest inhabitants. Naia's

DNA evidence demonstrated unbroken ancestry linking Ice Age populations to contemporary indigenous communities.

The cave environment that preserved Naia also contained remains of extinct Ice Age animals. Sabre-toothed cats, giant ground sloths, and gomphotheres had fallen into the same cavern system over thousands of years. The bone assemblage created a complete picture of Pleistocene ecosystems that existed in the Yucatan when the region was much drier than today.

Naia's skeleton provided crucial information about the lifestyle and physical capabilities of early Americans. Her bone chemistry revealed a diet based on land animals and plants rather than marine resources. Her muscle attachment points showed evidence of a physically demanding lifestyle that required strength and endurance. Her age at death, approximately 15-17 years, suggested she was already an adult by her society's standards.

The circumstances of Naia's death offered insights into early American behavior and environment. She was exploring caves during a period when the chamber was accessible from the surface. Her presence in the deep cavern suggested that Paleoindian populations possessed detailed knowledge of underground landscapes and were comfortable navigating complex cave systems.

Additional human remains in Hoyo Negro confirmed that cave exploration was a regular activity among early American populations. At least four other individuals died in the same chamber across several thousand years. The repeated human presence in dangerous underground environments suggested specific cultural practices that drew people into caves despite obvious risks.

The bone preservation at Hoyo Negro exceeded anything previously found in American Paleoindian sites. The underwater environment protected organic materials from decomposition and disturbance. Researchers recovered complete DNA sequences from bone samples that would have been destroyed in surface archaeological sites.

Radiocarbon dating of multiple bone samples confirmed the antiquity of human presence in the region. The dates pushed back the timeline for human occupation of the Yucatan Peninsula by several thousand years. Early Americans had reached the area and adapted to tropical environments much earlier than previous archaeological evidence suggested.

The discovery had implications beyond archaeology. Modern Maya communities recognized spiritual connections between ancient remains found in cenotes and their own traditional beliefs about ancestors dwelling in underwater realms. Naia's presence in the sacred cave system linked contemporary indigenous peoples to the earliest inhabitants through both genetic and spiritual continuity.

International collaboration between Mexican, American, and European researchers demonstrated the importance of Hoyo Negro's discoveries for global understanding of human migration. The skeleton provided crucial data points for models of how and when humans colonized the Americas. Naia became one of the most important archaeological discoveries of the 21st century.

The continuing exploration of Hoyo Negro and similar underwater cave systems promises additional discoveries about early American populations. Advanced diving techniques allow researchers to reach previously inaccessible chambers where more ancient remains may await discovery. The cenotes of the Yucatan Peninsula continue to yield secrets about the earliest chapters of human history in the Americas.

The protection of Hoyo Negro as an underwater archaeological preserve ensures that future research can continue without disturbing this crucial site. Mexican authorities established legal protections for the cave system and its contents. The underwater museum preserves Naia's legacy for both scientific research and public education about the deep history of indigenous peoples in the Americas.

# Chapter 12: Sunken Cities - Civilizations Beneath the Waves

## Cuban Sonar: 600-Meter-Deep Geometric Structures

Paulina Zelitsky adjusted the sonar controls aboard the research vessel Ulises. The Canadian marine engineer had spent months mapping Cuba's territorial waters for the government's oil exploration program. Her side-scan sonar equipment could penetrate deep ocean floors, revealing geological formations invisible to surface observation. On May 14, 2001, the sonar readings showed something impossible.

Six hundred meters beneath the Caribbean Sea, geometric patterns stretched across the ocean floor. Zelitsky stared at the monitor display. Straight lines formed perfect rectangles. Circular structures sat at precise intervals. Stone blocks appeared to be arranged in organized grids. The formations covered an area larger than downtown Havana.

"These cannot be natural," Zelitsky told her Cuban colleague, Manuel Iturralde. The geologist studied the sonar images with growing excitement. Ocean currents carve random patterns in seafloor sediment. Geological processes create irregular formations. Nothing in nature produces such systematic organization.

The Cuban Academy of Sciences authorized a follow-up expedition. Zelitsky's team deployed remotely operated vehicles equipped with high-resolution cameras. The underwater footage confirmed the sonar findings. Rectangular stone blocks lay arranged in orderly patterns. Circular structures showed evidence of deliberate construction. Smaller stones filled gaps between larger blocks, suggesting mortared joints.

One structure measured over 400 meters in length. Its walls rose 40 meters above the seafloor. Internal chambers divided the space into smaller rooms. Doorway-like openings connected different sections. The entire complex bore unmistakable signs of architectural planning.

Iturralde calculated the geological timeline. Post-glacial flooding had raised Caribbean sea levels approximately 120 meters since the last Ice Age. The structures now resting at a 600-meter depth would have been dry land 12,000 years ago. If humans built these formations, they predated all known Caribbean civilizations by thousands of years.

The discovery attracted international attention. National Geographic funded additional surveys. The Discovery Channel produced documentaries. Marine archaeologists requested access to the site. Then official silence descended. Cuban authorities restricted further exploration. International partners withdrew funding. The underwater city vanished from public consciousness.

Zelitsky continued her research privately. She identified pyramid-shaped structures within the complex. Stone pathways connected different buildings. Circular plazas created public spaces. The urban planning showed a sophisticated understanding of hydraulic engineering and architectural design.

Marine geologist Robert Ballard examined Zelitsky's data. The explorer famous for discovering the Titanic confirmed the artificial nature of the formations. "Someone built these structures," Ballard announced at a scientific conference in 2002. "The question is who and when."

Orthodox archaeologists rejected the implications. No known culture possessed the technology to construct such massive underwater installations. The depth made detailed excavation impossible with current equipment. Without artifacts or dating materials, the structures remained scientifically unproven.

Independent researchers proposed alternative explanations. Ancient Caribbean peoples might have developed advanced maritime civilizations before post-glacial flooding. Rising sea levels could have driven them to higher ground or extinction. Their cities sank beneath the waves, leaving only stone foundations as evidence of their existence.

Zelitsky documented additional anomalies throughout her surveys. Straight lines crossed the ocean floor for kilometers. Circular depressions showed uniform dimensions. Stone arrangements created geometric patterns visible only from above. The entire Caribbean seafloor appeared modified by intelligent design.

Satellite imagery revealed corresponding formations on nearby landmasses. Geometric earthworks dotted the Caribbean islands. Linear features crossed mountainous terrain. Ancient road systems connected

*Ancient American Civilizations*

coastal areas with inland settlements. The pattern suggested an integrated civilization spanning the entire region.

Local oral traditions supported these findings. Indigenous Taíno peoples spoke of ancestral cities swallowed by the sea. Cuban fishermen reported seeing stone walls beneath clear water during low tides. Haitian folklore described a golden age when land bridges connected the islands.

The Cuban discovery sparked searches for similar formations throughout the Caribbean. Sonar surveys off Jamaica revealed rectangular structures at 200-meter depths. Puerto Rican waters contained linear arrangements of megalithic blocks. Dominican Republic expeditions found circular stone platforms beneath coastal shelves.

Each new discovery strengthened the case for widespread ancient settlement. The Caribbean basin appeared to harbor the remains of a civilization extensive enough to construct cities across multiple islands. Rising sea levels had hidden their achievements beneath hundreds of meters of water.

Zelitsky's team identified specific architectural features within the Cuban complex. Stepped pyramids rose from central plazas. Perpendicular streets created organized districts. Aqueduct systems channeled water through urban areas. The city planning exceeded anything found in contemporary land-based sites.

Computer modeling reconstructed the ancient coastline configuration. During the last Ice Age, much of the current Caribbean seafloor formed exposed land. Broad plains connected islands. Rivers flowed through valleys now hundreds of meters underwater. The geography supported large human populations with extensive trade networks.

The implications stretched far beyond archaeology. If advanced civilizations flourished in the Caribbean 12,000 years ago, human cultural development followed different patterns than conventional models suggested. Maritime societies might have achieved urban sophistication earlier than land-based cultures. Island civilizations could have influenced continental developments through trade and migration.

# Bimini Road: Half-Kilometer Stone Causeway

Dr. Manson Valentine pushed through the crystal-clear waters off Bimini Island in September 1968. The marine archaeologist and his diving partner, Jacques Mayol, had been exploring Bahamian reefs for evidence of ancient human activity. Twenty feet beneath the surface, they found something that challenged everything they knew about Caribbean prehistory.

Massive limestone blocks stretched across the ocean floor in perfectly straight lines. Each block measured approximately fifteen feet in length and ten feet in width. The stones fitted together with minimal gaps, creating a continuous roadway extending over half a kilometer into the distance. Local fishermen called it "the Bimini Road," though none could explain its origin.

Valentine documented the formation's precise measurements. The roadway maintained a consistent width of thirty feet throughout its length. Stone blocks showed a uniform thickness of approximately two feet. Edges displayed cut marks and deliberate shaping. Natural limestone formations never exhibited such geometric regularity.

Geologist Dr. Eugene Shinn examined the site in 1978. He concluded the blocks were natural formations created by geological fracturing and erosion. Limestone bedrock splits along predictable patterns under pressure. Ocean currents can remove softer sediments between cracks, leaving rectangular blocks behind.

Valentine disputed Shinn's interpretation. He pointed to specific features inconsistent with natural formation. Corner blocks showed L-shaped cutting. Some stones bore chisel marks and tool scarring. Smaller rocks filled gaps between larger blocks, suggesting intentional construction. The overall pattern created a deliberate transportation corridor.

Underwater photographer Dimitri Rebikoff captured detailed images of the formation in 1975. His photographs revealed additional construction elements overlooked by earlier surveys. Anchor holes penetrated specific blocks at regular intervals. Stone ramps connected the main roadway to adjacent structures. Parallel walls created channels for water flow.

The controversy attracted attention from Edgar Cayce followers. The famous psychic had predicted the discovery of Atlantean ruins near

Bimini during the late 1960s. When Valentine announced his findings, Cayce supporters proclaimed vindication of their leader's prophecies. This association damaged the site's scientific credibility.

Marine archaeologist Dr. William Donato conducted systematic surveys throughout the 1990s. His team mapped additional stone structures beyond the main roadway. Circular formations created harbor facilities. Rectangular platforms suggested building foundations. Linear arrangements extended in multiple directions from the central causeway.

Donato's measurements revealed construction techniques inconsistent with natural processes. Stones showed evidence of quarrying and transportation from distant sources. Chemical analysis identified limestone varieties foreign to local geology. Carbon dating of organic materials trapped beneath blocks yielded ages of 12,000 to 19,000 years.

Critics questioned the dating methodology. Organic materials could have accumulated beneath the stones through natural processes long after formation. Carbon dates reflected the age of trapped debris, not construction activity. Without directly dating the limestone blocks themselves, the actual age remained uncertain.

Proponents highlighted architectural sophistication throughout the complex. The main roadway connected natural harbors on opposite sides of the island. Curved sections followed optimal navigation routes through shallow waters. Elevated construction allowed boat passage during high tides. The design showed intimate knowledge of local maritime conditions.

Underwater explorer Robert Ferro documented construction details invisible to surface observation. Individual blocks displayed mortise and tenon joints connecting adjacent stones. Keystone arrangements locked larger sections together. Drainage channels directed water flow away from the roadway surface. These features required advanced engineering knowledge.

Local Bahamian traditions supported ancient construction theories. Island elders described ancestral peoples who built stone roads beneath the sea. Fishing guides reported similar formations throughout the Bahama Banks. Archaeological surveys confirmed extensive megalithic structures scattered across the shallow platform.

The Bimini formation gained renewed scientific attention during the 2000s. Satellite imagery revealed the roadway as part of a larger complex spanning several square kilometers. Ground-penetrating radar detected buried structures extending inland. The discovered remains suggested a substantial ancient settlement.

Dr. Greg Little organized comprehensive surveys combining multiple investigation techniques. Sonar mapping revealed the full extent of underwater constructions. Side-scan imaging identified construction patterns invisible to direct observation. Sub-bottom profiling detected buried structures beneath sediment layers.

Little's team found evidence supporting human construction. Tool marks scarred stone surfaces. Quarry sites showed systematic extraction activities. Transportation channels connected construction areas with material sources. The logistics required organized labor forces and advanced planning.

Geological analysis complicated the interpretation. Bahamian limestone does fracture along predictable lines under specific conditions. Wave action can transport and arrange stones in linear patterns. Chemical weathering creates uniform block sizes over extended periods. Natural processes could theoretically produce formations resembling human construction.

The debate highlighted broader questions about Caribbean prehistory. If ancient peoples built stone roads beneath current sea levels, they possessed maritime capabilities exceeding conventional estimates. Island societies might have developed sophisticated technologies for underwater construction. Rising sea levels could have hidden extensive evidence of advanced cultures.

Archaeological evidence from surrounding areas supported ancient occupation. Stone circles dotted adjacent islands. Megalithic structures appeared throughout the Caribbean basin. Linear earthworks connected coastal sites with inland settlements. The regional pattern suggested widespread cultural activity during the post-glacial period.

# Post-Ice Age Sea Level Rise Impact

The ice began melting 19,000 years ago. Massive glacial sheets covering northern continents slowly retreated toward the poles. Billions of tons of frozen water returned to the oceans. Global sea levels rose steadily, ultimately climbing over 400 feet higher than Ice Age minimums. The transformation reshaped coastlines worldwide and potentially erased evidence of entire civilizations.

Dr. Richard Fairbanks studied this process through coral reef analysis in Barbados. Ancient corals grow only in shallow water near sea level. By drilling through reef formations and dating successive layers, Fairbanks reconstructed the timeline of rising seas. His research revealed the scope of post-glacial flooding.

Twelve thousand years ago, vast areas of the current seafloor formed dry land. The Bahama Banks extended as broad plains connecting today's islands. Caribbean basins contained river valleys and inland lakes. Continental shelves stretched hundreds of miles beyond present coastlines. The geography supported human populations now impossible to imagine.

Fairbanks calculated the rate of sea level change during critical periods. Between 14,000 and 8,000 years ago, oceans rose approximately one foot per decade. Coastal communities faced constant retreat from advancing waters. Settlements built near shorelines required frequent relocation. Entire regions disappeared beneath the waves within human lifespans.

The implications for archaeology were staggering. If ancient peoples preferred coastal environments, their settlements now rest underwater. Stone monuments, urban centers, and ceremonial sites could lie buried beneath hundreds of feet of ocean. Traditional land-based archaeology might miss the most significant evidence of early human achievement.

Marine geologist Dr. Cesar Emiliani proposed systematic surveys of drowned coastlines. His research team identified probable settlement areas on continental shelves. River deltas, protected harbors, and freshwater springs created optimal locations for human occupation. These sites now lay beneath 200 to 400 feet of seawater.

Underwater reconnaissance confirmed Emiliani's predictions. Submerged terraces showed evidence of human modification. Stone arrangements created harbors and breakwaters. Linear features suggested roads and aqueducts. Circular depressions indicated building foundations. The patterns extended across vast areas of the current seafloor.

*Ancient American Civilizations*

Archaeological surveys of drowned river valleys yielded additional discoveries. Sonar mapping revealed systematic landscape modification. Terraced hills created agricultural platforms. Straightened channels improved navigation. Stone causeways connected islands and peninsulas. The engineering required substantial populations and organized labor forces.

The Mediterranean provided a model for understanding post-glacial impacts. Black Sea research revealed how rapidly rising waters could transform entire regions. Around 5600 BCE, Mediterranean waters breached the Bosporus barrier. The resulting flood raised Black Sea levels by over 500 feet within decades. Coastal settlements vanished beneath the expanding waters.

Similar catastrophic flooding affected other global regions. The English Channel formed when rising seas breached chalk barriers connecting Britain to continental Europe. The Bering Strait opened as waters inundated the land bridge between Asia and North America. In each case, substantial areas of human habitat disappeared beneath advancing oceans.

Climate researcher Dr. William Ryan documented the human impact of these changes. Archaeological evidence from Mediterranean sites showed abrupt cultural disruptions coinciding with major flooding events. Settlement patterns shifted dramatically. Pottery styles changed suddenly. Population centers relocated to higher elevations. The archaeological record reflected massive social upheaval.

Caribbean flooding followed similar patterns. As post-glacial melting accelerated, rising seas advanced across low-lying areas at unprecedented rates. Island chains are separated into isolated fragments. Coastal plains transformed into underwater shelves. River valleys became submarine canyons. The changes forced major population movements and cultural adaptations.

Geophysical surveys revealed the extent of drowned landscapes. Side-scan sonar mapping identified submerged beach ridges, river channels, and valley systems. Seismic profiling detected buried soil layers and organic deposits, indicating previous terrestrial environments. The seafloor contained a complete record of pre-flood geography.

Dating techniques confirmed the timeline of environmental changes. Radiocarbon analysis of organic materials provided precise ages for different sea level stages. Coral growth patterns recorded annual variations in ocean conditions. Sediment cores contained pollen and other indicators of past climatic conditions. The data created detailed reconstructions of post-glacial transformations.

Archaeological implications extended beyond site preservation. Rising seas disrupted trade networks spanning ocean basins. Island-hopping routes required constant revision as stepping stones disappeared. Maritime technologies needed continuous adaptation to changing conditions. Cultural exchanges between distant regions faced increasing barriers.

Dr. Douglas Bailey studied how flooding affected human societies in southeastern Europe. His research showed that communities adapted to rising waters through technological innovation. Pile dwellings are elevated structures above flood levels. Boat construction evolved to handle rougher seas. Agricultural techniques accommodated changing drainage patterns. Social organization became more flexible and mobile.

Similar adaptations likely occurred throughout the Caribbean. Archaeological evidence suggests increasing reliance on maritime resources during the post-glacial period. Shell middens expand dramatically in size and complexity. Fishing technologies become more sophisticated. Boat construction incorporates ocean-going capabilities. The changes reflect successful adaptation to marine environments.

The cultural memory of these changes persisted in oral traditions. Flood myths appear in virtually all Caribbean indigenous cultures. Stories describe golden ages when islands were connected by land. Legends speak of cities swallowed by rising seas. Ancestral spirits dwell in underwater realms. These traditions might preserve actual historical memories of post-glacial flooding.

Modern researchers recognized the need for systematic underwater archaeology. Traditional excavation techniques required adaptation for marine environments. Remote sensing technologies provided new tools for site discovery. Underwater preservation offered unique opportunities for studying ancient materials. The submerged landscape represented an untapped archaeological frontier.

# Caribbean Archaeological Anomalies

Captain Don Rodocker guided his research vessel through the crystal waters northeast of Andros Island in the Bahamas. The experienced marine surveyor had spent three decades mapping Caribbean seafloors for commercial and scientific clients. His sophisticated sonar equipment could penetrate deep sediments and identify buried structures invisible to surface observation. On this expedition in 1996, his instruments detected formations that defied conventional explanation.

Geometric patterns stretched across the ocean floor at depths ranging from 100 to 300 feet. Perfectly circular features measured 100 to 200 meters in diameter. Linear arrangements extended for several kilometers in straight lines. Rectangular outlines suggested building foundations or ceremonial platforms. The formations appeared too systematic for natural creation.

Rodocker documented the coordinates and returned with underwater cameras. The footage revealed massive stone blocks arranged in organized patterns—individual stones measured 10 to 15 feet in length. Joints between blocks showed evidence of precise fitting. Smaller stones filled gaps in apparent mortared construction. The underwater structures resembled ancient architectural remains.

Marine archaeologist Dr. William Donato examined Rodocker's findings. The formations displayed construction techniques found nowhere else in the Caribbean region. Megalithic building methods typically associated with Mediterranean or Atlantic cultures appeared in tropical waters thousands of miles from their supposed origins. The discovery challenged fundamental assumptions about ancient maritime capabilities.

Donato organized systematic surveys of the Andros platform throughout the late 1990s. His team identified over 200 individual structures scattered across a 50-square-mile area. The features showed consistent construction methods and architectural planning. Circular plazas connected to linear roadways. Rectangular buildings clustered around central courtyards. The complex suggested a substantial ancient settlement.

Sonar mapping revealed additional anomalies throughout Bahamian waters. Linear features crossed the Grand Bahama Bank in perfectly straight lines. Circular depressions dotted the Tongue of the Ocean with

*Ancient American Civilizations*

uniform spacing. Rectangular patterns appeared near Eleuthera and Cat Island. The entire region contained evidence of systematic landscape modification.

Dr. Greg Little expanded the search to other Caribbean locations. His expeditions found similar formations off Cuba, Jamaica, and Puerto Rico. Each site displayed comparable construction techniques and architectural organization. The distribution suggested a widespread culture capable of major engineering projects across the entire Caribbean basin.

Geological analysis complicated the interpretation of the discoveries. Bahamian limestone does fracture along predictable patterns under specific conditions. Circular sinkholes form naturally through dissolution processes. Linear features can result from fault systems or erosion channels. Natural explanations existed for many observed formations.

However, specific details contradicted purely geological origins. Tool marks scarred stone surfaces at multiple sites. Quarry areas showed systematic extraction activities. Transportation channels connected construction zones with material sources. The evidence suggested human modification of natural formations rather than purely accidental creation.

Radiocarbon dating of organic materials trapped within the structures yielded ages between 8,000 and 12,000 years. These dates coincided with post-glacial sea level rise in the Caribbean region. If the formations represented human construction, they originated during the transition from Ice Age to modern climate conditions.

Local Bahamian knowledge supported ancient human activity. Island elders described traditions of underwater cities built by ancestral peoples. Fishermen reported seeing stone walls beneath clear waters during exceptionally low tides. Diving guides identified artificial structures throughout the Bahama Banks. The oral traditions suggested long-standing awareness of submerged archaeological sites.

Similar anomalies appeared in other Caribbean locations. Off the coast of Venezuela, sonar surveys detected linear arrangements of megalithic blocks extending for several miles. Dominican Republic waters contained circular stone platforms at 150-meter depths. Jamaican expeditions found rectangular structures near underwater cliff faces. The discoveries spanned the entire Caribbean Sea.

Each new site displayed comparable architectural features. Stepped platforms created elevated ceremonial areas. Circular arrangements focused attention on central points. Linear causeways connected different structural complexes. The consistency suggested shared cultural traditions or direct communication between distant communities.

Dr. Iturralde examined the Cuban offshore formations discovered by Paulina Zelitsky. His analysis identified specific construction techniques that require advanced engineering expertise. Interlocking stone layouts created earthquake-resistant foundations. Hydraulic systems regulated water flow through urban areas. Astronomical alignments aligned major structures with celestial events.

The sophistication of these features exceeded the capabilities typically attributed to Caribbean cultures during the post-glacial period. Orthodox archaeological models proposed simple hunter-gatherer societies inhabiting the islands until relatively recent times. The underwater discoveries suggested more complex cultural developments occurring thousands of years earlier.

Satellite imagery revealed corresponding terrestrial features throughout the Caribbean region. Geometric earthworks appeared on mountainous islands from Puerto Rico to Trinidad. Linear arrangements crossed valleys and ridgetops with engineering precision. Circular structures created ceremonial complexes in remote highland areas. The terrestrial sites complemented underwater discoveries.

Computer modeling reconstructed ancient coastline configurations during different sea level stages. The analysis showed how current underwater sites might have functioned as coastal settlements, harbors, or

ceremonial centers. Rising seas gradually submerged these facilities, preserving them beneath protective sediment layers.

The implications extended beyond regional archaeology. If advanced cultures developed throughout the Caribbean during the post-glacial period, human maritime capabilities exceeded conventional estimates. Island societies might have created extensive trade networks connecting distant continents. Rising sea levels could have hidden evidence of early trans-oceanic contact.

Independent researchers proposed connections to other anomalous archaeological sites. Mediterranean megalithic structures showed similar construction techniques to Caribbean underwater formations. Atlantic islands contained comparable circular and linear arrangements. The global distribution might reflect ancient seafaring cultures operating on oceanic scales.

# Andros Island: Submerged Symmetrical Formations

The Tongue of the Ocean drops suddenly from Andros Island's eastern shore. This underwater canyon plunges over 6,000 feet into oceanic depths, creating one of the Caribbean's most dramatic geological features. Along its edges, where the shallow Bahama Banks meet the deep blue void, lie formations so perfectly symmetrical they seem crafted by intelligent design rather than natural forces.

Marine biologist Dr. Mandy Joye first noticed the anomalies during a 2003 research expedition studying deep-water corals. Her submersible descended along the canyon walls, documenting marine life in different depth zones. At 200 feet, her lights illuminated circular depressions carved into the limestone shelf. Each circle measured approximately 150 meters across. Perfect geometric spacing separated them at 300-meter intervals.

Joye directed her pilot to investigate further. The submersible moved along the shelf edge, revealing dozens of identical formations. Every circle displayed the same dimensions and depth characteristics. Smaller circular features surrounded the larger ones in organized patterns. Linear channels connected different groups, creating a systematic network that extended for several kilometers.

Subsequent sonar mapping confirmed the extent of the formations. High-resolution side-scan imaging revealed over 300 individual circles distributed across a 20-square-kilometer area. Computer analysis calculated the mathematical precision of their arrangement. The spacing followed consistent geometric ratios. The orientations aligned with cardinal compass directions. The patterns suggested deliberate planning rather than random natural processes.

Dr. Paul Weinzweig joined the research team to investigate the formations' origins. The marine geologist had extensive experience studying Caribbean geology and underwater formations. His initial assumption favored a natural explanation through dissolution processes. Limestone regularly develops circular sinkholes through chemical weathering and groundwater action.

Nevertheless, detailed analysis revealed features incompatible with natural formation. The circles exhibited uniform depth profiles throughout their entire area. Walls showed smooth, vertical sides rather than irregular erosion patterns. Bottom surfaces contained organized arrangements of stone blocks. Connecting channels maintained consistent widths and slopes. The precision surpassed anything observed in natural sinkhole systems.

Underwater excavation within selected circles revealed further anomalies. Stone blocks were arranged in geometric patterns across the seabed. Individual stones showed signs of shaping and deliberate placement. Mortared joints linked adjacent blocks in organized sequences. Smaller stones filled gaps, indicating intentional construction techniques. The materials suggested purposeful placement rather than accidental accumulation.

Carbon dating of organic materials trapped between the stones yielded ages of 10,000 to 12,000 years. These dates corresponded to post-glacial sea level rise in the Caribbean region. The formations had been submerged as melting ice sheets raised ocean levels following the last Ice Age. If they represented human construction, the builders worked during the transition to modern climate conditions.

Geological surveys identified the source materials for the stone constructions. Chemical analysis traced the limestone blocks to quarry sites located several kilometers inland from current shorelines. During lower sea level periods, these quarries would have been accessible by land transportation. The evidence suggested systematic extraction and movement of building materials over substantial distances.

Remote sensing revealed additional features associated with the circular formations. Linear arrangements of stones created causeways connecting different circles. Rectangular platforms provided elevated surfaces within selected depressions. Curved walls created partial enclosures around ceremonial areas. The complexity suggested sophisticated architectural planning and construction techniques.

Dr. Charles Hapgood studied the mathematical relationships between different formation elements. His analysis identified consistent proportional ratios governing circle diameters, spacing intervals, and connecting channel dimensions. The ratios corresponded to geometric principles found in ancient architectural traditions worldwide. The precision required advanced mathematical knowledge and surveying capabilities.

Three-dimensional modeling reconstructed the formations' appearance during different sea level stages. When ocean levels stood 200 to 300 feet lower, the circles would have been dry land features elevated above the surrounding terrain. The connecting channels could have functioned as water management systems. The platforms might have supported ceremonial or residential structures.

Local Bahamian knowledge provided additional insights into the formations' significance. Andros Island traditions spoke of underwater cities built by ancestral peoples possessing advanced stone-working abilities. Fishing communities described circular structures visible beneath clear waters during calm conditions. Diving guides identified similar formations throughout the Bahama Banks region.

Archaeological surveys of nearby terrestrial areas revealed corresponding features on dry land. Circular earthworks appeared in the highland regions of Andros Island. Linear stone arrangements crossed valleys and ridgetops. Rectangular platforms created ceremonial complexes near freshwater sources. The terrestrial sites suggested cultural continuity between underwater and surface archaeological remains.

The discovery attracted attention from researchers investigating other anomalous Caribbean sites. The Andros formations showed architectural similarities to underwater structures off Cuba, Bimini, and other Bahamian islands. The consistency suggested shared cultural traditions or direct communication between ancient communities across the region.

Comparative analysis identified parallels with megalithic sites in other global locations. Mediterranean islands contained similar circular and linear stone arrangements. Atlantic archipelagos showed comparable architectural planning and construction techniques. The similarities raised questions about ancient maritime connections spanning oceanic distances.

Critics proposed alternative explanations for the formations' regular patterns. Geological processes could theoretically create circular features through systematic dissolution or volcanic activity. Ocean currents might arrange transported stones in organized patterns. Natural explanations remained possible for at least some observed characteristics.

However, the mathematical precision and architectural complexity of the Andros formations exceeded typical natural processes. The geometric relationships, construction techniques, and material sourcing suggested human planning and execution. The evidence supported interpretations favoring ancient cultural activity rather than purely geological origins.

The implications extended beyond Caribbean archaeology. If advanced cultures created systematic architectural complexes throughout the region 10,000 years ago, human maritime capabilities during the post-glacial period exceeded conventional estimates. Island societies might have developed sophisticated technologies for underwater construction and resource management.

Rising sea levels following the Ice Age could have submerged extensive evidence of early human achievement. Traditional archaeology, which focuses on terrestrial sites, might miss the most significant remains of ancient civilizations. The underwater formations suggested new directions for investigating human cultural development in maritime environments.

The Andros discoveries highlighted the need for comprehensive surveys of drowned coastlines worldwide. Similar formations might exist near other island chains or continental margins. Systematic exploration could reveal previously unknown chapters in human cultural history. The ocean floor represented an archaeological frontier containing evidence of lost civilizations.

Dr. Joye continued documenting the formations through multiple research expeditions. Each survey revealed additional architectural details and construction techniques. The complexity and sophistication of the underwater structures challenged fundamental assumptions about ancient human capabilities. The evidence suggested remarkable achievements by people whose names and stories had been lost beneath the rising seas.

# PART II
# IMPOSSIBLE
# STONEWORK

# Chapter 13: Tiwanaku and Pumapunku - The Impossible Engineering

## 13,000-Foot Altitude Construction Challenges

Eduardo Pareja climbed the last steep section of the trail leading to Pumapunku. His lungs burned in the thin air. At 12,600 feet above sea level, every step demanded extra effort. The Bolivian archaeologist had made this journey hundreds of times over the past fifteen years. He never got used to the altitude.

Pareja reached the edge of the ancient site and stopped. Scattered across the windswept plateau lay massive stone blocks arranged in geometric patterns. Some weighed over 100 tons. Others bore intricate cuts and angles that defied explanation. The sight always left him breathless, and not from the climb.

Constructing anything at this altitude poses significant challenges for modern construction crews. Heavy machinery struggles in the thin atmosphere. Concrete takes longer to cure. Workers need frequent breaks to avoid altitude sickness. Ancient builders faced these same problems without modern equipment or medical knowledge.

The Tiwanaku basin sits in one of the world's harshest construction environments. Winter temperatures drop below freezing. Summer storms bring hail and lightning. Winds sweep across the open plain without obstruction. Rain falls unpredictably, turning dust into mud that clings to everything.

Ancient engineers somehow transported multi-ton blocks across this unforgiving landscape. They lifted them into precise positions. They carved complex joints and channels. They created architectural complexes covering hundreds of acres. Modern observers struggle to understand how such work was possible.

The nearest quarries lie six miles away across broken terrain. No roads existed. No wheeled vehicles carried loads. No cranes lifted stones into position. No metal tools have shaped the hardest rock types known to geology. Ancient builders accomplished what seems impossible using methods we cannot identify.

*Ancient American Civilizations*

Oxygen levels at 13,000 feet drop to 68% of sea level concentrations. Workers tire quickly. Concentration becomes difficult. Physical exertion brings immediate fatigue. Building projects requiring years of sustained effort should have been nearly impossible to complete.

Archaeological evidence suggests thousands of people worked at Tiwanaku during its construction phases. They needed food, water, and shelter in an environment barely capable of supporting agriculture. Supply lines stretched across difficult mountain terrain. Everything required for massive construction projects had to be imported or created locally under harsh conditions.

Modern altitude physiology research shows that people need weeks to acclimatize to high elevation work. Ancient builders either possessed superior physical conditioning or developed adaptation techniques we have lost. Perhaps they understood how to work efficiently in low-oxygen environments through methods modern science has not rediscovered.

The construction timeline spans several centuries. Workers maintained consistent quality and precision across generations. Knowledge was transferred from master builders to apprentices without written documentation. Complex engineering decisions are coordinated across multiple work sites. The organizational capabilities required suggest sophisticated management systems.

# Andesite and Diorite: Stones Harder Than Steel

Geologist Robert Schoch ran his hand across the perfectly smooth surface of an H-shaped block at Pumapunku. The stone felt like glass under his fingers. No tool marks showed anywhere on the surface. The andesite had been shaped with precision that modern diamond-tipped tools would struggle to match.

Andesite ranks among the hardest rocks on Earth. It rates 7 on the Mohs scale, harder than steel files and most cutting tools. Diamond rates 10. Quartz rates 7. Only specialized industrial equipment can work andesite efficiently today. Ancient builders somehow achieved flawless results using unknown techniques.

Diorite blocks at the site present even greater puzzles. This igneous rock forms deep underground under intense heat and pressure. It contains crystals of feldspar and hornblende locked in an incredibly hard matrix. Modern stone workers avoid diorite because it rapidly destroys cutting tools. Shaping it costs more than most projects can afford.

Schoch examined block after block, searching for clues about construction methods. He found perfectly flat surfaces extending for yards without deviation. Right angles are measured exactly 90 degrees. Curved sections followed precise mathematical arcs. Internal corners showed sharp, clean edges. The workmanship exceeded what modern stonecutters produce with computer-controlled machinery.

Traditional explanations suggest ancient workers used harder stones to shape softer ones. This theory fails at Pumapunku. No stones exist harder than andesite and diorite, except diamonds and a few rare minerals. Ancient builders would have needed industrial diamonds in large quantities to achieve the observed results. No evidence supports such technology.

Some archaeologists propose that repeated heating and cooling made the stones easier to work. Fire followed by cold water can crack rock surfaces. Builders could then chip away fractured pieces to shape blocks gradually. Experiments with this technique produce rough, irregular surfaces, nothing like the precision work at Pumapunku.

Schoch discovered another impossibility. Many blocks show evidence of machine-like processing. Surfaces bear parallel ridges like those left by rotary cutting tools. Bore holes extend deep into solid rock with perfectly circular cross-sections. Internal channels follow complex three-dimensional paths carved with mathematical precision.

The site contains over 150 H-shaped blocks weighing 10 to 15 tons each. Every surface shows identical quality control. Measurements vary by fractions of an inch across hundreds of stones. This consistency demands standardized tools and techniques replicated across years of construction work.

Microscopic analysis reveals no trace of copper or bronze tools, the only metals available to ancient Andean cultures. Copper tools cannot cut andesite effectively. Bronze performs slightly better but wears away too quickly for major construction projects. Iron tools, harder than bronze, still struggle with andesite and diorite. Steel tools work better but show clear wear patterns after cutting such hard stones.

Chemical analysis found no evidence of acids or other substances that might soften rock surfaces. No unusual mineral deposits suggest special processing techniques. The stones appear to have been worked in their natural state using methods that left no physical traces of the tools involved.

# H-Shaped Blocks: CNC-Level Precision Cutting

Mechanical engineer Christopher Dunn spent three days at Pumapunku measuring H-shaped blocks with precision instruments. His digital calipers, laser levels, and surface measurement tools revealed construction accuracy that shocked him. The ancient blocks matched tolerances achievable only by computer-controlled machinery.

Each H-shaped block consists of a rectangular body with projecting flanges on opposite sides. The design allows multiple blocks to interlock like three-dimensional puzzle pieces. No mortar joins the connections. Perfect fit depends entirely on machining precision.

Dunn found surface flatness variations of less than two millimeters across blocks measuring 10 feet in length. Modern machine shops struggle to achieve such precision when working with steel. Stone cutting introduces additional challenges because rock contains internal stresses that cause unpredictable warping as material gets removed.

The projecting flanges show even more impressive accuracy. Each flange must align perfectly with the corresponding recesses in adjacent blocks. Angles must match exactly. Heights must coordinate precisely. Width dimensions must maintain consistency. Any error prevents proper assembly.

Dunn measured dozens of blocks and found remarkable standardization. Flange dimensions varied by less than 5 millimeters despite blocks being carved from separate pieces of stone. This consistency suggests either incredibly skilled craftsmen or mechanical systems that maintained precise measurements across extensive production runs.

Internal corners where flanges meet block bodies show sharp, clean edges without chips or rounded curves. Stone cutting typically leaves fractured edges because rock breaks unpredictably under stress. Achieving sharp internal corners requires controlled cutting techniques that prevent fracturing during the final cuts.

Several blocks contain channels and grooves carved into their surfaces. These features follow complex three-dimensional paths through solid stone. Channels maintain consistent width and depth over their entire length. Sharp corners show no signs of gradual carving or hand tool marks. The precision suggests machine cutting under computer control.

Dunn examined the bore holes drilled through many blocks. Circular holes extend deep into solid andesite with perfectly smooth walls and consistent diameters. No spiral marks indicate rotary drilling. No step patterns suggest piecemeal boring. The holes appear to have been cut in single operations using unknown techniques.

Some H-blocks show evidence of modification after initial shaping. Channels were added, holes were enlarged, or surfaces were refinished. These alterations maintain the same precision as the original work. Ancient builders could apparently modify completed blocks without losing accuracy or surface quality.

The engineering implications puzzle modern observers. H-shaped designs maximize interlocking strength for earthquake resistance. Bolivia sits in a seismically active zone where ground motion regularly damages buildings. Ancient designers created structural systems that remain stable after centuries of earth movement.

# Perfect Bore Holes Without Metal Tools

Archaeologist Alexei Vranich descended into the underground chambers beneath Akapana pyramid at Tiwanaku. His headlamp illuminated stone blocks bearing dozens of circular holes drilled with stunning precision. The sight never failed to amaze him, despite years of studying it.

The holes range from finger-sized to several inches in diameter. They extend deep into solid andesite blocks without deviation from perfectly circular cross-sections. No drill marks score the walls. No step patterns indicate piecemeal boring. The holes appear to have been cut in single continuous operations.

Vranich measured hole dimensions with precision instruments. Diameters remain constant over their entire depth. Wall surfaces show mirror-smooth finishes. Centers align with mathematical precision when multiple holes appear in single blocks. The accuracy exceeds that of modern masonry bits when drilling much softer stones.

Traditional archaeology explains these holes as anchor points for ropes used to move blocks during construction. This theory fails basic engineering analysis. Rope anchor holes need rough internal surfaces to provide grip. Smooth walls allow ropes to slip under load. The precision machining actually reduces functional effectiveness for rope attachment.

Experimental archaeologists have attempted to recreate similar holes using copper and bronze tools available to ancient Andean cultures. Copper pipes rotated with sand abrasive can slowly drill holes in softer stones. The process takes days for small holes and destroys multiple tools. Results show rough, irregular boring with visible tool marks and fractured edges.

Bronze hollow drills perform slightly better than copper but still require excessive time and tool replacement. Neither copper nor bronze maintains cutting edges long enough to drill the deep holes found at Tiwanaku. Ancient builders would have needed thousands of metal tools to complete observed drilling work.

Some holes show remarkable engineering features. Internal channels branch off from main bores, creating complex three-dimensional passages through solid stone. Branch angles maintain perfect geometry. Surface finishes remain consistently smooth throughout branching systems. No known hand tools could achieve such complex internal shaping.

Vranich discovered holes that were drilled partway through blocks from both sides. The holes meet perfectly in the center with no misalignment. This technique requires precise measurement and positioning of external block surfaces. Ancient builders somehow calculated internal meeting points with accuracy matching modern surveying methods.

Several blocks contain holes drilled at precise angles to block faces. The angles follow mathematical relationships that suggest careful engineering rather than random placement. Some holes align with astronomical orientations. Others coordinate with drainage systems or structural load paths. The positioning appears deliberately planned for specific functions.

Chemical analysis of hole walls reveals no residue from metal cutting tools or abrasive compounds. No copper oxide stains indicate bronze drill usage. The absence of quartz particles suggests sand abrasive techniques. The boring process left no chemical traces that might identify the tools or methods involved.

# 100-Ton Stone Transport Across Difficult Terrain

Bolivian engineer Jorge Miranda stood beside the largest block at Pumapunku, calculating the forces needed to move such a massive weight. His measurements showed the andesite monolith weighed approximately 131 tons. Moving it from the nearest quarry, six miles away, required overcoming obstacles that challenge modern heavy equipment.

The route from quarry to construction site crosses broken terrain with steep slopes, unstable soils, and seasonal flooding. No evidence exists of ancient road construction adequate for multi-ton loads. Modern engineers would need to build specialized roadways with reinforced foundations to transport such weights safely.

Traditional explanations suggest ancient builders used wooden rollers, rope systems, and human labor to move the blocks. Mathematical analysis reveals the impossibility of such methods. A 100-ton load requires forces beyond what hundreds of workers can generate using simple mechanical advantage systems.

Miranda calculated that moving a 131-ton block on wooden rollers would require over 2,000 people pulling simultaneously. Coordinating such large work crews across difficult terrain exceeds practical organizational limits. The rollers themselves would need replacement every few hundred yards as the immense weight crushed wood to splinters.

Archaeological surveys found no evidence of ancient transportation infrastructure adequate for such loads. No ramp systems, reinforced roadways, or bridge foundations appear between quarry and construction sites. Ancient builders transported massive blocks across natural terrain that barely supports modern all-terrain vehicles.

The blocks show no damage from transportation stress. Stone edges remain sharp and surfaces stay perfectly flat. Rough handling during transport typically chips stone corners and scratches surfaces. The pristine condition suggests transportation methods that protected blocks from impact and abrasion.

Some researchers propose that ancient builders used water transport during seasonal flooding. The theory requires artificial canal systems to carry floating platforms loaded with multi-ton blocks. No archaeological evidence supports extensive canal construction in the Tiwanaku region during the relevant time periods.

Experimental archaeology teams have attempted to recreate ancient transport methods using historically available technology. The largest stone successfully moved weighed 10 tons and required 180 people working on prepared surfaces. Extrapolating these results suggests that 100-ton blocks would need thousands of workers and extensive infrastructure preparation.

Miranda discovered additional complications in the transport puzzle. Many blocks were shaped at the quarry before transport. This sequence requires moving finished architectural elements rather than rough stone. Finished blocks cannot tolerate the stresses that rough stone might survive during difficult transport operations.

The quarry itself presents engineering mysteries. Ancient workers extracted blocks weighing over 100 tons from solid bedrock without creating access ramps or lifting systems visible in archaeological remains. Modern quarrying operations leave extensive infrastructure evidence that should survive for archaeological detection.

Several transported blocks show evidence of precision fitting adjustments made after reaching the construction site. This sequence suggests builders could modify multi-ton blocks as needed during assembly. The capability implies lifting and positioning systems sophisticated enough to allow fine-tuning of massive architectural elements.

Recent geological surveys identified multiple quarry sources for different stone types used at Tiwanaku. Builders transported andesite, diorite, and sandstone from separate locations across varying distances. Each material required different handling techniques due to weight, hardness, and fracture characteristics.

The transportation achievements become even more remarkable when considered across the entire construction timeline. Thousands of blocks were moved over several centuries of building activity. Ancient builders maintained consistent transportation capabilities across generations without written technical documentation to preserve methods.

Modern heavy transport equipment would struggle with similar challenges in the Tiwanaku environment. High altitude reduces engine performance. Seasonal weather limits operating windows. Remote location complicates equipment maintenance and fuel supply. Ancient builders overcame these obstacles using technologies that left no archaeological traces of their existence.

# Chapter 14: Inca Engineering - When Stone Becomes Art

## Sacsayhuamán: 120-Ton Interlocked Stones

The morning sun struck the massive stone walls above Cusco, casting shadows that revealed every precise joint and curve. Spanish chronicler Pedro Cieza de León climbed the steep path to Sacsayhuamán in 1548, three decades after Pizarro's conquest. What he saw defied every assumption about indigenous capabilities.

Enormous stones stretched before him like a frozen geological wave. Some blocks measured thirty feet in length and weighed more than 120 tons. Each stone fit perfectly against its neighbors. No gaps existed between the massive pieces. No mortar held them together. The Spanish had conquered the Inca Empire, but they could not explain how these monuments came to exist.

Cieza de León interviewed elderly Inca nobles who remembered the construction. They described thousands of workers quarrying limestone from distant mountainsides. Teams of men moved stones across ravines and up impossible slopes using only rope, wooden rollers, and human strength. Master stonemasons shaped each block to fit exact specifications. The work continued for over seventy years under three different Inca rulers.

Modern engineers have attempted similar projects using contemporary equipment. They failed to achieve the precision found at Sacsayhuamán. Laser measurements reveal tolerances measured in fractions of millimeters. The stones interlock in three dimensions, creating structural stability that has survived five centuries of earthquakes, colonial demolition attempts, and modern tourist traffic.

The construction process required unprecedented organization and technical knowledge. Workers quarried specific types of limestone from Waqoto and Rumiqolqa, sites located several miles from Sacsayhuamán. The different stone types were chosen for specific structural purposes. Darker, harder limestone formed the foundation courses. Lighter, more workable stone created the upper walls. The selection process showed sophisticated understanding of material properties.

Teams transported the quarried blocks across rugged terrain without wheels or draft animals. Inca roads included ramps, switchbacks, and carefully engineered grades to accommodate heavy loads. Workers constructed temporary earthen ramps to position stones at precise elevations. They used bronze crowbars, wooden levers, and rope systems to maneuver blocks weighing more than modern cranes can lift.

The shaping process remains the most mysterious aspect of construction. Each stone required custom cutting to fit against multiple neighbors simultaneously. The surfaces show tool marks consistent with bronze implements, but bronze tools cannot cut limestone with the precision found at Sacsayhuamán. Some researchers propose that Inca masons used harder stone tools or abrasive techniques to achieve the final finish.

Archaeological evidence suggests a different approach. Inca builders created full-scale models of wall sections using smaller stones before beginning work with the massive blocks. They tested joint patterns, structural loads, and earthquake resistance using these prototype walls. Once the design proved sound, they scaled up to full-size construction. This method reduced errors and minimized the need to move enormous stones multiple times.

The interlocking patterns follow mathematical principles that distribute seismic forces throughout the wall structure. Individual stones cannot shift independently during earthquakes. The walls move as unified systems, flexing rather than breaking when ground motion occurs. Spanish colonial builders never achieved similar seismic resistance using European masonry techniques.

# Earthquake-Resistant Wave-Curve Walls

The walls of Sacsayhuamán follow subtle curves that become apparent only when viewed from specific angles. Spanish observers initially dismissed these curves as an imperfect construction. Modern structural analysis reveals sophisticated earthquake engineering principles embedded in the seemingly irregular patterns.

Inca builders understood that straight walls concentrate seismic stresses at vulnerable points. Curved walls distribute earthquake forces across larger areas, reducing the likelihood of catastrophic failure. The curves also create interlocking patterns that bind individual wall sections together into unified structural systems.

The Great Earthquake of 1950 devastated Cusco and the surrounding areas. Modern buildings collapsed throughout the region. Colonial churches built with Spanish techniques suffered severe damage. The ancient walls of Sacsayhuamán remained intact. Observers documented minor settlement in some areas, but no structural failures occurred in the original Inca construction.

Each curve follows precise mathematical relationships based on the golden ratio and other geometric constants. The builders did not create random organic shapes. They applied systematic design principles that balanced structural requirements with aesthetic considerations. The curves appear natural but result from careful calculation and planning.

The wave patterns also serve functional purposes beyond earthquake resistance. The curved surfaces deflect wind and rain more effectively than flat walls. Water drainage follows predictable patterns that protect the stone foundations from erosion. The shapes create acoustic effects that amplify human voices at specific gathering points.

Construction crews marked curve patterns on the ground using stakes and rope systems before beginning stone placement. They maintained consistent curve radii across wall sections hundreds of feet in length. This precision required mathematical knowledge and surveying techniques comparable to modern construction methods.

The curves create visual effects that change throughout the day as sunlight strikes the walls from different angles. Morning light emphasizes the wave patterns, making them appear to flow like frozen water. Afternoon shadows reveal the precise joints between individual stones. Evening light transforms the walls into abstract sculptures that seem to move as observers change position.

# Machu Picchu: 2,430-Meter Altitude Precision

Hiram Bingham climbed through cloud forest on July 24, 1911, following an indigenous guide named Anacleto Arteaga up treacherous mountain paths. They had left their base camp before dawn, crossing the rushing Urubamba River on a log bridge and ascending nearly vertical slopes covered in dense vegetation. At 2,430 meters above sea level, they encountered one of archaeology's most extraordinary discoveries.

Machu Picchu stretched across a knife-edge ridge between two towering peaks. Terraced gardens cascaded down impossible slopes. Stone buildings perched on precipices that should have been uninhabitable. Water flowed through carved channels that followed the mountain's contours with mathematical precision. The city seemed to grow from the living rock rather than being imposed upon it.

The construction challenges at this altitude exceeded anything attempted by ancient civilizations elsewhere. Workers transported every stone, every timber, every tool up mountain paths that modern hikers find difficult to navigate. They built on slopes approaching sixty degrees in some areas. They created level platforms for buildings on terrain that offered no natural flat surfaces.

The granite used throughout Machu Picchu came from local quarries, but these quarries existed on cliffs that required rock climbing skills to access. Workers lowered quarried blocks down vertical faces using rope systems. They carved steps into cliff faces to create access routes. They built temporary bridges to span gaps between rock formations.

Each building follows the natural contours of its specific location. The architects studied every rock outcrop, every water source, every wind pattern before beginning construction. They integrated existing boulders into wall systems rather than removing natural obstacles. The result appears organic, as if the city had been shaped by geological forces rather than human hands.

The precision of individual buildings at Machu Picchu equals anything found at Sacsayhuamán, but this precision extends across an entire urban complex built on impossible terrain. The Room of the Three Windows maintains perfect alignment despite being constructed on a steep slope. The Intihuatana stone occupies the exact center of the city's astronomical observations. The Temple of the Sun follows curves that match the hillside's natural geometry.

Water management at Machu Picchu demonstrates sophisticated hydraulic engineering adapted to extreme mountain conditions. Sixteen fountains connect in sequence, each receiving water from the one above through carved stone channels. The system maintains consistent flow rates despite seasonal variations in precipitation. Springs located hundreds of feet above the city provide reliable water through drought periods that lasted multiple years.

The terracing system transforms steep slopes into workable farmland. Workers built level planting platforms by constructing retaining walls filled with carefully layered soil, gravel, and drainage materials. The terraces help prevent erosion during the heavy rains typical at this altitude. They also create microclimates that extend the growing season for crops such as maize and potatoes.

Construction crews worked without modern safety equipment on exposures where falls meant certain death. They built scaffolding systems using wooden poles and rope to support workers positioning stones on vertical surfaces. Evidence suggests they used counterweight systems to lift heavy blocks up the steepest sections. The human cost of construction must have been enormous, but no records survive to document casualties.

# No Mortar Construction Techniques

Inca masons achieved structural permanence without using any binding agents between stones. Modern construction relies on cement, concrete, or specialized adhesives to create strong joints. The Inca developed alternative techniques that proved more durable than European mortar-based systems introduced during the colonial period.

The key innovation involved precision cutting that created multiple contact points between adjacent stones. Each block touched its neighbors along carefully shaped surfaces that distributed loads across large areas. The joints formed mechanical connections rather than relying on chemical bonding agents.

Master craftsmen spent months shaping individual stones to achieve perfect fits. They used bronze tools, stone hammers, and abrasive techniques to remove material gradually. Trial-and-error processes required repeated testing as each stone neared its final dimensions. The time investment per block exceeded what modern construction schedules would consider economical.

The cutting process began with rough shaping at the quarry sites. Workers reduced stone blocks to approximate sizes before transportation to reduce the loads that construction crews needed to move. Final shaping occurred at the building location using templates and measuring devices to ensure precise fits against stones already in place.

Evidence from unfinished walls reveals the construction sequence. Builders placed cornerstones first to establish alignment and elevation references. They worked toward the center of each wall section, adjusting stone shapes to maintain consistent joint patterns. The final stones required the most precise cutting because they needed to fit precisely into spaces defined by surrounding blocks.

The lack of mortar created joints that respond flexibly to thermal expansion, seismic motion, and structural settlement. Mortar joints crack when subjected to differential movement. The Inca joints maintain contact even when walls shift during earthquakes. This flexibility explains why Inca construction has survived seismic events that destroyed later colonial buildings.

Seasonal temperature variations at high altitude create significant thermal stresses in stone walls. Mortar would crack and fail under these conditions. The Inca joints accommodate thermal movement without losing structural integrity. The walls expand and contract as unified systems rather than developing stress concentrations at rigid mortar lines.

Archaeological analysis of Inca quarries reveals a sophisticated understanding of stone fracture patterns and structural properties. Builders selected specific stone types for different structural applications. They oriented blocks to take advantage of natural grain directions and cleavage planes. The selection process showed knowledge equivalent to modern materials engineering.

# Astronomical Window and Doorway Alignments

The buildings of Machu Picchu function as a three-dimensional calendar that tracks celestial events throughout the year. Windows, doorways, and architectural features align with sunrise and sunset positions during solstices, equinoxes, and other astronomically significant dates. The city becomes an instrument for measuring time and predicting seasonal cycles.

The Room of the Three Windows faces east toward the rising sun. During the winter solstice, sunlight passes through the southern window and illuminates specific interior features. The summer solstice creates different light patterns through the northern window. The central window marks equinox events when day and night achieve equal length.

The Intihuatana stone serves as the focal point for astronomical observations throughout the complex. This carved granite outcrop functions as a sundial that tracks solar motion across the sky during different seasons. The stone's shadow points toward specific architectural features during key calendar dates, creating visual connections between celestial cycles and human activities.

Construction of astronomically aligned features required precise surveying and long-term observations before building began. Inca astronomers studied sunrise and sunset positions throughout multiple annual cycles to identify exact alignment directions. They used temporary markers and sighting devices to establish reference lines that guided construction crews.

The Temple of the Sun contains windows positioned to frame the Pleiades constellation during specific times of the year. These stars served as calendrical markers for agricultural activities and religious ceremonies. The window positions allow observers inside the temple to track stellar motion and predict optimal planting and harvesting dates.

Doorway alignments connect buildings across the entire urban complex into unified astronomical observation systems. Standing in specific doorways, observers can sight through multiple buildings to frame celestial events on the horizon. These sighting lines cross the city at calculated angles that maximize astronomical viewing opportunities.

The precision of these alignments approaches modern surveying accuracy. Measurements reveal angular tolerances measured in fractions of degrees. Achieving such precision required sophisticated mathematical knowledge and careful use of measuring instruments. The builders understood concepts of triangulation, angular measurement, and geometric calculation.

Modern astronomers have verified the accuracy of Inca celestial predictions based on Machu Picchu's architectural alignments. The city's features correctly track precession, seasonal variations, and lunar cycles across multiple centuries. The astronomical knowledge embedded in the construction exceeds what Spanish chroniclers attributed to indigenous peoples.

The alignments also serve practical functions related to agricultural scheduling and resource management. Accurate calendars enabled the prediction of rainy seasons, drought periods, and optimal times for planting different crops. This knowledge was essential for survival at high altitude, where weather patterns were unpredictable and growing seasons were short.

Hidden alignments exist throughout the complex that become visible only during specific astronomical events. Some windows reveal interior features only when particular stars or planets rise at precise times. These hidden elements suggest that Machu Picchu contained levels of astronomical knowledge accessible only to specialized priests or observers who understood the complete system.

The integration of astronomical functions with architectural beauty achieves a synthesis rarely matched in human construction. The buildings serve practical purposes of shelter, storage, and ceremony. They simultaneously function as scientific instruments for observing and predicting celestial events. The combination creates structures that operate as both art and technology, demonstrating a sophisticated understanding of how human needs and natural cycles could be harmonized through careful design and construction.

*Ancient American Civilizations*

# Chapter 15: The Olmec Mystery - Giants, Gods, and Vanished Peoples

## Colossal Basalt Heads: 50-Ton Sculptures

The machete blade struck something hard beneath the Mexican jungle floor. Stirling Dickey wiped sweat from his forehead and knelt to examine what his workers had found. The year was 1938. The location was Tres Zapotes in Veracruz. What emerged from the earth would transform our understanding of ancient Mesoamerica forever.

A massive stone face stared up from the excavation pit. The sculpture measured nearly six feet tall and weighed approximately eight tons. Carved from a single block of basalt, the head displayed remarkable artistic skill and engineering precision. The features were unmistakably human, yet unlike any known indigenous population in the region. Broad nose, full lips, and a distinctive helmet-like headdress marked this as something entirely unique.

Dickey had discovered the first of what would become twenty known colossal heads scattered across the Olmec heartland. Each sculpture told a story of technical mastery and cultural sophistication from over 3,000 years ago. The heads ranged in height from five to nearly ten feet. Their weights varied from eight to fifty tons of solid volcanic rock.

Archaeological teams working at La Venta uncovered four additional heads between 1940 and 1967. Each sculpture bore unique facial features, suggesting they depicted individual rulers or important figures rather than generic representations. The craftsmanship revealed intimate knowledge of human anatomy. Every wrinkle, every expression line, every subtle curve had been carefully planned and executed.

The largest head, designated Monument 1 at La Venta, dominated its ceremonial plaza like a silent sentinel. Workers needed heavy machinery to move it during excavation. Ancient sculptors had somehow transported, positioned, and carved this masterpiece using only stone tools and human labor. The technical achievement defied easy explanation.

*Ancient American Civilizations*

San Lorenzo yielded ten colossal heads during excavations led by Michael Coe in the 1960s. These sculptures displayed even greater variety in size and artistic style. Head 1 measured 9.4 feet tall and weighed an estimated 25 tons. Head 8 reached only 5.7 feet but showed the most refined carving techniques. Each piece required months of skilled labor to complete.

The heads were not randomly distributed across the landscape. They occupied positions of prominence within carefully planned ceremonial centers. At La Venta, the sculptures formed alignments with other monumental architecture. At San Lorenzo, they marked important plazas and ritual spaces. Their placement followed deliberate patterns that modern archaeologists are still working to understand.

Recent discoveries at La Cobata added three more heads to the known corpus. These sculptures, found in 1994, showed evidence of intentional burial. Ancient peoples had carefully covered them with earth and stone, perhaps during religious ceremonies or political transitions. The burial patterns suggested the heads held sacred significance beyond their artistic value.

Each sculpture displayed unique headdress designs. Some featured simple bands around the forehead. Others showed elaborate geometric patterns or symbolic motifs. A few included what appeared to be chinstraps, suggesting the headdresses were functional helmets rather than purely decorative elements. These variations might indicate different time periods, social ranks, or ritual purposes.

The faces themselves commanded attention through their powerful expressions. Some appeared serene and contemplative. Others showed stern authority or quiet strength. The sculptors had captured subtle emotional nuances that brought the stone portraits to life. Modern viewers often report feeling watched by these ancient eyes.

Surface details revealed the sophistication of Olmec carving techniques. Ear ornaments, nose plugs, and lip decorations were rendered with precise accuracy. Hair patterns followed natural growth lines. Even fingernails and skin textures received careful attention. The level of realism achieved with primitive tools demonstrated extraordinary skill.

Tool marks on the sculptures provided insights into construction methods. Pecking stones had been used to rough out the basic forms. Abrasive sands helped smooth the surfaces. Polishing stones created the final finishes. The entire process required intimate knowledge of basalt's working properties and years of specialized training.

Chemical analysis of the stone revealed additional mysteries. The basalt came from quarries in the Tuxtla Mountains, over sixty miles from the ceremonial sites where the heads were found. Moving fifty-ton sculptures across this distance without wheels, draft animals, or metal tools presented enormous logistical challenges.

# Quarry-to-Site Transportation Without Wheels

The Cerro Cintepec quarries in the Tuxtla Mountains show clear evidence of ancient basalt extraction. Archaeologist Carl Drucker first identified these sites in 1952 during systematic surveys of the Olmec heartland. The quarrying areas contained partially worked stone blocks, abandoned sculptures, and tool caches left by ancient workers.

Quarry sites revealed the Olmec selection process for suitable stone. Workers chose basalt with fine, even grain structure and minimal flaws. They tested blocks by breaking off small samples to examine internal quality. Rejected stones still litter the quarry floors, showing the high standards maintained for monumental sculptures.

The distance from quarries to ceremonial sites created massive transportation challenges. La Venta lay ninety miles from the nearest basalt sources. San Lorenzo stood sixty miles away. Tres Zapotes was positioned forty miles from the quarries. Every colossal head required moving tons of stone across difficult terrain without modern technology.

River transport offered the most practical solution for long-distance movement. The Coatzacoalcos River system connected the Tuxtla Mountains to major Olmec centers through a network of waterways. Experimental archaeology has shown that large basalt blocks could be floated on wooden platforms during high water seasons.

The construction of river rafts required sophisticated engineering. Balsa wood, abundant in the region, provided buoyancy for heavy loads. Multiple logs had to be lashed together with precise calculations of weight distribution. The rafts needed steering mechanisms to navigate river currents and shallow areas.

Seasonal timing became critical for water transport. The Coatzacoalcos reached maximum depth during the summer rainy seasons. Ancient logistics coordinators had to plan quarrying, raft construction, and transportation within narrow time windows. Missing the optimal season meant delays of an entire year.

Overland transport presented even greater difficulties. Wooden rollers could move heavy objects across level ground, but the Gulf Coast terrain included hills, marshes, and dense forests. Roads had to be cleared and maintained. Bridges were needed for stream crossings. The infrastructure requirements were enormous.

Experimental attempts to move large stones using ancient methods have provided valuable insights. A team led by archaeologist Rebecca Gonzalez successfully transported a two-ton basalt block using forty people, wooden rollers, and rope pulling systems. Scaling up to fifty-ton sculptures would require coordinated efforts by hundreds of workers.

Rope technology became essential for successful transportation. Henequen fibers, extracted from local agave plants, provided strong cordage. Archaeological remains show evidence of rope-making workshops near major Olmec sites. Specialized workers produced thousands of feet of rope for construction projects.

The logistics of feeding and organizing large work crews added complexity to transportation projects. Hundreds of workers required daily access to food supplies, fresh water, and shelter during multi-week hauling operations. Support systems had to be established along transportation routes.

Evidence from San Lorenzo suggests that some sculptures were partially carved at the quarries before being transported. This approach reduced weight and shipping difficulties. Rough shaping could remove excess stone, leaving final detailing work for arrival at the destination. Tool caches found along transport routes support this interpretation.

La Venta's location on an island in coastal marshlands created unique transportation challenges. The final approach to the ceremonial center required crossing several miles of shallow waterways. Special boats or causeways were necessary to bridge this last gap. Archaeological surveys have identified possible ancient landing sites.

*Ancient American Civilizations*

The organizational capabilities required for these transportation projects indicate sophisticated social structures. Planning, resource allocation, and workforce coordination demanded centralized authority and administrative systems. The colossal heads thus reflect not only artistic achievement but also political and economic complexity.

# African Facial Features in Mesoamerican Context

The facial characteristics carved into Olmec colossal heads sparked decades of scholarly debate and controversy. Dr. Alexander von Wuthenau first drew attention to these features in 1963 when he published detailed photographic comparisons between the sculptures and modern African populations. His observations launched discussions about possible transoceanic contact during ancient times.

Anthropologist Ivan Van Sertima expanded on these observations in his 1976 work examining Olmec sculptural traditions. Van Sertima noted the broad noses, full lips, and pronounced facial structure displayed in many colossal heads. He argued these features were more consistent with West African populations than with indigenous Mesoamerican peoples.

Physical anthropologists conducted detailed measurements of the sculptural features to test these claims. Dr. Andrzej Wiercinski used statistical analysis to compare Olmec head proportions with known population samples. His measurements suggested significant differences from typical Mesoamerican facial structures documented in other ancient art forms.

The debate intensified when researchers examined La Venta Monument 13, known as the "Ambassador." This basalt sculpture depicts a standing figure with clearly African facial features, elaborate headdress, and distinctive clothing. The figure appears to be interacting with another individual, showing more typical Mesoamerican characteristics.

San Lorenzo Head 1 displays particularly pronounced features that support the African comparison hypothesis. The sculpture's nose width, lip fullness, and overall facial proportions differ markedly from contemporary Maya or Zapotec artistic traditions. Computer modeling has been used to reconstruct the possible living appearance based on the stone features.

Critics of the African connection theory point to artistic conventions in Olmec sculpture. They argue the facial features reflect stylistic choices rather than ethnic representation. Some scholars suggest the broad noses and full lips resulted from technical limitations in basalt carving rather than attempts at realistic portraiture.

Archaeological evidence from Olmec sites has not yielded any clear indicators of African presence. No African artifacts, plants, or animals have been found in secure Olmec contexts. Genetic studies of modern populations in the Olmec heartland show no significant African ancestry from ancient times.

Alternative explanations focus on indigenous diversity within ancient Mesoamerica. Skeletal remains from Olmec sites show considerable variation in physical features. Some populations may have naturally possessed the facial characteristics depicted in the colossal heads without requiring external influence.

The "baby face" phenomenon in Olmec art provides another perspective on facial feature interpretation. Many Olmec sculptures show infant-like proportions with large heads, small features, and rounded faces. This artistic tradition might explain some perceived differences from typical adult representations.

Recent discoveries have added complexity to the facial feature debate. The 2018 excavation of Monument 6 at La Cobata revealed a colossal head with distinctly different facial characteristics from previously known examples. The sculpture shows more angular features and a different artistic style.

Experimental archaeology has explored the technical constraints of basalt carving. Working with stone tools limits the fine detail possible in sculptural work. Some features that appear "African" might result from these technical limitations rather than intentional ethnic representation. Stone hardness affects the achievable level of realism.

Chemical analysis of basalt sources has revealed interesting patterns in stone selection. Different quarries produced basalt with varying working properties. Sculptors might have chosen particular stone types based on their suitability for achieving desired artistic effects. This selection process could influence final appearance.

The cultural context of Olmec society provides important background for interpreting sculptural choices. If the heads depict rulers or important individuals, they might show idealized rather than realistic features. Royal portraiture in many cultures emphasizes power and authority through artistic convention rather than accurate representation.

Modern populations in the Olmec region show considerable physical diversity. Some individuals naturally possess features similar to those carved in the colossal heads. This contemporary variation suggests ancient populations might have included similar diversity without requiring external genetic input.

# La Venta Stela 3: Earliest American Writing

The discovery of carved symbols on La Venta Stela 3 reformed the understanding of early writing development in the Americas. Archaeologist Philip Drucker first documented this monument during his 1943-1944 excavations at the site. The stela contained a complex array of glyphs and symbols arranged in apparent sequential order.

Stela 3 stands over four feet tall and weighs approximately two tons. The basalt monument was carefully positioned within La Venta's ceremonial Complex A, suggesting it held special significance for ancient Olmec peoples. The carved surface shows evidence of deliberate planning and sophisticated compositional arrangement.

The symbol system on Stela 3 includes over thirty distinct glyphs arranged in apparent columns and rows. Some symbols appear to be logographic, representing entire words or concepts. Others seem phonetic, corresponding to sound values rather than meanings. This combination suggests a mature writing system rather than simple pictographs.

Epigraphist David Stuart conducted a detailed analysis of the Stela 3 inscriptions during the 1990s. Stuart identified recurring glyph combinations that might represent names, titles, or important concepts. His work suggested the symbols followed grammatical rules similar to those found in later Maya writing systems.

Carbon dating of organic materials associated with Stela 3 placed the monument's creation around 900 BCE. This dating makes the inscription significantly older than previously known American writing systems.

The Maya developed their elaborate hieroglyphic system several centuries after Stela 3 was carved.

Comparative analysis with other Olmec inscriptions revealed consistent symbol usage across multiple sites. The Cascajal Block, discovered in 1999, contains sixty-two symbols arranged in apparent sequential order. Many glyphs from this artifact match those found on Stela 3, suggesting a standardized writing system.

The directional reading of Olmec inscriptions remains debated among epigraphers. Some researchers argue for a left-to-right reading order based on symbol arrangements. Others propose top-to-bottom or even boustrophedon (alternating direction) reading patterns. The uncertainty reflects our limited understanding of Olmec linguistic structures.

Linguistic analysis has attempted to connect Olmec symbols with known language families. Some researchers propose links to Mixe-Zoquean languages still spoken in the region. Others suggest connections to broader Mesoamerican linguistic groups. The absence of bilingual texts makes definitive identification extremely difficult.

The subject matter of Stela 3 inscriptions appears to focus on calendrical and ceremonial information. Several glyphs resemble day signs found in later Mesoamerican calendar systems. Others might record important historical events or religious concepts. The monument could function as a permanent record of significant information.

Recent digital imaging techniques have revealed previously unnoticed details in the Stela 3 inscriptions. High-resolution photography using raking light has identified additional glyphs and symbol modifications. These discoveries continue to expand our understanding of Olmec writing complexity.

The preservation state of Stela 3 creates challenges for complete decipherment. Weathering has obscured some symbol details. Ancient modifications or repairs to the monument might have altered original meanings. Researchers must work with incomplete information when attempting translation.

The social implications of Olmec writing suggest sophisticated administrative and religious systems. Literacy required specialized training and social support. The presence of writing indicates complex societies with needs for permanent record-keeping, religious texts, or historical documentation.

Archaeological context provides important clues about Stela 3's original function. The monument was positioned to be visible during important ceremonies. Its location within the ceremonial center suggests public rather than private use. The writing may have been intended for a broader audience rather than specialized readers.

The artistic integration of text and imagery on Stela 3 shows sophisticated design sensibilities. Glyphs are arranged to complement carved figures and decorative elements. This integration suggests writing was considered an artistic as well as functional medium. The monument represents multimedia communication combining visual and textual information.

Experimental approaches to Olmec decipherment have yielded intriguing results. Computer analysis of symbol frequencies and distributions has identified potential grammatical patterns. Machine learning algorithms have been applied to identify recurring glyph combinations. These technological tools supplement traditional epigraphic methods.

# Cultural Foundation for Maya and Aztec Civilizations

The Olmec cultural legacy extended far beyond their temporal boundaries, shaping Mesoamerican civilization for over two millennia after their mysterious disappearance. Archaeological evidence reveals how later peoples adopted, adapted, and transmitted Olmec innovations across vast geographical distances. The influence flowed through trade networks, religious practices, and artistic traditions.

Calendar systems provide the clearest example of Olmec cultural transmission. The Long Count calendar, later perfected by the Maya, originated in late Olmec times. Stela C at Tres Zapotes bears the earliest known Long Count date, corresponding to 32 BCE. This calendrical system required sophisticated mathematical concepts including positional notation and the concept of zero.

The calendar's vigesimal (base-20) counting system became standard throughout Mesoamerica. Maya mathematicians would later develop this system into one of history's most accurate timekeeping methods. Aztec calendar wheels incorporated the same fundamental principles. The intellectual foundation laid by Olmec astronomers supported centuries of scientific advancement.

Religious iconography shows remarkable continuity from the Olmec to later cultures. The feathered serpent deity, known as Kukulkan to the Maya and Quetzalcoatl to the Aztecs, first appeared in Olmec art around 1000 BCE. La Venta Monument 19 depicts this supernatural being in recognizable form, establishing iconographic conventions that would persist for millennia.

The World Tree concept, fundamental to later Mesoamerican cosmology, originated in Olmec religious thought. This cosmic axis connected the underworld, earthly, and celestial realms through a great ceiba tree.

Maya creation myths incorporated this imagery extensively. Aztec cosmological diagrams placed the World Tree at the center of their universe.

Ballcourt games spread from the Olmec region throughout Mesoamerica, carrying religious and social significance far beyond simple sport. The earliest known ballcourt, dating to 1400 BCE, was constructed at Paso de la Amada in Chiapas. The game's ritual associations with death and rebirth became central to later Maya and Aztec religious practices.

Jade working techniques developed by Olmec artisans influenced luxury goods production across ancient America. The translucent green stone held sacred significance representing water, vegetation, and life force. Maya rulers wore elaborate jade regalia based on Olmec prototypes. Aztec emperors maintained jade workshops using traditional Olmec methods.

Urban planning principles pioneered at La Venta shaped later ceremonial center construction. The site's precise north-south axis, monumental pyramid placement, and integrated plaza systems became templates for Maya cities like Tikal and El Mirador. Aztec Tenochtitlan incorporated similar spatial organization concepts in its ceremonial core.

Artistic styles originating in Olmec workshops spread through trade and cultural exchange. The distinctive "Olmec blue" jade color became highly prized in later periods. Ceramic traditions, stone carving techniques, and decorative motifs flowed outward from the Gulf Coast heartland. Regional variations developed, but core stylistic elements remained recognizable.

Writing system development shows clear evolutionary connections from Olmec symbols to later scripts. Maya hieroglyphic writing incorporated numerous glyphs with apparent Olmec origins. The directional reading patterns, grammatical structures, and calendrical notations all show ancestral relationships to earlier Olmec inscriptions.

Political organization models established by Olmec rulers influenced subsequent Mesoamerican societies. The concept of divine kingship, monumental architecture as political expression, and centralized ceremonial centers became standard features. Maya ahau (rulers) and Aztec huey tlatoani (great speakers) inherited political traditions with deep Olmec roots.

The trade network organization pioneered by Olmec merchants created economic patterns that persisted for centuries. Obsidian distribution systems, cacao exchange routes, and luxury goods trafficking followed pathways first established during Olmec times. Maya and Aztec merchants operated within commercial frameworks inherited from their predecessors.

Astronomical knowledge accumulated by Olmec observers provided the foundation for later scientific achievements. Venus cycle calculations, eclipse prediction methods, and seasonal agricultural timing originated in Olmec ceremonial centers. Maya astronomers built upon this accumulated wisdom to create history's most accurate ancient calendars.

Educational systems necessary for transmitting complex knowledge were developed during Olmec times. Scribal schools, priestly training programs, and craft specialization workshops created institutional structures that later cultures inherited and expanded. The Maya established their renowned centers of learning using Olmec organizational models.

The mysterious Olmec disappearance created knowledge gaps that later cultures struggled to fill. Some traditions were lost entirely. Others survived in fragmentary form. Maya creation myths speak of previous world ages and forgotten peoples, possibly preserving memories of their Olmec predecessors.

Regional variations in Olmec cultural transmission created distinctive local traditions. The Pacific Coast Soconusco region developed its own synthesis of Olmec and local elements. Highland Mexican populations adapted Olmec innovations to different environmental conditions. These regional variations contributed to Mesoamerica's remarkable cultural diversity.

Archaeological evidence continues to reveal new connections between Olmec and later cultures. Recent excavations at Maya sites have uncovered Olmec-style artifacts in foundation deposits, suggesting deliberate cultural continuity acknowledgment. Aztec rulers collected Olmec jade pieces as precious heirlooms, recognizing their ancient significance.

The Olmec cultural foundation supported three millennia of Mesoamerican civilization development. Their innovations in astronomy, mathematics, writing, art, and political organization provided essential building blocks for all subsequent societies. Without this foundation, the remarkable achievements of Maya and Aztec civilizations would never have been possible.

# Chapter 16: Lost Technologies - Metals, Sound, and Sacred Science

## Tumbaga: Ancient Electroplating Techniques

The Moche master craftsman heated fermented cactus juice in a ceramic bowl. Steam rose from the acidic liquid as he lowered a copper-gold figurine into the solution. He understood something that modern science had taken centuries to rediscover. Organic acids could dissolve surface metals and leave behind pure layers underneath.

This process happened fifteen hundred years ago in workshops along Peru's northern coast. No electricity powered the operation. No chemical formulas guided the measurements. The artisan relied on knowledge passed down through generations, wisdom encoded in the careful selection of plants, the precise timing of reactions, and the patient observation of color changes in heated metal.

The figurine emerged from its acid bath transformed. Surface copper had vanished, revealing brilliant gold underneath. The piece appeared to be solid precious metal. In reality, it contained mostly copper with a thin gold coating. The Moche had invented electroplating without understanding electron flow or chemical reduction. They simply knew which combinations produced the desired results.

Spanish conquistadors discovered thousands of these objects in sacred tombs across the Andes. They melted most of the materials into ingots, destroying evidence of manufacturing techniques that would not be officially "invented" in Europe until 1805. The few surviving pieces continue to puzzle metallurgists. Modern analysis reveals alloy compositions and surface treatments that require precise control of temperature, acidity, and timing.

Dr. Heather Lechtman spent decades studying pre-Columbian metalwork at the Massachusetts Institute of Technology. Her laboratory analysis of Moche artifacts revealed technical sophistication that challenged assumptions about ancient capabilities. The tumbaga process required an understanding of chemical reactions, material properties, and heat management. Practitioners demonstrated knowledge that modern industrial chemistry is validated as scientifically sound.

The technique spread throughout South America. Chimu craftsmen refined the methods, producing objects with multiple layers of different metals. Ecuadorian artisans created figurines with contrasting colors achieved through selective acid treatment. Colombian metalsmiths developed variations using different plant acids and heating schedules. Each culture added innovations to a core technology that originated in unknown antiquity.

Archaeological evidence suggests tumbaga production centers operated at industrial scales. Workshops contained dozens of ceramic vessels, specialized heating chambers, and storage areas for raw materials. Masters trained apprentices in techniques requiring years to perfect. Quality control demanded consistent results across hundreds of finished pieces. These operations supplied objects for religious ceremonies, elite burials, and diplomatic exchanges across vast distances.

The raw materials told their own story of technical mastery. Gold and copper came from different mountain regions. Artisans learned to identify ore qualities, refine metals to the required purities, and create precise alloy ratios. They developed temperature indicators using visual cues from flame colors and metal surface appearances. They timed chemical reactions by observing bubble patterns and solution color changes.

Modern attempts to replicate tumbaga often fail. Industrial chemists with precise instruments struggle to match the surface quality achieved by ancient practitioners. Computer-controlled heating produces inferior results compared to objects made with wood fires and ceramic containers. The pre-Columbian masters possessed practical knowledge that formal education systems have not preserved.

# 1000°C Heat Achievement at High Altitude

The workshop stood at 3,800 meters above sea level near Lake Titicaca. Thin air contained forty percent less oxygen than found at sea level. Standard combustion should have been impossible. The Tiwanaku metalworkers solved this problem with engineering brilliance that modern science barely comprehends.

They built furnaces into natural rock formations where mountain winds created consistent airflow. Stone channels directed air currents through combustion chambers with mathematical precision. The design harnessed atmospheric pressure differentials and thermal updrafts to achieve temperatures exceeding 1000 degrees Celsius. No electric blowers powered the system. No fossil fuels supplemented the heat. Wood charcoal and natural wind circulation created infernos hot enough to melt bronze.

Archaeological excavations revealed ceramic fragments scorched at temperatures modern kilns require electric heating elements to achieve. Slag deposits contained metallic residues proving successful smelting operations. Tool fragments showed wear patterns consistent with high-temperature metalworking. The evidence revealed industrial-scale production in locations where conventional wisdom had claimed such operations were impossible.

The furnace designs revealed a profound understanding of fluid dynamics and thermodynamics. Air intake chambers were precisely sized to create optimal flow rates. Combustion spaces featured specific geometric proportions that maximized heat retention. Exhaust systems prevented heat loss through careful management of gas flow patterns. Each element worked together to overcome the challenges of high-altitude metallurgy.

Modern experiments attempting to replicate these achievements have largely failed. Industrial engineers, who use computer modeling and controlled conditions, struggle to match the temperatures achieved by ancient practitioners using stone tools and empirical knowledge. The pre-Columbian metalworkers possessed a practical understanding of physical principles that formal education has not preserved.

Fuel selection demonstrated additional technical sophistication. Different wood species produced specific heat characteristics. Charcoal preparation required precise timing and temperature control. Fuel-to-air ratios needed adjustment based on altitude, humidity, and seasonal variations. Masters developed methods for predicting optimal conditions based on wind patterns, atmospheric pressure, and other environmental factors.

The implications extend beyond metallurgy. If ancient peoples could achieve 1000-degree temperatures at high altitude, they possessed engineering knowledge applicable to many technical challenges. Ceramic production, glass working, and chemical processing all require similar temperature control. The metallurgical evidence suggests broader technological capabilities than archaeologists have recognized.

Workshop locations were carefully chosen based on geographic advantages. Mountain passes provided consistent wind patterns. Rocky outcroppings supplied construction materials for furnace walls. Water sources enabled rapid cooling of finished products. Fuel forests grew within reasonable transport distances. The sites demonstrated integrated planning that considered multiple technical requirements simultaneously.

# Acoustic Instruments: Precise Internal Geometries

The Nazca trumpet lay buried for eight centuries in Peru's desert sand. When archaeologist Anna Roosevelt lifted the copper instrument from its tomb, she held technology that challenged everything acoustics textbooks taught about ancient capabilities. The trumpet's internal bore varied in diameter with mathematical precision. Each section created specific resonant frequencies when combined with adjacent chambers.

Modern acoustic analysis revealed engineering principles that European instrument makers did not discover until the Renaissance. The bore geometry followed logarithmic curves that optimized sound wave propagation. Internal chambers functioned as resonators that amplified specific frequency ranges. The mouthpiece design created laminar airflow patterns that enhanced tonal clarity and volume projection.

Dr. Perry Cook brought the instrument to Stanford University's computer music laboratory. Digital analysis mapped internal dimensions with laser precision. Acoustic modeling software calculated resonant frequencies and harmonic relationships. The results showed technical sophistication rivaling modern brass instruments. Ancient craftsmen had created tools for sound production that demonstrated an advanced understanding of wave physics and materials science.

The trumpet belonged to a family of acoustic devices found across pre-Columbian America. Maya conch shells featured carved internal channels that modified natural resonance patterns. Peruvian ceramic whistles contained multiple chambers that produced complex harmonic series. Aztec bone flutes incorporated finger hole placements calculated to generate specific musical scales. Each culture developed instruments requiring precise mathematical relationships between physical dimensions and acoustic properties.

Manufacturing these instruments required skills that modern craftsmen find hard to imitate. Copper work needed careful heating and cooling cycles to avoid cracking during shaping. Internal boring required maintaining a consistent diameter through curved sections. Surface finishing influenced acoustic properties through microscopic texture differences. Quality control involved testing methods to confirm acoustic performance before ceremonial use.

Archaeological evidence suggests instrument production occurred in specialized workshops with master-apprentice training systems. Tool marks on surviving pieces show consistent techniques across multiple artifacts. Raw material selection followed standardized criteria for acoustic optimization. Production centers supplied instruments for religious ceremonies across vast geographic regions.

The instruments served purposes beyond entertainment. Acoustic properties created specific psychological effects during religious rituals. Infrasonic frequencies below human hearing thresholds induced altered consciousness states. Harmonic combinations produced standing wave patterns in enclosed ceremonial spaces. Sound became a technology for manipulating human perception and creating transcendent experiences.

Modern attempts to recreate these effects often fail because contemporary acoustics focuses on electronic amplification rather than natural resonance phenomena. Ancient practitioners understood how architectural spaces, human physiology, and acoustic frequencies interacted to create desired psychological states. This knowledge system integrated physics, psychology, and architecture in ways modern specialization has fragmented.

# Light-Reflective Temple Wall Applications

The morning sun struck the temple wall at Machu Picchu and transformed stone into liquid light. Dr. Johan Reinhard climbed the terraced steps as dawn illuminated metal sheets beaten so thin they were nearly transparent. The gold surfaces reflected and refracted sunlight into dancing patterns that seemed to breathe with divine energy.

This effect was not accidental decoration. Inca architects designed temples to function as light machines that marked astronomical events and created specific visual experiences. Metal foils covered strategic wall sections where reflected light would strike at precisely calculated angles during solstices and equinoxes. The buildings became calendars written in brilliant illumination.

The manufacturing process required technical mastery that modern metalworkers respect. Craftsmen hammered gold into sheets measuring less than one-thousandth of an inch thick without tearing the material. They achieved uniform thickness across large surfaces using only stone tools and human skill. The finished products were then attached to temple walls using adhesive compounds that have remained intact for centuries.

Chemical analysis of remaining foil fragments reveals alloy compositions tailored for reflective qualities. Gold content was adjusted to produce specific colors under different lighting conditions. Copper additions altered reflectance properties for particular wavelengths. Silver traces boosted surface brilliance during dawn and dusk illumination. Each piece was designed for its particular architectural role.

The adhesive compounds present their own technological mysteries. Organic binders held metal foils to stone surfaces through centuries of weather exposure, seismic activity, and temperature fluctuations. Modern structural adhesives often fail under similar conditions. Analysis reveals complex formulations combining plant resins, mineral additives, and possibly organic polymers produced through controlled fermentation processes.

Installation required precise geometric calculations to achieve the desired lighting effects. Craftsmen had to account for solar angles throughout the year, reflection coefficients of different materials, and architectural sight lines from specific viewing positions. The work demanded integrated knowledge of astronomy, optics, mathematics, and construction techniques.

Contemporary attempts to restore damaged temple sections struggle to match the original visual effects. Modern adhesives fail to provide the longevity of ancient formulations. Machine-produced metal foils lack the optical properties of hand-beaten sheets. Computer calculations cannot replicate the astronomical alignments achieved through empirical observation and practical experience.

The technology extended beyond religious architecture. Elite residences incorporated reflective surfaces that directed natural light into interior spaces. Administrative buildings used light effects to emphasize authority and create impressive visual displays. Defensive structures employed reflective signals for long-distance communication across mountainous terrain.

# Chemical Reactions Without Modern Equipment

The laboratory contained no glass beakers, no precision instruments, and no controlled atmosphere chambers. In a ceramic workshop beside Ecuador's Guayas River, Valdivian chemists created color-change glazes that shifted from red to blue depending on viewing angle and lighting conditions. They achieved these effects through chemical reactions that modern ceramics science struggles to explain or replicate.

The glazes required precise combinations of mineral oxides, organic compounds, and trace elements found only in specific geographic locations. Practitioners had to identify ore sources, purify raw materials, and combine ingredients in exact proportions. Temperature control during firing demanded an understanding of chemical reactions occurring at different heat levels. The finished products demonstrated mastery of complex physical and chemical processes.

Dr. Pamela Vandiver studied these ceramics at the Smithsonian Institution using electron microscopy and spectral analysis. Her research revealed a sophisticated understanding of materials science principles not officially discovered until the twentieth century. The ancient ceramicists had developed techniques for controlling crystal formation, managing thermal expansion, and creating composite materials with engineered properties.

Mineral processing began with ore selection based on visual and tactile characteristics. Practitioners learned to identify chemical compositions through practical experience with different rocks and earths. They developed methods for extracting useful compounds through crushing, heating, leaching, and other physical processes. Quality control relied on systematic testing of raw materials before use in final products.

Color development required an understanding of oxidation-reduction reactions occurring during high-temperature firing. Different atmospheric conditions in kilns produced different chemical environments that affected final colors. Practitioners controlled these conditions through careful management of fuel types, airflow patterns, and firing schedules. The results demonstrated practical knowledge of inorganic chemistry principles.

The kilns themselves represented sophisticated engineering achievements. Ceramic construction materials withstood repeated heating cycles without structural failure. Temperature distribution systems ensured uniform heating of multiple pieces simultaneously. Ventilation controls managed atmospheric conditions during different firing phases. Fuel feeding systems maintained consistent temperatures throughout extended firing periods.

Chemical knowledge extended beyond ceramics into medicine, agriculture, and materials processing. Plant-based dyes required the understanding of pH effects, mordant chemistry, and colorfast properties. Agricultural lime production involved controlled heating of limestone to produce calcium oxide for soil treatment. Metal refining used chemical processes to separate valuable elements from complex ore compositions.

Modern industrial chemistry validates many ancient practices as scientifically sound. Temperature ranges, reaction times, and ingredient proportions match optimal conditions determined through contemporary research. The ancient practitioners achieved results that modern processes replicate using expensive equipment and formal chemical knowledge.

The knowledge systems that produced these achievements remain largely mysterious. No written chemical formulas survived from pre-Columbian America. Technical knowledge was passed through master-apprentice relationships using practical demonstration and oral instruction. The loss of these knowledge systems means modern science must reverse-engineer ancient achievements without understanding the theoretical frameworks that guided their development.

Evidence from workshop sites suggests systematic experimentation and knowledge accumulation over generations. Tool fragments show wear patterns consistent with repetitive processing operations. Waste deposits contain failed experiments and practice pieces. Raw material storage areas reveal a systematic organization of different chemical inputs. These archaeological remains document scientific methodologies that preceded formal chemistry by centuries.

# Chapter 17: Nazca Lines - Messages to the Sky

## Geoglyphs Visible Only From Above

Maria Reiche arrived in Peru in 1932 as a young German mathematician seeking adventure in South America. She found something far more extraordinary than she ever imagined. Standing on a small hill overlooking the Nazca desert plateau, Reiche squinted through the blazing afternoon sun at strange markings etched across the barren landscape below. Dark stones had been carefully removed to reveal pale earth underneath. The patterns stretched for miles in perfectly straight lines that seemed to serve no practical purpose.

Local people called them the "lines of Nazca." They spoke of ancient spirits who had walked across the desert, leaving permanent footprints in the earth. Reiche saw something different. She recognized geometric precision that required advanced planning and mathematical knowledge. Someone had created these markings with deliberate intent. But why? And how could they achieve such accuracy across such vast distances?

Reiche spent the next five decades of her life trying to answer these questions. She lived in a simple house near the lines, sleeping in a tent when fieldwork demanded. Every morning before dawn, she walked out onto the desert with a measuring tape, a compass, and a notebook. She documented distances, calculated angles, and mapped the intricate network of lines that crisscrossed the Nazca plateau.

The work was exhausting. Desert temperatures soared above 100 degrees Fahrenheit during the day and dropped near freezing at night. Sandstorms buried equipment and erased delicate markings. Water had to be carried from distant villages. Reiche suffered from arthritis that made walking increasingly painful. She continued her research into her nineties.

What Reiche discovered defied explanation. The lines formed complex geometric patterns spanning hundreds of square miles. Straight lines ran for twelve miles without deviating more than a few yards from perfect alignment. Trapezoids covered areas larger than football stadiums. Spirals wound outward in mathematical progression. The precision exceeded anything achievable by ancient peoples using simple tools.

*Ancient American Civilizations*

But the lines were only part of the mystery. Scattered among the geometric patterns were enormous drawings of animals, plants, and human figures. These geoglyphs dwarfed anything humans had created before. The hummingbird measured 318 feet from beak to tail. The spider stretched 150 feet across. The monkey's tail curled into a spiral that was 330 feet long. Each figure was drawn with single continuous lines that never crossed themselves.

Reiche faced the same problem that puzzled everyone who studied the Nazca lines. The drawings could only be adequately seen from high above the desert floor. At ground level, they appeared as meaningless scratches in the dirt. Even standing on the highest nearby hills provided insufficient elevation to appreciate their full scope. The ancient Nazca people had created artwork that they themselves could never properly view.

This paradox sparked wild theories. Erich von Däniken claimed the lines were landing strips for ancient astronauts. Others suggested the Nazca had developed primitive hot air balloons to observe their creations from above. Archaeological evidence supported neither explanation. No runway-like features existed among the lines. No balloon materials or launch facilities had been discovered.

Reiche proposed a more grounded explanation. The lines served as a giant astronomical calendar. She documented alignments between specific lines and the rising or setting points of important stars. The summer solstice sun appeared directly over one major line. The constellation Orion aligned with another. Perhaps the Nazca used their desert observatory to track celestial cycles crucial for agriculture and religious ceremonies.

Dr. Anthony Aveni from Colgate University tested Reiche's theories using computer analysis. He found that only about 20 percent of the lines showed clear astronomical alignments. This percentage matched what statisticians would expect from random chance. The astronomical explanation could not account for the vast majority of Nazca lines.

Ground-penetrating radar revealed another clue. Many lines pointed toward underground water sources or ancient well sites. In the extremely arid Nazca desert, water meant survival. Perhaps the lines marked paths to crucial resources during drought periods. Travelers could follow the perfectly straight lines across the featureless desert to reach life-saving wells.

The animal figures presented additional mysteries. Why did the Nazca choose specific creatures for their giant drawings? The hummingbird appears frequently in local mythology as a messenger between earth and sky. The spider symbolized rain and fertility in Andean cultures. The monkey might have represented the jungle regions where Nazca traders obtained exotic goods.

Each animal was drawn with intimate knowledge of its anatomy and behavior. The hummingbird's proportions matched those of actual birds found in the region. The spider showed accurate details of leg segments and body structure. The monkey displayed characteristic postures and tail positions. Whoever created these geoglyphs observed their subjects carefully before translating them into massive desert artwork.

# Spider, Hummingbird, Monkey: Massive Animal Forms

The spider appeared first in 1927 when Peruvian archaeologist Toribio Mejía Xesspe spotted strange markings from a foothill overlooking the Nazca plateau. What he saw made no sense. Lines carved into the desert floor formed the unmistakable shape of an enormous spider. The creature measured 150 feet from front legs to rear abdomen. Every detail had been rendered with startling accuracy.

The spider's body showed the correct number of segments. Its eight legs displayed proper joint positions and proportional lengths. The abdomen featured the distinctive shape of a female spider carrying eggs. Most remarkably, the figure depicted a species found only in the Amazon rainforest, over 200 miles from the Nazca desert.

Creating this massive arachnid required extraordinary planning. The ancient artists worked without elevated vantage points to check their progress. They could not step back to see how the overall figure was developing. Each line had to be placed perfectly the first time. A single mistake would ruin months of careful work.

The process began with small-scale drawings on pottery or textiles. Archaeological excavations around Nazca have uncovered ceramics decorated with the same animal figures found in the desert. These pottery designs served as templates for the giant geoglyphs. Artists scaled up the small drawings using mathematical techniques that maintained proper proportions across vast distances.

Teams of workers removed dark desert stones to expose lighter soil underneath. The contrast created visible lines from great heights. The work required coordination among dozens of people following a master plan. Someone directed the overall project. Others measured distances and angles. Still others carried away countless tons of stones.

The hummingbird geoglyph demonstrated even greater sophistication. This figure measured 318 feet long and featured perfect symmetry in its wing positions. The bird's beak pointed directly toward sunrise on the December solstice. Its tail aligned with important star positions during the southern hemisphere winter. The Nazca had combined artistic expression with astronomical observation in a single monumental creation.

Local legends provided clues about the hummingbird's significance. Nazca mythology described tiny birds that carried messages between the human world and the realm of the gods. Hummingbirds could hover motionless in the air, suggesting supernatural powers. Their iridescent feathers shimmered with colors that changed depending on the viewing angle. These qualities made them perfect symbols for divine communication.

The monkey geoglyph told a different story. This figure sprawled across 370 feet of desert with its distinctive curled tail forming a perfect spiral. Monkeys lived hundreds of miles away in the Amazon basin, far from the arid Nazca region. Yet the desert artists knew enough about monkey anatomy to create an accurate representation of these distant creatures.

Trade networks linked the coastal Nazca culture with jungle societies that possessed exotic goods. Nazca ceramics have been found in Amazon settlements. Jungle products like jaguar teeth and tropical bird feathers appear in Nazca graves. The monkey geoglyph might have honored these important commercial relationships or served as a massive territorial marker visible to trading partners approaching from the east.

Creating the monkey required solving complex geometric problems. The tail's spiral followed mathematical curves that maintained consistent proportions throughout multiple revolutions. The body proportions matched those of real spider monkeys despite the enormous scale. The positioning of arms and legs showed the creature in a naturalistic pose that conveyed movement and life.

Each major animal figure required distinct artistic solutions. The condor, with its 443-foot wingspan, needed techniques to create smooth curves over large distances. The whale figure incorporated water imagery suitable for a desert people who relied on Pacific Ocean resources. The dog depicted domesticated animals that played vital roles in Nazca daily life.

The artistic achievement becomes even more impressive when considering the tools available to Nazca creators. They worked with wooden stakes, rope made from plant fibers, and simple measuring devices: no metal tools, no surveying equipment, no mechanical aids of any kind. Everything depended on human skill, mathematical knowledge, and careful planning.

Contemporary efforts to replicate Nazca-style geoglyphs have proven very challenging, even with modern tools. The Kentucky-based Nazca Project spent years developing methods for creating large-scale ground drawings. Despite using GPS devices, laser levels, and mechanised equipment, they found it difficult to match the accuracy and craftsmanship of the original ancient works.

The animal geoglyphs served multiple purposes simultaneously. They functioned as religious symbols connecting earthly and divine realms. They demonstrated cultural knowledge about distant regions and exotic creatures. They displayed mathematical and artistic capabilities that enhanced tribal prestige. They created permanent landmarks in a landscape that otherwise lacked distinctive features.

# Straight Lines Extending 12+ Miles

The longest Nazca line runs for more than twelve miles across desert valleys, over hills, and through rocky ravines without deviating from its course. Ancient surveyors achieved this incredible precision using tools no more sophisticated than wooden stakes and woven ropes. The accuracy challenges modern engineering capabilities.

Dr. Persis Clarkson from the University of Winnipeg spent years studying how the Nazca accomplished this feat. She discovered evidence of careful planning that began long before construction started. Teams of scouts walked potential routes, identifying obstacles and planning solutions. Surveyor stations were established at key points along each intended line. Signal fires or mirrors reflected sunlight to maintain alignment across long distances.

The work required unprecedented cooperation among different Nazca communities. Individual family groups controlled separate sections of the desert plateau. Creating lines that crossed multiple territories demanded negotiation and shared effort. Leaders had to coordinate labor contributions, resolve disputes, and maintain project momentum over many years.

Some lines connected important ceremonial centers separated by dozens of miles. Others linked water sources with residential areas. A few pointed toward sacred mountains where the Nazca people believed their ancestors resided. The longest lines might have served as pilgrimage routes followed during religious festivals.

Following these ancient pathways on foot reveals their remarkable engineering. The lines maintain constant width for their entire length. They climb steep hillsides and descend into valleys without losing their alignment. They cross areas where flash floods have scoured the landscape for centuries. In many places, they continue under modern roads and buildings, a testament to their original precision.

Creating such long, straight lines required advanced mathematical knowledge. Surveyors had to account for the earth's curvature over distances of ten miles or more. They needed to adjust for elevation changes that would throw off simple sight-line measurements. They had to maintain direction despite crossing terrain that blocked direct visual contact between the starting and ending points.

Recent research has revealed the specific techniques used by Nazca engineers. They established a series of intermediate points along each intended line. These stations were marked with piles of stones that served as permanent references. Surveyors could then create shorter straight segments between adjacent stations. When connected, these segments formed longer lines that appeared perfectly straight from any distance.

The intermediate stations also allowed for error correction during construction. If workers discovered they had drifted off course, they could realign their work using the nearest reference point. This system prevented small mistakes from compounding into major deviations that would ruin the entire project.

Some researchers have suggested that the Nazca possessed more advanced surveying tools than the archaeological record indicates. Bronze or copper instruments might have corroded away completely in the desert environment. Wooden tools could have been burned as fuel by later people who did not understand their significance. The absence of sophisticated equipment in Nazca graves does not prove it never existed.

However, ethnographic studies of traditional Andean cultures show that complex projects can be accomplished using only basic tools and accumulated knowledge. Quechua-speaking peoples in modern Peru still use similar techniques for aligning agricultural terraces and irrigation canals. They achieve remarkable precision through careful observation, mathematical understanding, and patient work.

The straight lines served purposes beyond simple transportation or religious symbolism. They created a permanent record of Nazca's mathematical and engineering capabilities. Other cultures in the region could observe these achievements and recognize Nazca's technical sophistication. The lines functioned as monuments to human ingenuity that would last for centuries.

Construction of the longest lines required several generations to complete. Fathers passed surveying knowledge to their sons. Techniques were refined through experience and tradition. What began as ambitious projects by individual leaders evolved into cultural practices that defined Nazca identity.

The investment in these monumental works suggests that Nazca society possessed considerable surplus labor and resources. People had to be fed and organized during construction. Materials had to be gathered and transported. Skilled supervisors had to direct the work. Such massive undertakings were only possible in a stable, prosperous culture with effective leadership.

# Astronomical and Water Source Alignments

Dawn broke over the Nazca desert on December 21, 378 CE. Priests climbed to observation platforms built on the highest hills surrounding the plateau. They carried bronze mirrors polished to perfect smoothness. As the sun's first rays struck the desert floor, the mirrors flashed signals to teams of workers positioned along the sacred lines.

This was the summer solstice in the southern hemisphere. The sun reached its northernmost point and began its journey back toward the south. For the Nazca people, this moment marked the beginning of their new year. Water sources that had dried during the preceding months would soon begin flowing again. Crops planted in river valleys would receive life-giving irrigation. The desert would briefly bloom with colorful flowers.

Dr. Gerald Hawkins from Boston University discovered that many Nazca lines pointed towards significant astronomical events. His computer analysis identified alignments with the rising and setting positions of important stars and constellations. The Pleiades star cluster, crucial for timing agricultural activities, aligned with several major lines. The Southern Cross, which guided navigation and religious ceremonies, matched the orientation of other geoglyphs.

But the most important alignments involved the sun's movement throughout the year. Nazca farmers depended on precise timing for their agricultural cycles. They planted crops in river valleys during brief flood seasons. They harvested fish from the Pacific Ocean when seasonal currents brought nutrients to coastal waters. They gathered wild plants from desert areas during rare rainfall periods.

Missing these narrow windows of opportunity meant starvation. The margin for error was extremely small in one of the world's most arid environments. Nazca survival depended on astronomical knowledge that allowed accurate prediction of seasonal changes.

The lines functioned as a massive solar calendar laid out across the landscape. Observers positioned at specific points could watch the sun rise or set directly over designated lines on important dates. The winter solstice sun appeared over one set of lines. The spring equinox aligned with others. Additional solar alignments marked planting and harvest times.

This system required no written records or complex calculations. Farmers could determine the correct timing for crucial activities simply by observing where the sun appeared relative to familiar lines on the horizon. The desert itself became a giant timekeeping device that functioned with perfect accuracy year after year.

Water sources played an equally important role in Nazca line alignments. Dr. David Johnson from the University of Massachusetts used satellite imagery to map underground aquifers beneath the Nazca plateau. His research revealed that many lines pointed directly toward springs, wells, and seasonal water sources.

The Nazca had developed sophisticated techniques for locating underground water in the desert environment. They dug funnel-shaped wells called puquios that tapped into aquifers flowing beneath the surface. These wells provided reliable water supplies during dry seasons when surface sources disappeared.

Many Nazca lines connected residential areas with distant puquios. Travelers could follow the perfectly straight paths across the featureless desert without becoming lost. The lines served as permanent navigation aids that guided people to life-saving water sources during emergencies.

Some lines pointed toward sacred springs located in mountain valleys, many miles from the desert plateau. These water sources held special religious significance for the Nazca people. Pilgrimages to mountain springs were important ceremonies that renewed spiritual connections between human communities and the natural world.

The combination of astronomical and water source alignments created a landscape filled with meaning and practical information. Every major line served multiple purposes simultaneously. Religious ceremonies, agricultural timing, and resource location were integrated into a single comprehensive system.

Constructing this system required detailed knowledge of local geography, astronomy, and hydrology accumulated over many generations. Nazca priests and engineers had to understand seasonal weather patterns, underground water flow, and celestial mechanics. They synthesized this information into permanent monuments that served their descendants for centuries.

The precision of these alignments suggests that Nazca astronomical knowledge rivaled that of other advanced ancient cultures. They achieved accuracy comparable to Mayan calendar calculations or Egyptian pyramid alignments using only naked-eye observations and simple tools.

Modern astronomers have confirmed that Nazca alignments remain accurate after 1,500 years. The lines still point toward the same star positions and solar events that guided ancient observers. The desert's stable climate has preserved these astronomical monuments in perfect condition.

# Desert Preservation: 1,500+ Years Unchanged

The Nazca desert has unique environmental conditions that have preserved ancient geoglyphs with almost supernatural precision. Rainfall averages less than one inch annually across the entire plateau. Winds blow consistently from the same direction, preventing sand build-up. The dark desert stones form a protective layer over lighter soil that resists erosion.

Temperature fluctuations between day and night create a natural preservation system. The intense daytime heat causes surface materials to expand. Cool nights cause them to contract. This daily cycle locks stones into stable positions that remain undisturbed for centuries. Even earthquake tremors rarely shift the carefully arranged surface materials.

The chemical composition of the Nazca desert soil contributes to the lines' preservation. High salt content prevents vegetation growth that would obscure the markings. Iron oxide gives the surface stones their dark color and helps them form protective crusts. The underlying pale soil contains minerals that resist wind erosion and water damage.

Francisco Atahualpa Vargas, a Nazca resident born in 1925, remembered his grandfather's stories about the ancient lines. The old man claimed his own grandfather had seen the markings exactly as they appeared in modern times. Four generations of the same family had observed no significant changes in the geoglyphs' appearance or condition.

This remarkable preservation allowed researchers to study Nazca engineering techniques in pristine detail. Maria Reiche could examine how ancient workers placed individual stones to create smooth curves and precise angles. She found evidence of repair work carried out by the original builders when weather or accidents damaged their creations.

Carbon dating of organic materials found along the lines provided accurate age estimates. Plant fibers used as measuring tools during construction dated to between 400 and 600 CE. Wooden stakes marking survey points showed similar ages. The evidence confirmed that most major geoglyphs were completed during the classic Nazca period.

The preservation is so complete that modern visitors can walk along the ancient pathways and see them exactly as their creators intended. Footprints left by Nazca workers are still visible in protected areas. Tool marks show where they scraped away surface stones. Even the sequence of construction can be determined by observing which lines cross over others.

This extraordinary preservation creates both opportunities and challenges for modern researchers. Scientists can study Nazca techniques with unprecedented detail. But the lines are also extremely fragile despite their apparent durability. A single footstep or vehicle track can cause permanent damage, destroying centuries of preservation.

Tourist activity poses the greatest threat to the lines' continued survival. Thousands of visitors arrive annually to see the geoglyphs from small aircraft or observation towers. Some attempt to walk on the lines themselves, leaving footprints that will remain visible for decades. Others remove stones as souvenirs, gradually erasing portions of the ancient artwork.

The Peruvian government has established strict protection measures around the most important geoglyphs. Fences prevent unauthorized access to sensitive areas. Guards patrol the desert to prevent vandalism. Aircraft routes are regulated to minimize noise and exhaust pollution. Research activities require special permits and careful oversight.

Climate change represents a new threat to Nazca preservation. Changing weather patterns could bring increased rainfall to the desert. Flash floods might scour away protective surface layers. Stronger winds could shift stones that have remained stable for centuries. Temperature fluctuations might alter the preservation chemistry that has protected the lines.

International conservation efforts are working to document and protect the Nazca lines for future generations. High-resolution satellite imagery provides permanent records of current conditions. Ground-penetrating radar maps subsurface features that are invisible from above. 3D scanning technology creates detailed digital models of individual geoglyphs.

Educational programs teach local communities about the lines' historical and scientific importance. School children learn about their ancient heritage and the need for careful preservation. Tourism guides receive training in conservation techniques and visitor management. These efforts help ensure that preservation knowledge passes to new generations.

The Nazca lines stand as testimony to human creativity and environmental stability working together across vast spans of time. Ancient artists created monuments intended to last forever. The desert environment fulfilled their vision by preserving their work in perfect condition. Modern humans bear the responsibility of protecting this irreplaceable legacy for the future.

The preservation of the Nazca lines offers hope that other ancient sites might survive with proper care and protection. Archaeological treasures around the world face threats from development, tourism, and environmental change. The Nazca example shows that cooperation between local communities, researchers, and government authorities can successfully preserve irreplaceable cultural heritage.

Standing on the Nazca plateau at sunset, with ancient lines stretching toward distant mountains, visitors experience a direct connection with people who lived fifteen centuries ago. The preservation is so complete that time seems to collapse. The desert becomes a bridge linking past and present across the endless sweep of human history.

# Chapter 18: Messages in Earth - The Effigy Mounds

## Animal-Shaped Earthworks: 60-300 Feet Long

Theodore Lewis climbed the wooden observation tower in 1883, camera equipment strapped to his back. Below him stretched rolling hills and farmland across southern Wisconsin. Lewis had spent months walking these fields, noting strange rises in the earth. Local farmers complained about plowing around the mysterious bumps. From ground level, the shapes made no sense.

The view from above changed everything. Lewis stared down at a massive bird outlined in grass and soil. Its wings stretched 200 feet from tip to tip. The head pointed directly toward the summer solstice sunrise. Lewis had discovered something unprecedented in American archaeology - earthworks designed to be seen from the sky.

Lewis and his partner, Frederic Ward, documented over 1,000 similar earthworks across Wisconsin, Minnesota, Iowa, and Illinois during their decade-long survey. Bears prowled across hillsides in permanent earth and stone. Turtles basked on prairie ridges. Serpents wound through river valleys for hundreds of feet. Humans with outstretched arms welcomed the dawn from elevated meadows.

Each effigy required careful planning. The builders had to visualize massive forms that they could never see completed. They worked from mental maps passed down through generations. Master architects directed teams of workers carrying earth in baskets woven from prairie grass. The construction process took years, sometimes decades.

The bird effigy that amazed Lewis required moving approximately 2,000 tons of soil. Workers dug clay from nearby streambanks. They gathered stones from riverbeds miles away. Every basketload was carried by human hands and shaped according to precise specifications. The wing curves followed mathematical proportions. The head alignment matched astronomical observations accurately to within degrees.

Modern surveys using ground-penetrating radar reveal internal structures within the mounds. Stone foundations anchor critical points. Clay layers create drainage systems, preventing erosion. Charcoal deposits mark ceremonial fires burned during construction phases. These were not random earthpiles but engineered monuments built to survive centuries.

The effigy builders understood their landscape intimately. They chose locations where natural topography enhanced artificial forms. Bear mounds occupied defensive positions overlooking river crossings. Bird effigies were placed on the highest ground for maximum visibility. Serpent forms followed natural ridge lines, extending organic curves into geometric precision.

Size varied dramatically across the region. Small effigies, measuring 60 feet long, were suitable for family or clan ceremonies. Massive constructions reached 300 feet, requiring coordinated labor from multiple communities. The largest bird effigy near Madison, Wisconsin, spans nearly 400 feet, making it visible from several miles away on clear days.

Construction techniques evolved over seven centuries. Early builders created simple outlines filled with local soil. Later architects developed sophisticated internal structures. They incorporated stone foundations, drainage systems, and ceremonial chambers. The final generation added astronomical alignments and complex symbolic elements.

Archaeological evidence suggests construction happened in seasonal bursts. Spring floods provided clay from swollen riverbanks. The summer drought made it easier to transport. Fall harvests freed workers from agricultural duties. Winter ceremonies consecrated completed sections. Each effigy grew incrementally through multiple construction seasons.

The builders left no written records explaining their motivations. They communicated through the earthworks themselves. Animal forms conveyed messages about spiritual relationships, seasonal cycles, and cosmic connections. The shapes functioned as three-dimensional books, accessible to those who understood the symbolic language.

European settlers recognized the artificial nature of the mounds but misunderstood their purpose. Some dismissed them as natural formations. Others attributed them to vanished races unrelated to Native Americans. Most farmers simply plowed them under to create flat fields suitable for agriculture.

# Woodland and Mississippian Construction: 500-1200 CE

Morning mist rose from the Wisconsin River as Walks-with-Eagles selected the perfect clay. The master builder knelt beside the streambank, testing soil consistency with experienced fingers. This clay would form the bear's powerful hindquarters. The mixture had to hold its shape through decades of rain and frost.

Behind him, thirty workers waited with woven baskets. Each person came from a different village scattered across the river valley. They spoke similar languages but maintained distinct customs. The great bear effigy would unite their separate communities under one protective spirit.

Walks-with-Eagles had apprenticed under his grandmother, learning the sacred mathematics of earth shaping. She taught him how animal forms channeled spiritual energy from the sky world down to human settlements. Bears protected villages from winter hardships. Birds carried prayers to the thunder beings. Serpents controlled the underwater spirits dwelling in deep pools and hidden springs.

The construction project began with purification ceremonies. Spiritual leaders burned sage and sweetgrass while chanting prayers in the ancient tongue. They marked the bear's outline using wooden stakes and braided cordage. Each measurement followed traditional proportions passed down through generations of earth builders.

Different craftsmen specialized in particular aspects of construction. Clay workers understood how various soil types behaved during freeze-thaw cycles. Stone carriers knew which rocks provided the best drainage. Grass specialists selected prairie plants whose root systems would prevent erosion. Astronomical observers calculated precise alignments with seasonal star positions.

The bear took three years to complete. Each construction season brought different challenges. Spring rains softened the earth, but they also made transportation difficult. Summer heat baked clay surfaces too quickly, causing cracks. Fall provided ideal conditions for final shaping and finishing work. Winter provided an opportunity to plan the following year's progress.

Workers developed efficient transportation systems. They built temporary wooden ramps for moving heavy loads up steep slopes. They

*Ancient American Civilizations*

created relay stations where carriers could rest and refresh themselves. They established tool-making areas where broken baskets could be repaired and new implements crafted from local materials.

Quality control was essential. Master builders inspected every basketload of earth before placement. They rejected soil containing too much sand or organic matter. They required specific clay-to-stone ratios for different parts of the effigy. They enforced precise compaction standards to ensure structural integrity.

The Woodland peoples who started this tradition lived in small villages along major riverways. They engaged in seasonal farming complemented by hunting and gathering. Their social structure focused on extended family groups with shared ceremonial duties. Effigy construction became a way to strengthen bonds between related communities.

Competition drove innovation in effigy design. Different river valleys developed unique styles and techniques. The Wisconsin River groups specialised in bird forms. The Mississippi Valley creators made intricate serpent effigies. The Great Lakes communities focused on human and geometric shapes.

Trade networks spread construction knowledge across great distances. Master builders travelled hundreds of miles to share techniques and oversee major projects. They carried specialised tools, seeds for ceremonial plants, and sacred earth from remote power spots. These exchanges created regional styles recognisable to modern archaeologists.

The Mississippian peoples who inherited this tradition around 1000 CE expanded the scale and complexity of earthwork construction. They organized larger labor forces and developed more sophisticated planning methods. Their effigies incorporated multiple animal forms into single compositions covering acres of carefully shaped landscape.

Religious beliefs evolved alongside construction techniques. Earlier builders created effigies for local spiritual needs. Later generations connected their earthworks to continent-wide ceremonial networks. Animal forms became parts of larger cosmic diagrams mapping the relationships between earthly and heavenly realms.

# Serpent Mound: 1,300-Foot Astronomical Alignment

Sarah Winchell Morris stood at the serpent's head on a cold December morning in 1886. The Harvard-trained archaeologist had traveled from Boston to investigate reports of a giant snake-shaped earthwork in rural Ohio. Local farmers called it the "great serpent," but Morris suspected something far more significant.

The morning sun climbed above the eastern horizon, casting long shadows across the serpent's curves. Morris watched the light creep along the earthwork's sinuous body. At the precise moment of winter solstice sunrise, sunbeams aligned perfectly with the serpent's gaping jaws. The ancient builders had created a solar calendar written in earth and stone.

Morris spent three weeks measuring and mapping the serpent's dimensions. The earthwork stretched 1,348 feet from tail to head, making it the longest effigy mound in North America. The body averaged four feet in height and twenty feet in width. Seven distinct curves followed mathematical proportions found in spiral formations throughout nature.

The serpent's head faced the summer solstice sunset. Its tail pointed toward the winter solstice sunrise. The body curves aligned with the northernmost and southernmost moonrise positions during the 18.6-year lunar cycle. This astronomical knowledge required generations of careful sky observation by trained specialists.

Construction began around 1000 CE during the height of Mississippian cultural influence. The builders selected a naturally elevated plateau overlooking Brush Creek valley. The location provided clear sightlines to horizon points where celestial bodies reached their extreme positions. The serpent became a three-dimensional observatory functional for predicting seasonal changes.

Archaeological investigations reveal the serpent's internal structure. A foundation of stones and clay supports the entire length. Drainage channels prevent water accumulation. Carefully selected soils resist freeze-thaw damage. The builders understood engineering principles necessary for long-term preservation in Ohio's variable climate.

Carbon dating of charcoal found within the mound confirms the construction timeline. Small fires burned at specific points during building phases. These ceremonies probably consecrated completed sections and invoked spiritual protection for the work. The fires also provided practical lighting for night construction during optimal astronomical conditions.

The serpent holds an oval object in its mouth. Early investigators called this the "egg," assuming it portrayed a snake swallowing prey. Modern astronomical analysis suggests it maps the position of Halley's Comet as visible around 1066 CE. The oval's orientation matches historical records of the comet's appearance from North American viewing locations.

Chemical analysis of the serpent's soil reveals exotic materials imported from distant sources. Clay from the Ohio River valley mixed with sand from Lake Erie beaches. Mica fragments came from Appalachian mountain deposits 200 miles away. These materials created specific colors and textures visible from observation points around the mound's perimeter.

The serpent's builders demonstrated sophisticated surveying skills. They maintained consistent proportions across the entire 1,300-foot length. They created smooth curves without modern measuring instruments. They achieved accurate astronomical alignments despite working on irregular terrain. This precision required mathematical knowledge and practical experience rarely acknowledged in ancient American cultures.

Frederic Ward Putnam of Harvard's Peabody Museum led the first scientific excavation in 1887. His team uncovered evidence of earlier earthworks beneath the serpent. Circular and square forms preceded the snake construction by several centuries. The serpent builders incorporated these older structures into their design, creating a palimpsest of sacred earthworks.

Putnam's excavations also revealed burial mounds near the serpent's tail. These contained cremated human remains along with ceremonial objects made from copper, mica, and carved stone. The artifacts showed connections to the Adena culture, which flourished in Ohio between 800 BCE and 100 CE. The serpent's builders maintained continuity with much older regional traditions.

Modern preservation efforts have revealed previously unknown details about the serpent's construction. Ground-penetrating radar shows stone alignments beneath the visible earthwork. These internal structures likely guided the builders during construction, helping to maintain the serpent's shape over centuries of weathering.

*Ancient American Civilizations*

The serpent attracts thousands of visitors annually during the solstice periods. Modern sky watchers can observe the same astronomical alignments that guided the ancient builders. The earthwork continues functioning as a calendar and observatory more than 1,000 years after its completion.

# Cosmic Cosmogram: Sky, Earth, Underworld Symbols

Three Crows painted the final red ochre stripe across her cheek before climbing the sacred hill. As the senior sky-keeper for the river valley communities, she alone possessed the authority to begin the great turtle's consecration ceremony. The earthwork had taken five years to complete. Tonight, under the full moon of the autumn equinox, the turtle would receive its animating spirit.

The massive turtle effigy spread across two acres of carefully sculpted prairie. Its shell incorporated seven distinct domes, each aligned with specific star groups visible during different seasons. The head pointed toward the constellation known to Three Crows' people as the Great Bear. The four legs stretched toward cardinal directions, marking solstice and equinox positions.

Three Crows understood the turtle's symbolic meaning within the cosmic order her ancestors had mapped across the landscape. Turtles dwelt at the intersection of three worlds - swimming in earthly waters, breathing sky air, and hibernating in underground dens. The turtle effigy channeled power flowing between these realms.

The ceremony began at sunset with sage burning and drum songs. Representatives from twelve villages gathered around the turtle's perimeter. Each group brought sacred earth from their own territories. These soil offerings would be mixed into the turtle's shell during the night-long ritual.

Star knowledge passed down through generations of sky-keepers guided the earthwork's design. Three Crows had learned the sacred star maps from her grandmother, who received them from her grandmother before her. The knowledge stretched back to the first people who emerged from the earth and learned to read the sky's messages.

The turtle shell's seven domes corresponded to star clusters visible during crucial agricultural periods. The central dome aligned with the Pleiades, whose spring return signaled corn planting time. Side domes marked the positions of other star groups important for hunting, harvesting, and ceremonial activities throughout the year.

Underground chambers within the turtle contained offerings linking earth spirits to celestial powers. Copper ornaments shaped like thunderbirds represented messengers of the sky realm. Shell beads carved into water symbols honored underwater spirits. Stone pipes and ceramic vessels held tobacco and sacred plants, connecting all three worlds.

The builders had spent months choosing the ideal spot for their cosmic turtle. The location offered views of the entire river valley where their communities lived and farmed. Natural springs provided access to underground water sources. Elevated ground offered clear sky views for astronomical observations.

Construction required coordinating multiple types of specialized knowledge. Astronomers calculated star positions and seasonal alignments. Engineers designed drainage systems and structural supports. Artists determined proportions and symbolic elements. Religious leaders supervised ceremonial aspects of the building process.

The turtle's internal geometry reflected sophisticated mathematical understanding. The shell dimensions followed proportions found in spiral patterns throughout nature. The dome heights matched acoustic requirements for ceremonial chanting and drum music. The leg positions created sight lines to important landmarks across the surrounding landscape.

Different animal effigies served specific cosmic functions within the regional earthwork system. Eagles and hawks connected communities to the upper sky realm, where thunderbirds controlled weather patterns. Bears and wolves channeled earth realm powers related to hunting success and territorial protection. Serpents and water spirits linked settlements to the underwater realm, governing springs, rivers, and rainfall.

Human effigies occupied special positions in the cosmic hierarchy. They typically appeared at elevated locations where the earth and sky realms intersected. These earthworks honored deceased leaders who had achieved spiritual transformation, becoming mediators between living communities and ancestral spirits dwelling in the star world.

The geometric precision of many effigies reflected beliefs about cosmic order and mathematical harmony. Circular forms captured the cyclical nature of seasons, life stages, and celestial movements. Square and rectangular shapes marked the four directions and their associated spirits. Complex combinations created three-dimensional maps of spiritual geography.

Regional variations in effigy styles indicated local adaptations of continent-wide religious concepts. Great Lakes communities emphasized water and sky symbols reflecting their aquatic environment. Prairie builders focused on bison and eagle forms, connecting them to grassland spirits. River valley peoples created diverse animal assemblages reflecting the rich biodiversity of their territories.

The cosmic diagram encoded in effigy earthworks extended far beyond individual mounds. Entire landscapes became sacred texts readable by those possessing the appropriate knowledge. Travel routes connected related earthworks across hundreds of miles. Pilgrimage journeys reinforced social bonds and shared spiritual understanding among distant communities.

# Hand-Carried Construction: Basket by Basket

Dawn broke over the Mississippi River bluffs as Singing Badger lifted her burden basket and began the day's work. The woven container, crafted from river willow and reinforced with deer sinew, could hold forty pounds of clay-rich earth. Today marked the beginning of her third season helping build the great bird effigy overlooking the river valley.

Singing Badger had woven her own basket according to specifications passed down through her family line. The bottom used tightly coiled techniques, creating a foundation strong enough to support heavy loads. The sides flared outward for easy filling and emptying. Carrying straps positioned the weight across her shoulders and back for maximum efficiency during long walks.

The clay pit lay a quarter-mile from the bird effigy construction site. Workers had selected this location after extensive testing of local soil conditions. The clay contained the right mixture of fine particles and sand to create stable earthworks. It held its shape when wet but did not crack excessively during dry periods.

Singing Badger joined the procession of women and men walking between the clay pit and the construction site. Each person carried a different type of material needed for that day's work. Some baskets held pure clay for detailed shaping. Others contained sand for drainage layers. Still others carried small stones for internal reinforcement.

The walking rhythm developed naturally as the group moved across the prairie. Experienced carriers set the pace to prevent exhaustion during the long workday. They followed established paths that avoided steep grades and muddy areas. Rest stops occurred at predetermined locations where water and food were available.

Loading procedures had been refined through years of experience. Workers used wooden paddles to fill baskets with measured amounts of material. They tested each load for proper consistency and weight distribution. Improperly mixed soil was rejected and returned to the preparation areas for reprocessing.

The bird effigy required approximately 10,000 basketloads of earth to complete. With thirty workers carrying loads daily during favorable weather, the construction process extended across multiple seasons. Each person made an average of eight trips between the clay pit and the building site during a typical workday.

Quality control began at the clay pit and continued through final placement. Master builders inspected materials before loading. They rejected earth containing too much organic matter or inappropriate stone content. They maintained strict standards for moisture levels and particle size distribution.

Transportation efficiency improved through collective problem-solving. Workers developed better basket designs, reducing spillage during transport. They created temporary bridges across streams and wet areas. They established relay stations where carriers could rest without disrupting the overall workflow.

The actual placement of earth required careful coordination between multiple craft specialists. Basket carriers worked alongside shapers who positioned materials according to the effigy's design specifications. Tool makers maintained a supply of wooden paddles, stone hammers, and measuring devices needed for construction activities.

Seasonal weather patterns determined optimal construction periods. Spring provided ideal clay consistency when winter frost had broken down soil particles. Summer heat dried surfaces too quickly, necessitating regular water applications. Fall offered stable conditions for final shaping and finishing work.

Children learned construction techniques by participating in simplified tasks appropriate to their strength and skill levels. They carried small loads of special materials, such as coloured clays and decorative stones. They helped maintain tools and preparation areas. They absorbed knowledge about earthwork construction through direct participation.

Construction camps developed around major effigy projects. Workers built temporary shelters near building sites during intensive work periods. They established cooking areas, tool-making shops, and storage facilities for materials and equipment. These camps became social centers, strengthening community bonds through shared labor.

The physical demands of earthwork construction shaped the bodies and stamina of the builders. Archaeological studies of skeletal remains show evidence of strong back and shoulder muscles developed through heavy lifting. Wear patterns on bones indicate repetitive motions associated with digging, carrying, and shaping activities.

Accidents and injuries occurred despite careful safety procedures. Workers developed practical medical knowledge for treating sprains, cuts, and exhaustion. They used plant-based medicines and healing techniques. Serious injuries sometimes forced temporary work stoppages until injured persons could recover or be replaced.

Completion ceremonies celebrated the collective achievements of entire communities. Workers who had contributed labor received recognition through feasting, gift-giving, and social advancement. The finished earthwork became a permanent monument to their dedication, skill, and spiritual commitment.

Modern experiments in earthwork construction using traditional methods have shown the enormous labour requirements involved. Building even small effigies takes thousands of person-hours. Large monuments like Serpent Mound would have required coordinated effort from hundreds of workers over several years. The achievement becomes even more impressive when considered within the context of societies without metal tools, draft animals, or wheeled vehicles.

# PART III
# LOST EMPIRES

*Ancient American Civilizations*

# Chapter 19: The Aztec Inheritance - Blood, Gold, and Borrowed Glory

## Teotihuacan Discovery: Already Ancient Ruins

Moctezuma Ilhuicamina stood at the edge of the ancient city in 1450. Grass grew tall between massive stone blocks. Vines crept up pyramid walls weathered by centuries of abandonment. The Aztec ruler gazed across the Avenue of the Dead, trying to comprehend the scale of what his ancestors had found in this valley.

The city stretched beyond the horizon. Pyramids rose like artificial mountains from the valley floor. Stone apartment complexes housed no one. Ceremonial plazas echoed with wind instead of voices. Whatever civilization had built this marvel had vanished completely. No oral traditions survived. No written records explained who these builders were.

Moctezuma's priests whispered stories about the ruins. They called it Teotihuacan - the place where gods were born. Divine beings had supposedly constructed these monuments before humans walked the earth. The Aztecs could not imagine mortal hands creating such architectural perfection. Only gods possessed such power and knowledge.

Archaeological evidence tells a different story. Human footsteps had worn smooth the stone stairs leading up to the Pyramid of the Sun. Cooking fires had blackened apartment walls. Obsidian workshops contained half-finished blades abandoned by their makers. Real people had lived, worked, and died in this city. They had disappeared before the Aztecs arrived.

The scale overwhelmed Aztec comprehension. Teotihuacan at its peak housed between 100,000 and 200,000 people. The city covered eight square miles of carefully planned urban development. Residential districts surrounded ceremonial centers. Markets connected neighborhoods through networks of stone-paved streets. Aqueducts supplied fresh water to every quarter of the metropolis.

Aztec engineers studied the construction techniques. They examined how massive stones fit together without mortar. They traced water channels that still functioned after centuries of neglect. They measured astronomical alignments connecting pyramids to celestial events. Everything they learned influenced their own building projects in Tenochtitlan.

The Pyramid of the Sun presented the greatest mystery. This artificial mountain rose 213 feet above the valley floor. Its base measured 738 feet on each side. Builders had moved over 1.2 million tons of stone and earth to complete the structure. No crane had ever lifted these blocks into position. No wheeled vehicle had transported materials from distant quarries.

Spanish chronicler Bernardino de Sahagún later recorded Aztec accounts of their ancestors' first encounter with Teotihuacan. Warriors returning from northern campaigns reported discovering "houses of gods" in an empty valley. Scouts brought back obsidian blades sharper than any their craftsmen could produce. Artists sketched architectural details unlike anything in the Aztec experience.

Moctezuma ordered his architects to visit the ruins. They spent months measuring buildings and recording construction details. The Avenue of the Dead ran perfectly straight for over two miles. Side streets intersected at precise right angles. Drainage systems directed rainwater through carefully calculated channels. Every aspect showed planning and execution beyond Aztec capabilities.

The discovery transformed Aztec identity. They began calling themselves inheritors of divine civilization. Their empire gained legitimacy through connection to these ancient builders. Aztec priests incorporated Teotihuacan's astronomical alignments into their own ceremonial calendar. Architects borrowed construction techniques for new temples in Tenochtitlan.

But questions haunted Aztec leaders. What had caused such a magnificent civilization to disappear? Disease, warfare, internal collapse, or divine judgment - any explanation seemed inadequate for such complete abandonment. The ruins offered no answers. Empty buildings kept their secrets locked in stone.

Teotihuacan's influence shaped Aztec religious thinking. If gods had once walked the earth and built cities, they might return. The Aztecs developed complex prophecies about divine beings arriving from the east. These beliefs would prove fatally vulnerable when Spanish conquistadors appeared on Mexico's shores.

The ruined city also inspired Aztec architecture. The Templo Mayor in Tenochtitlan mirrored design elements from Teotihuacan's pyramids. Aztec palaces featured courtyards based on those in the ancient ruins. Even residential buildings adopted construction techniques perfected by the vanished civilisation.

# Fifth Sun Cosmology and Solar Maintenance

Dawn broke over Tenochtitlan on the morning of the New Fire ceremony in 1507. Aztec priests climbed the steps of the Templo Mayor carrying sacred implements for the most important ritual in their religious calendar. Every 52 years, they performed this ceremony to prevent the end of the world. Their cosmology demanded constant vigilance to keep the universe functioning.

The Aztecs believed they lived in the Fifth Sun, the current age of the world. Four previous worlds had existed and perished before their time. Each collapse resulted from divine anger or cosmic imbalance. The First Sun ended when jaguars devoured humanity. Wind destroyed the Second Sun. Fire consumed the Third Sun. Floods obliterated the Fourth Sun. The Fifth Sun faced destruction by earthquakes unless humans maintained their cosmic obligations.

This worldview drove every aspect of Aztec civilization. Religious ceremonies followed astronomical calendars designed to support the sun's daily journey across the sky. Political decisions considered cosmic implications. Military campaigns timed themselves to celestial events. Individual lives gained meaning through participation in universal maintenance.

The sun required nourishment to continue its path from east to west. Aztec priests taught that Tonatiuh, the sun god, had sacrificed himself to create the Fifth Sun. His divine blood gave life to the world as we know it. Human blood must now sustain his daily rebirth. Without this sacrifice, darkness would swallow the earth forever.

Every morning brought renewed anxiety. Would the sun rise again? Aztec astronomers tracked celestial movements with mathematical precision. They calculated eclipse dates decades in advance. They mapped planetary cycles and correlated them with earthly events. Their observations convinced them that cosmic balance hung by threads requiring constant attention.

The Twenty Day Count and the 365-day solar calendar intersected to create the Sacred Round of 260 days. This cyclical system guided agricultural activities, religious festivals, and social obligations. Specific days favored warfare, others demanded fasting. Births on certain dates were predicted to influence individual destinies. The calendar became a blueprint for organizing human life according to cosmic rhythms.

Aztec creation myths explained why sacrifice was necessary. The gods had assembled at Teotihuacan during the cosmic darkness between the Fourth and Fifth Suns. Two divine beings volunteered to become the new sun and moon. Nanahuatzin, covered in sores and rags, leaped bravely into the sacred fire. His courage transformed him into the brilliant sun. Tecuciztecatl, adorned in gold and jewels, hesitated before jumping. His cowardice made him the pale moon.

The newly created sun refused to move across the sky. Divine sacrifice alone could set celestial mechanisms in motion. All the gods offered their hearts and blood to start the solar movement. Their example established the pattern human beings must follow. Regular sacrifice would keep the sun moving and prevent universal collapse.

This cosmology justified the Aztec empire's constant warfare. Military campaigns captured prisoners for sacrificial ceremonies. The more prisoners taken, the stronger the cosmic support for solar movement. Warriors who died in battle joined the sun's daily journey, becoming divine guardians of celestial order. Death in combat guaranteed eternal glory and cosmic service.

The Aztecs calculated that approximately 18,000 people needed to die annually to maintain universal balance. Major festivals required hundreds of simultaneous sacrifices. The dedication of the Templo Mayor in 1487 reportedly involved 20,000 victims over four days. These numbers seem impossible to modern observers. Contemporary Spanish accounts may have exaggerated for propaganda purposes. But archaeological evidence confirms that human sacrifice occurred on a massive scale.

Different types of sacrifice served specific cosmic functions. Heart extraction powered solar movement. Drowning children brought rain.

Flaying victims encouraged agricultural fertility. Warriors fought ritual combats to honor celestial battles between day and night. Each ceremony addressed particular aspects of universal maintenance.

The Sacred Round determined when specific sacrifices should occur. Certain days demanded offerings to rain gods. Others required honoring agricultural deities. Military victories called for thanking war gods. Individual life events - births, marriages, deaths - all needed cosmic approval through appropriate sacrifices.

Aztec poets composed hymns explaining the necessity of cosmic maintenance. They described the universe as a delicate mechanism requiring constant adjustment. Human beings served as cosmic mechanics, providing the energy and attention needed to keep celestial systems functioning. Without their vigilance, creation would collapse into primordial chaos.

# Blood Sacrifice: Cosmic Balance Philosophy

The obsidian knife gleamed in torchlight as High Priest Tlacaelel raised it above the captive warrior's chest. The prisoner from Tlaxcala stared at the predawn sky over Tenochtitlan, his body stretched across the sacrificial stone atop the Templo Mayor. Drums echoed across the silent city. Thousands of Aztec citizens gathered in the plaza below, waiting for the ceremony that would ensure the sun's rebirth.

Tlacaelel had dedicated his life to understanding the cosmic mechanisms that kept the world functioning. His grandfather had been present when Aztec astronomers first calculated the exact amount of human blood needed to maintain universal balance. The numbers came from careful observation of celestial cycles and agricultural patterns. Too little sacrifice brought droughts and famines. Too much caused floods and earthquakes. Perfect balance required precise measurements.

The captive warrior understood his role in this cosmic drama. Tlaxcalan priests taught similar beliefs about divine sacrifice and solar maintenance. His death would not be murder but a transformation. His heart would join the sun's daily journey across the sky. His blood would nourish the earth and ensure another day of life for all humanity. He had prepared for this moment since childhood.

Aztec sacrifice differed fundamentally from random violence or political terror. Elaborate ceremonies preceded every offering. Priests purified themselves through fasting and bloodletting. Victims received fine clothes, abundant food, and ritual preparation. Musicians composed songs honoring their courage. Artists created masks representing their transformation into divine beings. Death became a cosmic celebration rather than simple execution.

The philosophy behind sacrifice is connected to the Aztec understanding of energy exchange throughout the universe. Nothing existed in isolation. Every action created consequences in other realms. Human blood contained the life force that linked earth to sky, mortality to divinity, present to future. The willingness of brave individuals to make sacrifices could influence cosmic processes and benefit entire civilizations.

Different forms of sacrifice served specific functions in maintaining universal balance. Heart extraction provided direct nourishment for solar movement. The organ was removed while still beating and held toward the sun as it consumed the fresh blood. Priests burned hearts in sacred braziers, sending smoke and essence skyward to feed celestial fires. The victim's body was then consumed in ritual meals that shared divine energy with the community.

Drowning children served a different cosmic purpose. Their tears resembled raindrops. Their innocence appealed to the rain gods who controlled agricultural fertility. During drought years, hundreds of children were taken to sacred cenotes and submerged until they drowned. Their sacrifice supposedly brought monsoons that ended famines and sustained crop production throughout the empire.

Flaying rituals honored Xipe Totec, the god of agricultural renewal and seasonal change. Victims were skinned alive, and priests wore their flesh like clothing for twenty days. This ceremony symbolized the earth shedding its winter covering to reveal spring growth beneath. Fields began producing crops again after successful flaying ceremonies. The agricultural cycle depended on regular renewal through sacrifice.

Gladiatorial combat satisfied war gods who needed evidence of human courage and martial skill. Captured warriors fought multiple opponents while tethered to circular stones. They received wooden swords embedded with obsidian blades. Their Aztec opponents used full metal weapons and shields. Victory was nearly impossible, but a brave performance earned divine favor for both warrior and empire.

The scale of Aztec sacrifice reflected their understanding of cosmic needs. Major festivals required hundreds of simultaneous offerings. The dedication of renovated temples involved thousands of victims over multiple days. Spanish chroniclers reported seeing skull racks containing tens of thousands of heads outside Tenochtitlan's ceremonial center. These numbers may be exaggerated, but archaeological evidence confirms large-scale sacrificial practices.

Timing mattered as much as scale. The Sacred Round calendar identified specific dates when particular types of sacrifice would be most effective. Solar eclipses demanded immediate offerings to prevent cosmic catastrophe. Planetary alignments required special ceremonies honoring celestial movements. Seasonal transitions needed rituals marking natural cycles. Military victories called for thanksgiving sacrifices to war gods.

# Borrowed Symbols from Earlier Civilizations

Nezahualcoyotl walked through the ruins of Tula in 1430, studying carved stone pillars that depicted warriors and divine beings. The Aztec architect had come to the abandoned Toltec capital seeking inspiration for new temples in Tenochtitlan. His rulers wanted their buildings to reflect the glory of previous civilizations. But the symbols he examined here were far older than Toltec culture.

The feathered serpent motif appeared on every major structure in Tula. Massive columns supported temple roofs with their coiled bodies. Wall carvings showed the deity flying between earth and sky. Priests' costumes incorporated feathered designs representing divine transformation. But Nezahualcoyotl knew this symbol predated Toltec civilization by many centuries.

Earlier visits to abandoned ruins had revealed the same imagery. Teotihuacan temples featured identical feathered serpent carvings. Olmec sites along the Gulf Coast contained the oldest known versions of this symbol. Maya cities throughout the Yucatan worshipped the same deity under different names. Kukulkan, Quetzalcoatl, Gukumatz - the feathered serpent had inspired reverence across Mesoamerica for over two thousand years.

Nezahualcoyotl sketched architectural details and symbolic elements that would enhance Aztec temples. He copied proportions from Toltec pyramids. He measured astronomical alignments that connected buildings to celestial events. He recorded color schemes that decorated religious artwork. Every element he documented had been borrowed from earlier cultures and adapted to serve new purposes.

The process of cultural borrowing had accelerated since the Aztecs established their empire. Each conquered territory contributed artistic traditions, religious symbols, and architectural techniques to the growing synthesis. Aztec craftsmen learned pottery styles from Cholula. Metalworkers adopted gold working techniques from Oaxaca. Astronomers incorporated calendar systems from Maya territory.

But the deepest influences came from civilizations that had disappeared long before Aztec expansion began. The symbols adorning Tenochtitlan's temples traced their origins to Olmec ceremonial centers built over three thousand years earlier. Jaguar gods, rain deities, astronomical alignments, and mathematical concepts had passed through dozens of cultures before reaching the Aztecs.

The concept of divine kingship followed similar patterns of transmission. Olmec rulers had first claimed to channel cosmic forces through their persons. Maya kings developed elaborate ceremonies demonstrating their connections to celestial deities. Toltec legends described priest-kings who could transform into animal spirits. Aztec emperors inherited these traditions and adapted them to support their own claims to divine authority.

Architectural elements showed the most unmistakable evidence of cultural borrowing. The step-pyramid form had originated in Olmec territory over two millennia before Aztec construction began. Each subsequent civilization had modified the basic design. Maya builders added astronomical observation chambers. Toltec architects incorporated warrior imagery. Aztec engineers scaled everything up to unprecedented proportions.

Religious iconography demonstrated even more complex patterns of transmission. The rain god Tlaloc appeared in Aztec ceremonies with attributes borrowed from multiple earlier cultures. His goggle eyes came from Teotihuacan traditions. His jaguar fangs reflected Olmec influences. His association with mountains derived from highland Maya beliefs. His agricultural functions incorporated traditions from across Mesoamerica.

Calendar systems provided the most sophisticated example of cultural synthesis. The 260-day Sacred Round had originated in Olmec territory around 600 BCE. Maya astronomers had refined it into complex long-count calculations. Zapotec scholars had added mathematical innovations. Aztec priests inherited the complete system and used it to organize their empire's religious and administrative activities.

Nezahualcoyotl understood that Aztec civilization's greatness came partly from its ability to absorb and improve upon earlier achievements. His architectural plans for Tenochtitlan incorporated design elements from every major Mesoamerican culture. The resulting temples would surpass their models in scale and grandeur, but their fundamental concepts traced back through centuries of cultural evolution.

The borrowing process continued throughout the Aztec expansion. Each new conquest brought fresh artistic traditions and religious concepts into the imperial synthesis. Aztec merchants traveled thousands of miles gathering exotic materials and learning foreign techniques. Diplomatic missions brought back detailed reports of architectural innovations and ceremonial practices.

# 1521 Rapid Collapse Under Spanish Contact

Hernán Cortés stood on the causeway connecting Tenochtitlan to the mainland on November 8, 1519. The Spanish conquistador gazed across the vast lake system surrounding the Aztec capital. Cities rose from artificial islands connected by stone bridges. Gardens floated on the water surface. Canoes filled channels between neighborhoods like water taxis in an aquatic metropolis. Nothing in European experience had prepared him for this sight.

Moctezuma Xocoyotzin waited in his palace, paralyzed by prophecies that had shaped Aztec religious thinking for centuries. The empire's priests had predicted the return of Quetzalcoatl, the feathered serpent god, in the year Ce Acatl (One Reed). Their calculations placed this divine return precisely in 1519. Spanish ships had appeared on Mexico's eastern shores exactly when prophecy demanded. The bearded strangers rode unknown animals and commanded thunder weapons. Everything matched ancient descriptions of returning gods.

The collision between two worlds began with mutual incomprehension. Cortés sought gold and territorial conquest for the Spanish crown. Moctezuma saw divine beings fulfilling cosmic prophecy. Spanish soldiers viewed Aztec ceremonies as demonic rituals requiring immediate suppression. Aztec priests interpreted Spanish demands as divine tests of human faithfulness. Neither side understood the other's fundamental motivations.

Disease preceded military conquest. Smallpox, typhus, and measles swept through indigenous populations with no previous exposure to Old World pathogens. Tenochtitlan's population crashed from approximately 200,000 to fewer than 50,000 within two years. Entire neighborhoods emptied as families died in their homes. Administrative systems collapsed when bureaucrats succumbed to epidemics. Agricultural production ceased as farmers abandoned their fields.

The speed of demographic collapse terrified survivors. Aztec medicine had no remedies for European diseases. Traditional healing ceremonies proved powerless against alien pathogens. Religious explanations failed as gods seemed to abandon their people. The cosmic balance that had sustained the Fifth Sun appeared to be breaking down catastrophically.

Military confrontation followed epidemiological disaster. Spanish steel weapons and firearms gave conquistadors significant advantages in direct combat. But their ultimate victory came through indigenous alliances rather than superior technology. Tlaxcalans, traditional enemies of the Aztec empire, provided thousands of warriors eager to overthrow their imperial oppressors. Totonacs, Cholulans, and other subject peoples joined the rebellion against Aztec rule.

The siege of Tenochtitlan lasted 93 days in 1521. Spanish brigantines controlled the lake system, cutting off supplies to the island capital. Aztec resistance continued under Cuauhtémoc, the last Emperor, even as starvation weakened defenders and disease decimated the population. Street-by-street fighting destroyed much of the city before final surrender came on August 13, 1521.

Cultural destruction accompanied political conquest. Spanish priests burned thousands of indigenous codices containing astronomical calculations, historical records, and religious knowledge accumulated over centuries. They demolished Aztec temples and used the stones to build Catholic churches. They prohibited indigenous ceremonies and imposed European religious practices throughout the former empire.

The collapse revealed fundamental vulnerabilities in Aztec imperial structure. The empire's legitimacy depended on successful cosmic maintenance through sacrifice and ceremony. When the Spanish conquest prevented traditional rituals, divine support appeared to withdraw. Subject peoples who had accepted Aztec rule because of its supernatural sanction quickly transferred their allegiance to the apparently more powerful Spanish gods.

Archaeological evidence from this period shows rapid abandonment of ceremonial centers throughout central Mexico. Teotihuacan, already ruined when the Aztecs found it, received no more pilgrimage offerings after 1521. Tula and other sacred sites lost their caretaker populations. The entire religious landscape that had connected Mesoamerican cultures for millennia disappeared within a single generation.

Spanish chronicles describe the psychological impact of conquest on surviving Aztecs. Many believed the Fifth Sun had indeed ended and the world was entering a new cosmic age. Some integrated Christian symbols with traditional beliefs, creating syncretic religious practices that survive today. Others retreated into remote areas where they could maintain ancestral customs away from Spanish surveillance.

The speed of imperial collapse surprised even the conquistadors. They had expected years of guerrilla warfare and gradual territorial control. Instead, the entire political and religious system disintegrated once its cosmic foundations lost credibility. The empire that had claimed divine sanction could not survive the appearance of apparently more powerful gods carrying superior weapons and immunity to disease.

But Aztec cultural influences survived the political collapse. Architectural techniques, agricultural methods, astronomical knowledge, and artistic traditions continued in modified forms throughout the colonial period. The synthesis of symbols and ideas that had defined Aztec civilization became part of the complex cultural heritage that shapes Mexican identity today. The borrowed glory had ended, but its legacy endured.

# Chapter 20: Maya Mastery - Writing, Time, and the Language of the Gods

## Hieroglyphic Script: Phonetic and Symbolic Encoding

Father Diego de Landa watched the flames consume centuries of Maya knowledge. The Spanish priest had ordered the burning of twenty-seven Maya books in the plaza of Maní on July 12, 1562. Smoke rose from bark paper covered in intricate symbols. The Maya people wept as their written history turned to ash.

"We found a large number of books in these characters," de Landa wrote later, "and, as they contained nothing in which were not to be seen as superstition and lies of the devil, we burned them all." The priest believed he was destroying pagan artifacts. He had actually destroyed one of the world's most sophisticated writing systems.

Only four Maya codices survived the Spanish conquest. These bark paper books contain fragments of what was once a vast literary tradition. Modern scholars spend decades deciphering individual pages. Each glyph reveals layers of meaning encoded by scribes whose training took decades to complete.

Maya writing started with symbols carved into stone. The earliest examples date back to the third century BCE. Scribes painted the same symbols on pottery, carved them into jade ornaments, and inlaid them with precious stones in temple walls. The system became more intricate over time as scribes added new signs and refined existing ones.

A young Maya scribe began training around age seven. Noble families selected the most intelligent children for this honored profession. The boy learned to recognize hundreds of individual glyphs. He memorized their sounds, meanings, and proper combinations. He practiced painting on bark paper with brushes made from animal hair. His hand had to be steady enough to create characters smaller than a thumbnail with perfect precision.

The writing system combined three different approaches. Some glyphs represented sounds, like letters in our alphabet. Others pictured the things they described - a jaguar head meant jaguar. The most sophisticated glyphs carried abstract meanings that required deep cultural knowledge to understand. A single text might use all three methods simultaneously.

Maya scribes could spell the same word in multiple ways. They might use pure sound symbols, pure meaning symbols, or combinations of both. This flexibility allowed scribes to create visual puns, embed hidden meanings, and demonstrate their educational sophistication. Reading Maya texts required not only literacy but a profound understanding of Maya culture, history, and religious beliefs.

The scribes held honored positions in Maya society. They served kings as record keepers, advisors, and historians. They painted murals in royal palaces showing courtly ceremonies and diplomatic meetings. They carved monument inscriptions commemorating military victories and royal birthdays. Their work preserved Maya civilization for posterity.

Kings valued scribes so highly they took them as prisoners during warfare. A captured scribe could read enemy documents, write propaganda, and teach the winner's children. Some prisoners received better treatment than captured nobles because their skills were irreplaceable.

Maya writing encoded information at multiple levels simultaneously. The surface meaning told stories of gods and kings. Deeper meanings revealed mathematical relationships, astronomical calculations, and prophetic interpretations. The deepest level contained mystical knowledge accessible only to the highest-ranking priests.

Scribes organized their texts in columns, reading from left to right and top to bottom. They grouped glyphs into blocks containing one to five individual symbols. Each block usually conveyed one word or concept. The blocks formed sentences and paragraphs describing events, people, and places with remarkable precision.

Royal scribes signed their work with personal glyphs identifying their names and titles. Some added self-portraits showing themselves presenting books to rulers. These signatures reveal individual personalities behind the formal texts. Scribes took pride in their craft and wanted recognition for their achievements.

The writing system could express any concept in the Maya language. Scribes wrote about agriculture, astronomy, medicine, history, and prophecy with equal facility. They recorded tribute payments, legal disputes, and marriage contracts. They composed poetry, epic stories, and religious hymns. No topic lay beyond their system's reach.

Maya glyphs carried aesthetic beauty equal to their informational content. Scribes shaped each character with artistic sensibility. They balanced positive and negative space, created rhythmic patterns across pages, and used color to emphasize important passages. Reading a Maya codex provided visual pleasure along with intellectual stimulation.

The complexity of Maya writing meant literacy remained limited to the elite. Perhaps five percent of the population could read and write fluently. This exclusivity gave scribes tremendous power as gatekeepers of knowledge. They controlled access to historical records, religious texts, and legal documents.

Spanish colonization ended this intellectual tradition within a generation. Missionaries destroyed most Maya books and forbade children from learning the ancient script. Within decades, no one could read the glyphs covering thousands of monuments throughout Maya territory. The writing system died with its last literate practitioners.

Modern decipherment began in the 1950s when scholars realized Maya glyphs functioned as a complete writing system rather than simple picture symbols. Russian linguist Yuri Knorosov proved that many glyphs represented sounds rather than ideas. American archaeologist Tatiana Proskouriakoff demonstrated that monument inscriptions recorded historical events rather than purely religious concepts.

These breakthroughs opened Maya texts to modern readers for the first time in four centuries. Scholars can now read about royal dynasties, warfare campaigns, and political alliances recorded by ancient scribes. The stones speak again, telling stories preserved in hieroglyphic script carved by masters whose names we are beginning to learn.

# Calendar Precision: 0.002-Day Solar Year Accuracy

High Priest Itzamnaaj knelt before the stone altar as Venus appeared in the pre-dawn sky. He had calculated this moment would arrive exactly 584 days after the planet's last morning appearance. The mathematical tables carved into the temple wall confirmed his prediction. Venus followed its cosmic pattern with clockwork precision, guided by forces the Maya understood better than any people on Earth.

The priest began his daily ritual of time measurement. He counted days since the current world began - over one million days ago, according to Maya calculations. He noted the position in the 260-day ritual calendar and the 365-day solar calendar. He checked which of the nine Lords of Night ruled this day. All these cycles interlocked like gears in a cosmic machine.

Maya understanding of time surpassed that of every contemporary civilization. Their astronomers calculated the length of the solar year as 365.2422 days - accurate to within 0.002 days of the true figure. Modern measurements using atomic clocks give 365.2422 days. The Maya achieved this precision through naked-eye observations conducted over centuries.

Maya timekeepers recognized that calendar systems must account for the solar year's extra fraction of a day. European calendars remained inaccurate until Pope Gregory XIII instituted reforms in 1582. The Gregorian calendar still accumulates errors requiring periodic adjustments. Maya calculations needed no such corrections.

The Maya developed multiple interlocking calendar systems to track different aspects of time's passage. The ritual calendar, called Tzolkin, combined twenty day names with thirteen numbers to create a 260-day cycle. The solar calendar, called Haab, contained eighteen months of twenty days plus five extra days considered unlucky. These two calendars meshed together to create a 52-year cycle called Calendar Round.

Beyond these basic systems, Maya astronomers maintained the Long Count, a linear calendar that measured days from the creation of the current world. This system used place notation similar to our decimal system but based on multiples of twenty rather than ten. The Maya could express any date in history or predict far future events using Long Count notation.

Maya Calendar Round ceremonies occurred every 52 years when both calendars returned to the same starting position. These occasions required elaborate rituals to ensure the world's continuation. Priests extinguished all fires, destroyed pottery, and conducted renewal ceremonies. The population fasted and performed penance. Only after proper rituals could the new cycle begin safely.

The Long Count enabled Maya historians to record precise dates for historical events occurring centuries before their time. Stone monuments throughout Maya territory display Long Count dates with accuracy spanning over two millennia. These inscriptions create a chronological framework for Maya civilization more precise than records from most ancient cultures.

Maya astronomers tracked celestial cycles with extraordinary accuracy. They calculated the lunar month as 29.53020 days, which is slightly less than the actual figure of 29.53059 days. They determined the synodic period of Venus as 583.92 days, which is the same as the true period. They measured Mars' cycle as 780 days, exactly matching astronomical observations.

These calculations required sophisticated mathematical techniques. Maya scribes used zero as a placeholder centuries before this concept reached Europe. They performed complex calculations involving millions of days using only addition and subtraction. Their mathematical notation enabled precise record-keeping across vast time periods.

Eclipse prediction demanded the highest levels of astronomical sophistication. Maya tables could foretell solar and lunar eclipses decades in advance. The Dresden Codex contains eclipse tables spanning over 400 years. These predictions account for seasonal variations and geographic differences in eclipse visibility.

Maya astronomers understood that celestial cycles repeat in predictable patterns. They identified the 405-month eclipse cycle, the 819-day Mars cycle, and complex Venus patterns lasting multiple centuries. This knowledge enabled them to create perpetual calendars requiring no adjustments for millennia.

Venus held special importance in Maya astronomy and religion. The planet's movements determined optimal times for warfare, coronations, and religious ceremonies. Maya armies timed attacks to coincide with Venus' first appearance as morning star. Kings scheduled their coronations when Venus reached maximum brightness.

The Maya tracked Venus through its complete 584-day cycle from morning star to evening star and back. They recorded the exact number of days for each phase: 236 days as morning star, 90 days invisible in superior conjunction, 263 days as evening star, and 8 days invisible in inferior conjunction. These observations achieved accuracy equal to modern telescopic measurements.

Maya calendar systems integrated astronomy, mathematics, and religion into unified worldview. Time was not an abstract concept but a living force that shaped human destiny. Each day carried specific characteristics determined by its position in multiple overlapping cycles. Success in any endeavor depended on choosing the proper time according to cosmic patterns.

Priests consulted almanacs indicating favorable days for planting, harvesting, marriage, travel, and warfare. These guides combined astronomical calculations with traditional knowledge accumulated over generations. Maya civilization synchronized its activities with celestial rhythms to an extent never achieved by any other culture.

The calendar's complexity required professional astronomers to maintain accurate records. These specialists were trained for decades to master the intricate calculations. They observed celestial events from stone platforms atop pyramids, recording data in books that preserved centuries of accumulated knowledge. Their work made Maya civilization the most time-conscious society in human history.

# Cascajal Block: 1000 BCE Earliest American Writing

María del Carmen Rodríguez pushed through the jungle undergrowth near La Venta, Mexico. The sweltering heat in Veracruz made every step exhausting. She searched for Olmec artifacts in areas disturbed by road construction. Local workers had reported finding carved stones, but most discoveries from this region disappeared into private collections before archaeologists could study them.

Rodríguez noticed an unusual stone block partly buried in excavated earth. The carved surface displayed rows of organized symbols, unlike anything she had en before. She carefully dug out the artefact, photographing each step of the process. The stone measured 36 centimeters long, 21 centimeters wide, and 13 centimeters thick. Its surface featured sixty-two distinct symbols arranged in horizontal rows.

The discovery occurred in 1999, but academic politics delayed publication for seven years. Critics argued the symbols were natural marks or modern fakes created to deceive researchers. Others questioned whether the artifact came from a secure archaeological context. The heated debate reflected deeper tensions about the origins of writing in the Americas.

Carbon dating of organic materials embedded in the stone's surface provided a date range of 1200 to 900 BCE. This made the Cascajal Block significantly older than any accepted American writing system. If authentic, it predated Maya hieroglyphic inscriptions by several centuries and rivaled the earliest Chinese and Mediterranean scripts.

The symbols on the Cascajal Block show clear organizational principles indicating systematic writing rather than random decoration. The marks repeat in patterns suggesting grammatical rules. Some symbols appear frequently in specific positions like prepositions or articles in modern languages. Others occur only at row beginnings or endings like punctuation marks.

Analysis reveals approximately sixty-two distinct symbols carved into the block's surface. This number falls within the range typical of logosyllabic writing systems, where symbols represent both sounds and meanings. Purely alphabetic systems use fewer symbols. Purely logographic systems use many more. The Cascajal Block's symbol count suggests sophisticated linguistic encoding.

The symbols themselves show clear artistic relationships to other Olmec art forms. Several resemble motifs found on Olmec sculptures, pottery, and jade ornaments. This consistency supports the artifact's authenticity and places it within established Olmec cultural traditions. The symbols were not random inventions but part of a coherent symbolic system.

Some symbols on the block clearly represent recognizable objects. A corn plant appears multiple times in different contexts. An insect, possibly a bee, occurs in several rows. These pictographic elements suggest the writing system began with picture-writing that gradually became more abstract over time, following patterns observed in other early scripts worldwide.

The arrangement of symbols in horizontal rows, reading left to right, matches writing conventions eventually adopted by Maya scribes. This consistency suggests the Cascajal Block inscription follows linguistic rules rather than decorative patterns. The symbols were meant to be read in sequence to convey meaningful information.

Repetition patterns within the inscription indicate grammatical structure. Certain symbol combinations occur multiple times in similar positions within different rows. These patterns suggest the presence of grammatical elements like determinatives, phonetic complements, or syntactic markers found in mature writing systems.

The Cascajal Block's discovery location near La Venta, one of the most important Olmec ceremonial centers, supports its authenticity. This site produced numerous other Olmec artifacts, including colossal stone heads, altars, and jade figurines. The cultural context matches what archaeologists would expect for early Olmec writing experiments.

Microscopic analysis of the carved symbols reveals weathering patterns consistent with genuine archaeological age. The cuts show signs of natural aging, mineral deposits, and erosion that would be difficult to fake convincingly. Modern tool marks would leave different traces than ancient carving techniques using stone and wooden implements.

The Cascajal Block represents a transitional stage between picture-writing and full phonetic literacy. Many symbols retain pictographic qualities, making them partially understandable even without knowing the underlying language. This accessibility suggests early writing served public communication rather than purely esoteric religious purposes.

If genuine, the Cascajal Block demonstrates that Olmec civilization achieved literacy centuries before previously documented. This discovery pushes back the origins of American writing systems to compete chronologically with the earliest scripts in China, Egypt, and Mesopotamia. The Americas independently invented writing as early as any region on Earth.

The block's inscription length - sixty-two symbols in multiple rows - indicates substantial content rather than simple labeling or decoration. The text appears to record information requiring extended written communication. This suggests that Olmec society had developed administrative, religious, or historical recording needs that demanded permanent written records.

Critics continue to question the block's authenticity despite growing evidence supporting its genuineness. Academic resistance reflects deeper issues about accepting paradigm-shifting discoveries that challenge established chronologies. The debate over the Cascajal Block mirrors earlier controversies about Maya decipherment and other archaeological breakthroughs.

Recent discoveries of other early Olmec inscriptions support the Cascajal Block's authenticity. Additional carved symbols have been found on pottery vessels and stone monuments from securely dated Olmec contexts. These finds create a growing body of evidence for early Olmec literacy that becomes harder to dismiss as coincidence or fraud.

The Cascajal Block inscription may never be fully deciphered without additional texts for comparison. Single inscriptions rarely provide enough context for complete linguistic analysis. However, its existence proves that American civilizations began experimenting with written communication far earlier than previously recognized, laying the foundations for the sophisticated scripts that would later flourish throughout Mesoamerica.

# Eclipse Prediction Without Telescopes

Akbal-Na peered through the narrow window of the Caracol observatory at Chichen Itza. The circular stone building rose above the jungle canopy, its precisely oriented openings designed to frame specific celestial events. Tonight, he would witness the climax of calculations that had occupied Maya astronomers for generations. The moon would pass through Earth's shadow in a total lunar eclipse predicted centuries before his birth.

The priest had spent decades learning to read the cosmic signs. His teachers passed down knowledge accumulated over a millennium of careful observation. Every eclipse, every planetary alignment, every stellar cycle had been recorded in bark paper books and carved into temple walls. The Maya possessed the most accurate astronomical records in the ancient world.

Maya eclipse predictions began with recognizing the fundamental rhythm underlying all eclipse events. Solar and lunar eclipses follow an 18-year, 11-day cycle called the Saros by modern astronomers. The Maya discovered this pattern through centuries of meticulous observation and called it by their own name. They realized that eclipses occurring 6,585 days apart shared similar characteristics.

The Dresden Codex, one of four surviving Maya books, contains eclipse tables spanning 405 lunar months - nearly 33 years of predictions. The tables account for seasonal variations, lunar orbit irregularities, and geographic differences in eclipse visibility. Maya astronomers achieved this accuracy using only naked-eye observations and mathematical calculations.

Maya observers noted that eclipses occur only during specific lunar months when the moon's path crosses the sun's apparent path through the sky. They identified these danger periods when eclipses became possible and calculated precisely when they would occur. This knowledge enabled priests to prepare proper rituals and warn populations of impending cosmic events.

The Maya understood that not every potential eclipse would be visible from their territory. They calculated which eclipses would be total, partial, or completely invisible from specific locations. These refinements required a sophisticated understanding of Earth's spherical shape and the moon's varying distance from our planet.

Eclipse calculations demanded the highest levels of Maya mathematical sophistication. Astronomers worked with cycles involving hundreds of thousands of days spanning multiple centuries. They used vigesimal (base-20) notation to handle these enormous numbers, developing computational techniques that would not be equaled in Europe for centuries.

The Palenque tablets contain eclipse records dating back over 1,500 years before the inscriptions were carved. These retrospective calculations demonstrate Maya ability to project astronomical cycles far into the past with extraordinary accuracy. They could determine the exact dates of eclipses that occurred during the reigns of long-dead kings.

Maya eclipse prediction served both practical and religious purposes. Solar eclipses posed perceived dangers to rulers whose power derived from solar symbolism. Priests needed advance warning to conduct protective ceremonies and reassure panicked populations. Accurate predictions enhanced priestly authority and demonstrated divine favor.

Lunar eclipses provided different challenges and opportunities. These events lasted longer than solar eclipses and were visible from entire hemispheres simultaneously. Maya priests used lunar eclipse predictions to coordinate ceremonies across far-flung cities and validate their astronomical expertise to distant populations.

The Maya recognized that eclipse cycles interlocked with other celestial rhythms in complex patterns. Venus cycles, Mars cycles, and eclipse cycles all influenced each other in ways requiring centuries of observation to understand fully. Maya astronomers created unified models encompassing all these interactions.

Eclipse tables in Maya codices include correction factors accounting for small variations in lunar orbit speed and eclipse frequency. These refinements prevented prediction errors from accumulating over long time periods. The Maya achieved greater chronological accuracy than European eclipse predictions until well into the Renaissance period.

Maya astronomers distinguished between different types of eclipses with remarkable precision. They calculated the duration of totality, the maximum eclipse magnitude, and the precise timing of different eclipse phases. Their predictions matched modern calculations to within hours despite having no mechanical timepieces.

The Maya developed warning systems to alert populations about upcoming eclipses. Messengers carried eclipse predictions to outlying settlements. Local priests prepared appropriate rituals and assembled communities for group observations. These coordinated responses demonstrate sophisticated communication networks spanning Maya territory.

Eclipse observations required specially trained personnel positioned at multiple locations throughout Maya lands. These observer-priests recorded precise timing data and reported their measurements to central astronomical centers. The collaborative approach enabled more accurate predictions than any single observatory could achieve alone.

Maya eclipse records preserve information about historical eclipses that modern astronomers use to study long-term changes in Earth's rotation rate. The precision of ancient Maya observations provides data for understanding how tidal friction has gradually slowed our planet's spin over the past two millennia.

The psychological impact of accurate eclipse predictions cannot be overstated. Populations living in constant fear of cosmic catastrophe gained confidence from priests who could foretell celestial events years in advance. This predictive power enhanced Maya civilization's stability and rulers' legitimacy throughout the classical period.

# Venus Cycle and Planetary Movement Tracking

K'inich Janaab Pakal I climbed the steep stone steps of the Palace Tower at Palenque as Venus blazed in the pre-dawn sky. The Maya ruler had timed his coronation ceremony to coincide with the planet's heliacal rising - its first appearance as morning star after a period of invisibility. According to Maya belief, Venus in this phase possessed maximum power to bless new rulers and ensure successful reigns.

The king's astronomers had calculated this moment with extraordinary precision. They knew Venus would remain visible as the morning star for precisely 236 days before disappearing into superior conjunction with the sun. After 90 days of invisibility, the planet would return as the evening star for 263 days. Then came eight days of inferior conjunction before the cycle repeated. This 584-day pattern governed Maya political and military activities for over a millennium.

Maya Venus observations began long before Pakal's reign. Priests at sites throughout Mesoamerica had tracked the planet's movements for centuries, recording data in books and stone inscriptions. They discovered that five Venus cycles exactly matched eight solar years - a relationship they called the Venus-solar correlation. This 2,920-day period enabled precise long-term predictions.

The Dresden Codex contains the most sophisticated Venus tables from the ancient world. These calculations span 384 years and account for the slight discrepancy between Venus cycles and solar years. Maya astronomers realized that using exactly 584 days for each Venus cycle would accumulate errors over time. They developed correction factors maintaining accuracy across centuries.

Venus held profound religious significance for the Maya. They identified the planet with their god Kukulkan, the feathered serpent who brought both creation and destruction. Venus, as the morning star, symbolised resurrection and new beginnings. Venus, as evening star, foretold warfare and sacrifice. The planet's eight-day disappearance during inferior conjunction represented death and underworld journey.

Maya armies timed major military campaigns to coincide with Venus events. Attacks launched during the planet's first appearance as morning star supposedly gained divine support. The Maya believed enemy cities became vulnerable when Venus reached maximum brightness or began

*Ancient American Civilizations*

its descent toward the western horizon. These astronomical warfare tactics appear throughout Maya historical records.

Kings scheduled important ceremonies according to the positions of Venus. Coronations, royal marriages, and temple dedications occurred when the planet occupied auspicious phases. The Maya coordinated political events across their entire civilization using Venus as a cosmic clock visible from any location.

Predicting Venus requires understanding the planet's complex behaviour patterns. Maya astronomers noted that Venus does not always become visible immediately after calculated conjunction dates. Atmospheric conditions, seasonal weather, and the planet's varying brightness affect visibility timing. Maya tables account for these variables with remarkable sophistication.

The Maya tracked other planets besides Venus with impressive accuracy. They determined Mars' synodic period as 780 days - exactly matching modern measurements. Jupiter's 399-day synodic period appears in Maya calculations. These outer planet observations required decades of patient recording since their cycles span multiple years.

Maya planetary astronomy reached its peak during the classical period between 250 and 900 CE. Observatories at sites like Chichen Itza, Palenque, and Copan conducted coordinated observations sharing data across hundreds of miles. This collaborative approach enabled more accurate measurements than individual sites could achieve alone.

The Caracol observatory at Chichen Itza contains windows precisely aligned with Venus' extreme positions. The planet reaches its maximum northern and southern positions every eight years, and the building's openings frame these events exactly. Similar architectural alignments exist at sites throughout Maya territory.

Maya Venus records provide modern astronomers with valuable historical data. The precision of ancient observations enables scientists to study small changes in planetary orbits over long time periods. Maya measurements help verify computer models of solar system evolution spanning multiple millennia.

Venus iconography appears throughout Maya art and architecture. The planet's glyph decorates temple facades, pottery vessels, and royal regalia. Venus symbols often accompany depictions of warfare, sacrifice, and royal power. The visual record confirms Venus' central importance in Maya cosmology and political ideology.

Maya Venus calculations required mathematical techniques not developed in Europe until the Renaissance. They used sophisticated interpolation methods to handle fractional day values. They developed algorithms for converting between different calendar systems. They created computational shortcuts enabling the rapid calculation of planetary positions.

The Maya understood that planetary cycles interconnect in complex patterns. Venus cycles correlate with eclipse cycles, lunar cycles, and Mars cycles in relationships that require centuries to fully observe. Maya astronomers created unified models encompassing all these interactions - an achievement not matched in other ancient civilizations.

Maya planetary astronomy continued after the classical collapse but gradually declined during the post-classical period. The Spanish conquest destroyed most astronomical records and killed the priestly specialists who maintained this knowledge. European missionaries viewed Maya astronomy as pagan superstition deserving elimination.

Modern decipherment of Maya astronomical texts reveals the full sophistication of their planetary observations. Computer analysis confirms that Maya Venus predictions achieved accuracy comparable to modern ephemeris tables. Their achievement stands as one of humanity's greatest intellectual accomplishments, created by patient observation and mathematical genius over many generations of dedicated sky watchers.

# Chapter 21: Lake Titicaca - Secrets Beneath Sacred Waters

## 2000 Underwater Archaeological Discovery

The diving equipment felt heavy against Lorenzo Epis's shoulders as he descended into Lake Titicaca's crystalline waters. March 15, 2000 marked his first expedition beneath Bolivia's sacred lake surface. Epis, a veteran underwater archaeologist from Argentina, had spent months preparing for this moment. The Bolivian government had finally granted permission for systematic exploration of the world's highest navigable lake.

Thirty feet below the surface, something impossible appeared in Epis's diving lights. Stone walls rose from the lake bed like ancient skyscrapers frozen in time. The blocks were massive, precisely cut, and fitted together without mortar. Each stone showed tool marks indicating careful shaping by human hands. The walls extended far beyond the reach of the light beams.

Epis surfaced and radioed his Cuban colleague, Iturralde Vinent, who was coordinating surface operations. "We have structures down here," Epis reported through his communication device. "Major architectural foundations. This is not a geological formation."

The joint Bolivian-Cuban expedition had originally planned to search for Inca gold offerings reportedly thrown into the lake during the Spanish conquest. Local indigenous communities had preserved oral traditions about underwater temples and sunken cities. Most archaeologists dismissed these stories as folklore mixed with wishful thinking about hidden treasures.

The reality proved far more significant than any golden artifacts. Over the following weeks, the diving teams mapped extensive underwater ruins covering several square kilometers of the lake bed. They discovered stone walls standing twenty meters tall, paved roadways disappearing into deeper waters, ceremonial platforms, and what appeared to be residential foundations arranged in organized patterns.

*Ancient American Civilizations*

Photography proved challenging in the lake's depths. The high altitude affected underwater lighting equipment. Sediment clouds reduced visibility when divers approached the structures. Camera equipment frequently malfunctioned in the thin atmosphere at 12,507 feet above sea level. Despite these obstacles, the team documented over 200 individual architectural features spread across the underwater site.

Radiocarbon dating of organic materials found within the structures provided preliminary age estimates. The results pointed to construction between 1,000 and 1,500 years ago, coinciding with the height of Tiwanaku civilization. This pre-Inca culture had dominated the Titicaca basin long before the Inca Empire expanded northward from the Cusco valley.

The discovery attracted international attention from underwater archaeology specialists. Dr. Franck Goddio, famous for exploring Alexandria's sunken harbor, offered technical assistance. The Belgian Navy contributed specialized diving equipment designed for high-altitude operations. UNESCO expressed interest in protecting the site from potential treasure hunters.

Local indigenous communities reacted with a mixture of vindication and concern. Aymara elders had maintained for generations that their ancestors built underwater temples to commune with lake spirits. The archaeological confirmation validated traditional knowledge often dismissed by academic institutions. However, community leaders worried about increased tourism disturbing sacred waters.

Bolivian authorities struggled to protect the site from unauthorized diving expeditions. Lake Titicaca's vast size made comprehensive surveillance impossible. Rumors of gold artifacts attracted treasure hunters willing to risk dangerous diving conditions. Several drowning incidents occurred when inexperienced divers attempted to reach the underwater ruins without proper equipment or training.

The initial expedition established protocols for future research. Diving operations required government permits, professional supervision, and strict artifact preservation standards. Any objects recovered went directly to La Paz National Museum for scientific study. Photography and mapping took priority over artifact collection to preserve the site's archaeological integrity.

Scientists began developing theories about how the structures came to be underwater. Rising lake levels could have submerged buildings originally constructed on dry land. Geological activity might have caused subsidence, lowering entire settlements below current water levels. Climate changes during the medieval period could have increased precipitation, raising Lake Titicaca beyond its historical boundaries.

The underwater city challenged conventional understanding of Tiwanaku civilization's relationship with Lake Titicaca. Previous archaeological work had focused on land-based sites around the lake's perimeter. The discovery suggested ancient peoples designed their settlements to incorporate both terrestrial and aquatic environments as integrated sacred landscapes.

# 20-Meter-Deep Stone Walls and Foundations

The stone blocks beneath Lake Titicaca's surface defied easy explanation. Each piece weighed several tons, carved from local andesite and sandstone quarried from lakeside cliffs. The precision cutting matched the finest examples found at surface Tiwanaku sites. Underwater visibility allowed detailed examination of construction techniques thought impossible without modern equipment.

Corner joints displayed the sophisticated interlocking patterns characteristic of pre-Columbian Andean architecture. No mortar held the stones together. Each block was shaped to fit perfectly against its neighbors, creating walls capable of withstanding earthquakes and water pressure. The underwater environment had actually preserved the stonework better than many exposed ruins subjected to centuries of weathering.

Measurements revealed walls reaching heights of twenty meters in some locations. The foundations extended another ten meters into lake bed sediments, indicating the builders had dug extensive footings to support their massive construction. This level of planning required detailed knowledge of soil conditions, water table levels, and structural engineering principles.

The wall orientations followed precise geometric patterns. Main structures aligned with cardinal directions within margins of error matching other Tiwanaku sites. Subsidiary buildings maintained consistent angular relationships to the primary axis. The overall layout suggested comprehensive urban planning rather than random construction over time.

Underwater surveys identified distinct architectural zones within the submerged complex. Residential areas featured smaller foundations arranged in rectangular compounds. Ceremonial precincts contained larger platforms and open plazas suitable for public gatherings. Storage facilities included chambers with drainage systems designed to manage water flow through the structures.

The craftsmanship rivaled the finest examples of ancient Andean stonework. Surface textures showed evidence of careful finishing with bronze tools. Edges were beveled to create shadow lines, enhancing the visual impact of the walls. Decorative elements included carved step-fret patterns and geometric designs matching motifs found at terrestrial Tiwanaku sites.

Preservation conditions varied throughout the underwater complex. Structures in deeper water showed excellent stone preservation due to protection from temperature fluctuations and mechanical weathering. Shallow areas had suffered more damage from wave action and ice formation during the winter months. Some walls retained original plaster coatings invisible at surface sites.

The engineering challenges of underwater construction seemed insurmountable for ancient builders. Moving multi-ton stone blocks required sophisticated lifting and transport systems. Placing foundations at precise depths demanded understanding of water levels and seasonal variations. Achieving the documented construction quality while working underwater pushed ancient capabilities beyond previously recognized limits.

Archaeological evidence suggested the builders had indeed worked in dry conditions. Tool marks on the stones showed no signs of underwater cutting or shaping. Mortar remnants contained terrestrial plant materials rather than aquatic organisms. Foundation designs assumed drainage of surface water rather than accommodation of permanent submersion.

This evidence pointed to dramatic changes in Lake Titicaca's water levels since the structures were built. The lake had risen at least twenty meters, possibly more, to reach current levels. Such changes could result from climate shifts, geological events, or human modifications to natural drainage patterns.

*Ancient American Civilizations*

Comparative analysis with other Tiwanaku sites revealed architectural evolution over time. The underwater structures shared characteristics with the earliest phases of Tiwanaku development. Construction techniques, decorative motifs, and urban planning concepts matched patterns found at Pukará and other early centers in the region.

The discovery forced reconsideration of Tiwanaku civilization's relationship with Lake Titicaca. Previous models treated the lake as a sacred boundary or resource to be exploited. The underwater city suggested instead that Tiwanaku architects integrated aquatic and terrestrial environments into unified ceremonial landscapes where water itself became part of the sacred architecture.

# Tiwanaku Culture: Pre-Inca Submerged Structures

The Tiwanaku people dominated the Lake Titicaca region for over a thousand years before Inca armies ever marched northward from Cusco. Their civilization peaked between 400 and 1000 CE, controlling trade routes across the high Andes and establishing cultural influence from northern Chile to southern Peru. The underwater structures in Lake Titicaca revealed new dimensions of their architectural achievements.

Tiwanaku builders created their first settlements around Lake Titicaca's shores approximately 2,000 years ago. Early sites like Pukará featured modest stone platforms and terraced compounds. Over centuries, the architecture grew more complex and monumental. The classic Tiwanaku style developed distinctive characteristics still visible in the underwater ruins.

The submerged buildings exhibited hallmarks of advanced Tiwanaku construction. Massive stone blocks were fitted together with mathematical precision. Trapezoidal doorways and windows were designed to evenly distribute structural loads. Platforms were built to specific modular dimensions based on ancient Andean measurement systems. These features confirmed the underwater complex as authentic Tiwanaku work.

Pottery fragments recovered from the lake bed confirmed the cultural attribution. Ceramic shards showed typical Tiwanaku decorative patterns, including stepped geometric designs, condor motifs, and stylized human figures. The pottery styles matched examples from the Tiwanaku ceremonial center, fifteen kilometers away. Carbon dating of organic materials embedded in the ceramics provided age estimates consistent with Tiwanaku's mature period.

The underwater site's urban planning reflected Tiwanaku organizational principles. Residential compounds surrounded central ceremonial areas. Storage buildings occupied strategic locations for controlling resource distribution. Workshop areas contained evidence of specialized craft production. The layout mirrored terrestrial Tiwanaku cities but adapted to aquatic environmental conditions.

Religious iconography found underwater matched the symbolic system used at all Tiwanaku sites. Stone carvings depicted the Staff God, a central deity in Tiwanaku mythology associated with agricultural fertility and cosmic order. Feline figures symbolized power and transformation. Bird motifs connected earthly and celestial realms. These images linked the underwater structures to broader Tiwanaku spiritual beliefs.

The scale of the underwater construction implied significant social organization and economic resources. Moving thousands of multi-ton stone blocks required coordinated labor forces. Feeding and housing the workers demanded extensive agricultural surplus. Organizing such projects indicated centralized political authority and sophisticated administrative systems.

Tiwanaku engineers had solved complex technical problems in creating the underwater city. They developed techniques for cutting and shaping massive andesite blocks using bronze tools and stone hammers. They created lever systems for moving heavy stones across difficult terrain. They designed foundation systems capable of supporting megalithic superstructures on potentially unstable lake bed soils.

The discovery revealed Tiwanaku's relationship with water as more complex than previously understood. Traditional interpretations focused on the culture's agricultural innovations, including raised field systems and irrigation networks. The underwater city showed that Tiwanaku architects also designed ceremonial spaces specifically for aquatic rituals and water-based spiritual practices.

Evidence suggested the underwater structures served specialized functions within Tiwanaku society. The building layouts differed from typical residential or administrative architecture. Ceremonial platforms, ritual pools, and offering chambers indicated religious purposes. The location beneath Lake Titicaca's sacred waters would have enhanced the spiritual significance of activities conducted there.

The submersion of these buildings marked a turning point in Tiwanaku history. Rising lake levels forced the abandonment of major ceremonial centers. Population centers shifted to higher ground. Trade networks connecting the underwater city to distant regions became disrupted. The loss of these important religious sites may have contributed to Tiwanaku civilization's eventual decline.

Climate reconstructions suggested the flooding occurred during a period of increased precipitation across the Andean region. Tree ring data from nearby areas indicated above-average rainfall for several consecutive decades. Glacier cores from regional ice fields confirmed unusual moisture levels during the late Tiwanaku period. These climate changes could have raised Lake Titicaca beyond its historical boundaries.

The underwater ruins provided insight into Tiwanaku's final centuries before the Inca conquest. Artifact distributions suggested continued ritual use of accessible areas even after partial submersion. Offerings of pottery, textiles, and metal objects accumulated in shallow waters. Local communities apparently maintained spiritual connections to the drowned ceremonial center.

Archaeological evidence indicated knowledge of the underwater city persisted through the Inca period and into colonial times. Spanish chronicles mentioned indigenous reports of buildings beneath Lake Titicaca's surface. Colonial priests recorded attempts to prohibit native ceremonies conducted over the submerged ruins. The cultural memory survived even as the physical structures disappeared beneath the water.

# Islands of Sun and Moon: Sacred Temple Complex

The sun barely touched the horizon when Inca priests began their daily ascent to the Island of the Sun's highest temple. Each dawn brought the same ritual procession across stone terraces carved into the island's steep slopes. The priests carried offerings of coca leaves, chicha beer, and finely woven textiles to honor Inti, the sun god born from these sacred waters according to Inca creation mythology.

The Island of the Sun, called Isla del Sol by Spanish colonizers, rises from Lake Titicaca's waters like a natural pyramid. Its rocky shores stretch nearly ten kilometers from north to south. Pre-Inca peoples had recognized the island's sacred character long before Inca armies reached Lake Titicaca. Tiwanaku builders had constructed the first ceremonial platforms on the island's windswept plateaus over a thousand years earlier.

Archaeological excavations revealed multiple construction phases spanning centuries of continuous use. The earliest structures dates to the Tiwanaku period, featuring massive stone foundations and platform complexes characteristic of that civilization's monumental architecture. Inca builders later expanded these foundations, adding their distinctive trapezoidal doorways and precisely fitted stone walls.

The Pilco Kaima complex occupied the island's southern peninsula. This extensive ceremonial center included residential quarters for priests, storage rooms for ritual offerings, and terraced gardens for growing sacred crops. The main temple faced east toward the rising sun. Its stone walls incorporated astronomical alignments marking important dates in the Inca agricultural and ceremonial calendar.

The Sacred Rock formation dominated the island's northern section. Human hands had modified this natural stone outcropping into a stepped altar complex. Inca stonemasons had carved channels, pools, and platforms directly into the bedrock. These features channeled rainwater and offerings through the sacred stone, creating a living altar where water and rock merged in ritual practice.

The Inca Trail crossed the island from south to north, connecting major ceremonial sites through carefully engineered stone pathways. These roads required extensive engineering to traverse the island's difficult terrain. Staircases carved directly into cliff faces allowed access to elevated temple platforms. Stone bridges spanned ravines and stream beds. Rest stops provided shelter for pilgrims making the sacred journey.

The Island of the Moon, located eight kilometers northeast of its larger neighbor, served as the feminine counterpart in Inca cosmology. The island housed the Iñak Uyu temple complex, dedicated to Mama Quilla, the moon goddess. This rectangular structure featured some of the finest Inca stonework found anywhere in the empire. The precision of the joints between massive andesite blocks exceeded even the famous examples at Machu Picchu.

Chosen Women, called acllas in Quechua, lived in cloistered compounds on the Island of the Moon. These selected females dedicated their lives to serving the moon goddess through weaving, brewing chicha, and maintaining temple ceremonies. Spanish chroniclers described the acllas as the most skilled textile producers in the empire, creating cloth so fine it seemed to glow in moonlight.

The islands' ceremonial calendar synchronized with astronomical events visible from Lake Titicaca. Solar observations determined the timing of planting and harvest festivals. Lunar cycles governed female initiation ceremonies and textile production schedules. Star positions marked important dates for pilgrimages and large-scale ritual gatherings involving thousands of participants from across the empire.

Pilgrims traveled enormous distances to reach the sacred islands. Archaeological evidence documents visitors from coastal regions over 500 kilometers away. Highland communities sent annual delegations carrying locally produced offerings. The islands became meeting points where diverse ethnic groups within the Inca Empire gathered for shared religious experiences.

The logistics of supporting large pilgrimage gatherings required extensive infrastructure. Agricultural terraces on both islands produced surplus crops for feeding temporary populations. Stone storage facilities preserved food supplies for distribution during ceremonies. Harbor areas provided secure mooring for the distinctive reed boats used for lake transportation.

The Spanish conquest brought dramatic changes to the islands' sacred character. Colonial administrators established encomienda grants, converting indigenous lands to private estates. Catholic missionaries built churches directly over Inca temple foundations. Traditional ceremonies faced suppression under colonial policies designed to eliminate indigenous religious practices.

However, indigenous communities maintained connections to the islands despite colonial pressure. Archaeological excavations have recovered post-conquest offerings buried in traditional locations. Oral traditions preserved knowledge of sacred sites and appropriate ritual practices. The islands retained spiritual significance for Aymara and Quechua-speaking peoples even under Spanish rule.

Modern archaeological investigations have revealed the complexity of pre-Columbian island settlements. Ground-penetrating radar detected buried structures beneath the current ground levels. Excavations uncovered sophisticated drainage systems, underground storage chambers, and defensive works protecting harbors from seasonal storms. The islands supported much larger populations than previously recognized.

Carbon dating of organic materials from multiple excavation contexts provided refined chronologies for the islands' occupation. The earliest evidence of human presence dated to 2,000 years ago, contemporary with early Tiwanaku expansion into the Lake Titicaca region. Occupation was continuous through the Inca period and into colonial times.

The islands' museum collections contain thousands of artifacts recovered from systematic excavations. Stone sculptures depict deities, animals, and geometric patterns reflecting different cultural traditions. Ceramic vessels show technological innovations in pottery production techniques. Metal objects demonstrate sophisticated metallurgical knowledge, including bronze alloy production and gold working.

# Cosmic Axis: Physical-Spiritual Boundary Dissolution

Lake Titicaca functioned as more than a geographical feature in ancient Andean cosmology. Indigenous peoples conceived the lake as the axis mundi, the cosmic center where heaven, earth, and underworld intersected. This sacred geography influenced every aspect of how cultures around the lake organized their settlements, conducted ceremonies, and understood their place in the universe.

The concept of Lake Titicaca as cosmic axis originated in creation mythologies shared across different Andean cultures. According to these traditions, the world began when divine beings first emerged from the lake's depths. The sun god Inti rose from the waters near the Island of the Sun. The moon goddess Mama Quilla appeared from beneath the Island of the Moon. Stars, mountains, and rivers received their powers through contact with the sacred lake.

This mythological framework influenced how ancient peoples designed their built environments around Lake Titicaca. Settlements were aligned with astronomical observations made from lakeside sites. Temple orientations included sight lines across the water towards important islands or mountain peaks. Urban planning adhered to principles that linked earthly architecture with celestial movements observed from the lake's surface.

Tiwanaku civilization developed the most sophisticated expression of these cosmic principles. Their ceremonial center at Tiwanaku, located fifteen kilometers southeast of the lake, incorporated water symbolism throughout its monumental architecture. Stone channels carried water through temple complexes. Sunken courts represented earthly connections to underground water sources. Platform temples elevated ritual activities toward celestial realms.

The underwater structures discovered in Lake Titicaca took these symbolic relationships to their logical conclusion. By building directly in the sacred waters, Tiwanaku architects eliminated the boundary between physical architecture and spiritual landscape. The submerged buildings existed simultaneously in the earthly realm of human construction and the divine realm of cosmic waters.

Inca civilization inherited and expanded these cosmic concepts when it incorporated the Lake Titicaca region into its empire. The Inca recognized the lake as the birthplace of their dynastic founder, Manco Capac, and his sister-wife Mama Ocllo. Imperial ceremonies conducted on the sacred islands renewed the royal family's divine authority by connecting them to their cosmic origins.

Pilgrimage practices demonstrated how physical journeys became spiritual transformations through engagement with the sacred landscape. Pilgrims traveled for weeks across difficult mountain terrain to reach Lake Titicaca's shores. The journey itself prepared participants for encountering the divine through physical hardship, social bonding, and a gradual approach to increasingly sacred locations.

The islands of Sun and Moon functioned as transitional spaces between the terrestrial world of daily life and the aquatic realm of divine power. Visitors underwent purification ceremonies before boarding boats to cross the water. Landing on the sacred islands required additional rituals acknowledging entry into divine territory. Return journeys reversed these processes, allowing pilgrims to carry spiritual benefits back to their home communities.

Water itself became the medium through which spiritual transformation occurred. Ceremonial bathing in Lake Titicaca's waters conveyed purification and renewal. Offerings thrown into the lake carried prayers and petitions to divine beings dwelling beneath the surface. The underwater ruins provided permanent sacred architecture where human offerings could reach the divine realm directly.

The integration of natural and constructed elements created seamless sacred landscapes where spiritual experiences could occur at multiple levels simultaneously. Surface ceremonies on island temples connected participants with solar and lunar deities. Underwater offerings reached the deeper powers associated with earth fertility and agricultural abundance. The lake's vast expanse provided space for large-scale rituals involving thousands of people.

Archaeological evidence documents the practical implementation of these cosmic principles in ancient settlement patterns. Communities around Lake Titicaca positioned their residential areas, agricultural fields, and ceremonial sites according to complex symbolic geographies. Distance from the lake shore indicated hierarchical relationships between more or less sacred spaces.

The Spanish conquest disrupted but could not entirely eliminate these cosmic relationships. Colonial authorities recognized the lake's importance to indigenous religious practice and attempted to control access to sacred sites. Catholic churches built on former temple locations sought to redirect spiritual energy toward Christian purposes. However, indigenous communities developed strategies for maintaining traditional relationships with the sacred landscape.

Modern archaeological investigations have revealed the sophistication of ancient Andean cosmic concepts. Ground-penetrating radar surveys detect buried structures aligned with astronomical phenomena. Excavations uncover artifact distributions reflecting complex ritual geographies. Ethnographic studies document the persistence of traditional knowledge about sacred relationships between human communities and Lake Titicaca's spiritual landscape.

The lake continues to function as a cosmic axis for contemporary indigenous peoples living around its shores. Aymara and Quechua communities maintain ceremonial calendars synchronized with astronomical events observed from lakeside locations. Traditional medicine practitioners conduct healing ceremonies incorporating water from sacred springs feeding the lake. Cultural festivals celebrate the lake's role in creation mythologies and community identity.

Contemporary environmental challenges threaten the lake's sacred character and practical functions. Climate change affects water levels and seasonal patterns important for traditional ceremonies. Pollution from mining activities contaminates waters used for ritual purposes. Tourism pressure on sacred sites disrupts indigenous access to traditional ceremonial locations.

The underwater archaeological discoveries add new dimensions to understanding how ancient peoples conceptualized the relationship between physical and spiritual realms. The submerged structures suggest that cosmic axis concepts influenced architectural practice at the most fundamental levels. Buildings designed to exist beneath sacred waters represented the ultimate integration of human construction with divine landscape.

These discoveries challenge modern distinctions between natural and cultural heritage. The underwater ruins cannot be separated from their aquatic environment without losing their essential spiritual significance. Conservation efforts must address both archaeological preservation and maintenance of the lake's sacred character for contemporary indigenous communities who continue to find spiritual meaning in these ancient waters.

# Chapter 22: Quipu - The Language of Knots

## Inca Empire Administration Without Writing

Chuya Sullca ran her fingers along the twisted cords with practiced precision. The young woman knelt in a stone chamber deep within Cusco's administrative complex, her hands moving across hundreds of knotted strings. Each knot told a story. Each color carried meaning. Each twist of fiber held information vital to governing an empire spanning thousands of miles.

The year was 1520. Spanish conquistadors had not arrived in the Inca heartland. Francisco Pizarro still sailed along the Pacific coast, gathering intelligence about this mysterious mountain empire. Within these quiet chambers, a civilization administered itself through an information system more sophisticated than anything Europeans had imagined possible.

Chuya belonged to an elite class of record keepers known as quipucamayocs. Her training had begun in childhood. She learned to read information with her fingertips. Her eyes were secondary tools. The real knowledge lived in the texture of fibers, the tension of knots, the spacing between cords. She could decode population records, tax assessments, tribute obligations, and historical chronicles without ever seeing a written symbol.

The Inca Empire controlled territories from modern Colombia to Chile. Over twelve million people lived under imperial rule. Roads crossed deserts, climbed mountain passes, and bridged raging rivers. Warehouses stored food supplies for emergency distribution. Military units moved according to coordinated commands. Tax collectors gathered tribute from hundreds of ethnic groups speaking dozens of languages.

All of this happened without paper. Without ink. Without alphabetic writing. The Inca had developed something different. Something uniquely their own.

Chuya's morning began with updating census records from the southern provinces. A chasqui runner had arrived before dawn carrying fresh quipu bundles. The messages contained birth records from Cusco's satellite communities. Three healthy males were born in Ollantaytambo.

Two females were delivered safely in Pisac. One stillbirth in Machu Picchu. Each event required recording in the imperial database.

She selected a primary cord colored deep red, the shade reserved for population matters. From this main strand, she suspended pendant strings in specific sequences. Brown fiber for males. White for females. Yellow for deaths. Black for complications. The combinations created a three-dimensional code readable by any trained quipucamayoc across the empire.

The morning's work continued with tribute assessments. Highland communities owed llama wool to imperial warehouses. Coastal peoples provided fish and seashells. Forest tribes contributed medicinal plants and exotic feathers. Each obligation had been calculated according to community resources and population capacity. The quipu recorded not arbitrary demands but carefully balanced requirements.

Chuya's hands moved with fluid confidence. She had memorized the color codes years earlier. Red indicated humans and sacred matters. Yellow meant gold and divine authority. Green-designated agricultural products. Blue marked religious ceremonial items. White showed silver and lunar associations: black recorded time and historical events.

Color was only the beginning. Knot placement mattered equally. Knots near the main cord indicated higher values. Those toward the pendant ends showed smaller quantities. Simple knots meant ones. Figure-eight knots signified tens. Complex clustering marked hundreds and thousands. The decimal system allowed calculations reaching into millions.

A veteran quipucamayoc entered the chamber carrying an ancient bundle. The elderly man's name was Qhapaq Runa. His scarred hands had recorded imperial history for four decades. Today he would share knowledge passed down through generations of cord keepers.

"The Sapa Inca requires historical information," Qhapaq announced. "The European strangers ask about our origins. How long have we ruled these lands? What victories did our ancestors achieve? Which kings expanded the empire to its current borders?"

Chuya watched as Qhapaq unrolled a massive quipu containing thousands of cords. The bundle stretched across the stone floor like a multicolored textile map. This was not a simple record. This was the imperial chronicle, the official history of Tawantinsuyu preserved in fiber and knot.

The old keeper's fingers traced specific cord sequences. "Here is Manco Capac, our first ruler. These knots record his emergence from Lake Titicaca. This section shows the conquest of the Chancas under Pachacuti. These cords detail Tupac Inca's campaigns in the northern territories."

Each ruler's reign occupied distinct cord groupings. Military victories appeared in red and yellow combinations. Architectural projects used brown and green sequences. Religious reforms were encoded in complex white and blue patterns. The entire history of the empire was entwined within these twisted fibers.

Qhapaq continued his lesson. "Spanish scribes demand written records. They cannot understand our system. They see only colored string. They cannot recognize the knowledge these cords contain. We must translate centuries of history into their strange markings on flat surfaces."

The challenge was immense. Quipu encoded three-dimensional information. Relationships between data points existed in physical space. Cords hung in specific orders. Knots clustered in meaningful patterns. Colors blended in sophisticated combinations. Reducing this complexity to linear writing would inevitably lose crucial details.

Moreover, quipu contained layers of meaning beyond simple data. Religious significance infused every cord. Astronomical relationships guided color choices. Mathematical principles structured the entire system. The Spanish alphabet could capture facts, but never the deeper wisdom embedded in the physical arrangement of fibers.

# Decimal-Based Numerical Recording System

Numbers were the foundation of Inca administration. Population counts determined labor obligations. Agricultural yields guided food distribution. Military strength calculations influenced campaign planning. Distance measurements enabled road construction. Time calculations coordinated religious festivals.

The Inca developed a numerical system based on powers of ten. Simple knots represented single digits. Groups of knots indicated tens. Cluster arrangements signified hundreds. Cord sections denoted thousands. Large bundles could encode numbers reaching into millions with mathematical accuracy surpassing many European methods of the time.

Chuya demonstrated the counting system to a young apprentice. She began with a single cord, dying it yellow to indicate corn tribute from valley communities. At the cord's top, she tied three simple knots close together. These represented three thousand baskets of dried corn delivered to imperial warehouses.

Moving down the cord, she created a cluster of seven figure-eight knots. These indicated seven hundred additional baskets collected during the harvest festival. Further down, she added four single knots for forty more baskets from smaller communities. At the cord's bottom, she tied two simple knots for two individual baskets offered as ceremonial gifts.

The total appeared clearly to trained fingers: 3,742 baskets of corn tribute. Any quipucamayoc could read this number instantly. The information could be updated as new deliveries arrived. Multiple cords could be combined to show regional totals. The system allowed calculations across the entire empire.

But numbers were more than administrative tools. They carried sacred significance in Inca cosmology. Certain quantities held religious power. Ritual offerings required specific amounts of precious materials. Ceremonial dates followed numerical patterns based on astronomical observations. Festival participants gathered in symbolically meaningful numbers.

The decimal system reflected divine order. Ten fingers represented the human connection to earthly tasks. Ten toes grounded people in the physical world—multiples of ten created harmony between human actions and cosmic forces. Mathematical calculations became spiritual exercises connecting administrators to universal principles.

Seasonal records demonstrated this integration of practical and sacred functions. Chuya worked with agricultural quipu tracking planting and harvest cycles. Spring planting required coordinating labor gangs across multiple ecological zones. Summer cultivation demanded precise irrigation scheduling. Autumn harvests generated tribute obligations. Winter storage ensured survival until the next growing season.

Each season's activities appeared in distinct cord sections. Spring cords used green fibers indicating new growth and agricultural potential. Summer cords were yellow like the sun, providing energy for crop development. Autumn cords appeared brown and gold, reminiscent of mature grain and harvested fields. Winter cords were white and blue, reminiscent of snow and cold mountain peaks.

The agricultural calendar synchronized with religious observances. Inti Raymi, the winter solstice festival, marked the beginning of a new agricultural year. Quipu recorded the ceremony's requirements: specific numbers of llamas for sacrifice, precise quantities of gold and silver ornaments, exact amounts of chicha beer for ritual consumption.

These calculations required mathematical sophistication. Llama requirements had to match the number of participating communities. Precious metal offerings reflected each region's tribute capacity. Chicha production depended on corn harvest yields and fermentation scheduling. Getting the numbers wrong could disrupt the entire ceremony.

Chuya's calculations extended beyond simple addition and subtraction. She performed multiplication when scaling regional data to imperial totals. Division helped distribute resources proportionally among communities. Fractional relationships appeared when calculating partial tribute obligations. The quipu system accommodated all of these operations.

# Quipucamayocs: Professional Knot Readers

The training began early. Children who showed aptitude for tactile learning were selected by master quipucamayocs. Their fingers developed sensitivity to slight variations in fiber texture. Their memory strengthened through constant practice with color sequences. Their understanding deepened as they absorbed the cultural significance underlying the technical system.

Amaru was eight years old when Qhapaq Runa chose him for advanced instruction. The boy came from a family of provincial administrators. His father supervised tribute collection in highland communities. His mother managed textile production for religious ceremonies. Amaru had grown up surrounded by quipu bundles and administrative discussions.

The first lessons focused on basic cord preparation. Amaru learned to select appropriate fibers from llama and alpaca wool. Different animals produced distinct textures suitable for specific types of records. Llama fiber was stronger and better for permanent chronicles. Alpaca wool was softer and ideal for frequently updated documents. Wild vicuña produced the finest fiber reserved for the most sacred records.

Dyeing came next. Amaru memorized the plants and minerals producing each color. Cochineal insects created deep reds for population and military records. Indigo plants yielded blues for religious and ceremonial information. Turmeric roots were used to generate yellow hues for solar associations and royal matters. Iron oxides producing browns were used for agricultural and construction data.

The colour system conveyed emotional and spiritual significance beyond mere coding functions. Red represented life force, blood, and vital energy. Blue implied water, sky, and spiritual realms. Yellow related to solar power, divine authority, and imperial legitimacy. Green signified growth, fertility, and agricultural abundance. Each shade held cultural meanings that apprentices needed to fully understand.

Knot tying required years of practice. Amaru's small fingers learned to create consistent tension across multiple cords. Loose knots could unravel and lose information. Tight knots became difficult to read and update. Perfect tension maintained data integrity over decades of handling and storage.

Different knot types served distinct functions. Simple overhand knots recorded basic numerical values. Figure-eight knots indicated higher decimal positions. Clove hitches marked special categories requiring additional attention. Complex clusters created mathematical relationships between different data sets. Master craftsmen developed personal variations readable only within specific regional traditions.

Spacing mattered as much as knotting technique. Regular intervals between knots improved reading accuracy. Consistent cord lengths helped organize complex bundles. Standardized pendant arrangements enabled quick navigation through extensive records. These physical conventions ensured any trained quipucamayoc could interpret any properly constructed quipu.

Memory training formed the core of advanced education. Apprentices memorized vast amounts of historical, geographical, and cultural information. They learned genealogies of royal families stretching back generations. They absorbed details of territorial boundaries, natural resources, and ethnic group characteristics. They studied religious calendar cycles, astronomical observations, and mathematical principles.

This memorized knowledge provided context for interpreting quipu records. Raw numerical data meant nothing without cultural understanding. Population figures gained significance when connected to historical migration patterns. Tribute records made sense only in relation to regional resource availability. Military statistics required an understanding of strategic geography and political alliances.

Amaru's education included extensive travel throughout the empire. He visited communities in all four suyus, the cardinal regions of Tawantinsuyu. He observed local customs, learned regional dialects, and practiced reading provincial quipu variations. This exposure taught him to adapt the central system to diverse cultural contexts.

Each region had developed distinctive conventions within the standard framework. Highland communities emphasized altitude-related agricultural cycles. Coastal peoples focused on fishing seasons and maritime resource management. Forest tribes prioritized hunting patterns and medicinal plant collection. Desert populations stressed water resource conservation and caravan trade relationships.

Advanced apprentices learned to create specialized quipu for specific administrative functions. Military records required different organizational principles than population censuses. Religious ceremony planning involved distinct coding systems from agricultural tribute collection. Historical chronicles followed narrative structures unlike contemporary statistical reports.

The most skilled quipucamayocs could compose new information systems for unprecedented situations. When Spanish conquistadors arrived, some cord keepers developed innovative methods for recording European technologies, animal species, and cultural practices. These experimental quipu preserved indigenous perspectives on the colonial encounter.

Master status required demonstrated ability to read, create, and teach the complete quipu system. Candidates faced rigorous examinations by panels of senior practitioners. They had to decode ancient chronicles, compose complex statistical reports, and train new apprentices in proper techniques. Success brought lifelong responsibilities for maintaining imperial records.

# Tactile Information Storage and Retrieval

Information lived in the fingers of quipucamayocs. These specialists developed extraordinary tactile sensitivity through years of handling fine fibers and small knots. They could distinguish cord materials by texture alone. Their fingertips detected minute variations in knot tension and spacing. Their hands read information in complete darkness with perfect accuracy.

Chuya worked in the pre-dawn hours before administrative duties began. She preferred the quiet chamber in the early morning when her concentration was sharpest. Llama-fat candles provided minimal light. She relied primarily on touch to navigate complex quipu bundles containing thousands of individual cords.

Her fingers moved systematically across the main horizontal cord supporting pendant strings. Each position held a specific meaning in the organizational scheme. Royal genealogy occupied the left section. Military records appeared in the center. Religious information filled the right portion. Administrative data hung from secondary support cords attached at regular intervals.

Finding specific information required following established pathways through the three-dimensional structure. Population records for Cusco's northern districts began with the third pendant from the left side. Chuya's fingers located this starting cord by counting tactile landmarks. She traced downward through subsidiary cords until reaching the appropriate data cluster.

The search was refined step by step. District-level cords branched into community subdivisions. Community cords divided into family group records. Family cords identified individual household members by age, gender, and occupation. The hierarchical structure guided her fingers through thousands of data points to specific pieces of information.

Texture variations helped identify different types of records. Smooth llama fiber indicated permanent information unlikely to change frequently. Coarser alpaca wool showed temporary data requiring regular updates. Finest vicuña fiber marked sacred records accessible only to the highest-ranking officials. These material differences were immediately recognizable to trained hands.

Knot characteristics conveyed additional layers of meaning. Fresh knots felt firm and retained clear geometric shapes. Older knots developed softer edges and looser tension over time. This aging process helped quipucamayocs estimate when specific information had been recorded and how often it had been accessed for updates or verification.

Reading speed increased dramatically with experience. Beginning students spent minutes decoding simple numerical sequences. Advanced practitioners could scan hundreds of cords in the same time period, extracting relevant information and identifying patterns requiring further investigation. Master quipucamayocs developed reading speeds comparable to literate scholars working with written documents.

Memory integration was crucial for effective information retrieval. Raw data meant nothing without contextual knowledge connecting individual records to broader imperial concerns. Population figures gained significance when compared to previous census results. Tribute totals made sense only in relation to community production capacity and seasonal variations. Military statistics required understanding of strategic threats and defensive requirements.

Chuya had memorized vast amounts of reference information supporting her tactile reading skills. She knew the names and characteristics of all ethnic groups throughout the empire. She understood seasonal patterns affecting agricultural production in different ecological zones. She recognized historical precedents for handling unusual administrative situations.

This background knowledge allowed rapid interpretation of quipu data. When her fingers encountered population decreases in specific communities, she immediately considered possible causes: disease outbreaks, labor mobilization for imperial projects, migration to new territories, or conflicts with neighboring groups. The quipu provided numbers, but experience supplied explanations.

Complex calculations required manipulating multiple cord bundles simultaneously. Tribute assessment for the upcoming harvest festival involved comparing current population levels with historical averages, adjusting for recent territorial acquisitions, and incorporating special religious requirements for the ceremony. Chuya's hands moved between different quipus while her mind performed the necessary mathematical operations.

Error detection relied on consistency checking across related records. Population totals had to match the sum of individual community counts. Tribute assessments needed to reflect actual resource availability. Military deployment numbers could not exceed available personnel. Experienced quipucamayocs developed intuitive sense for detecting inconsistencies requiring investigation.

Information updates followed systematic procedures to maintain data integrity. Changes were never made to the original records without creating backup copies. New information was verified through multiple sources before incorporation into official bundles. Historical records were preserved unchanged even when superseded by more recent data.

The most challenging aspect was encoding narrative information beyond simple numerical data. Historical chronicles, legal decisions, and religious teachings required sophisticated techniques for converting verbal content into knot patterns. Master quipucamayocs developed personal methods for capturing complex conceptual relationships in three-dimensional form.

# Spanish Conquest: Mass Destruction of Cord Records

The morning of November 16, 1532, changed everything. Francisco Pizarro's small force of conquistadors confronted Inca Emperor Atahualpa in the plaza of Cajamarca. What followed was not a battle but a massacre. Spanish horses and steel weapons destroyed thousands of Inca warriors in minutes. Atahualpa became a prisoner in his own empire.

The capture of the Sapa Inca sent shock waves throughout Tawantinsuyu. Administrative systems that had functioned smoothly for generations suddenly faced unprecedented challenges. Local governors waited for instructions from Cusco. Tax collectors suspended tribute collection. Army commanders received no strategic guidance. The communication network built on chasqui runners and quipu records began breaking down.

Spanish conquistadors had no understanding of the information systems they were destroying. Fray Vicente de Valverde, the expedition's priest, examined quipu bundles found in Cajamarca's administrative buildings.

He saw colored strings and meaningless knots. The cords contained no recognizable writing. They displayed no Christian symbols. They obviously served some pagan purpose.

Valverde ordered the quipu bundles burned. His soldiers gathered hundreds of carefully preserved records and fed them to bonfires in the plaza. Decades of imperial history vanished in smoke. Population censuses, tribute assessments, military records, and religious chronicles were reduced to ash in a few hours.

Similar destruction occurred throughout the conquered territories. Spanish administrators replaced indigenous governance with European systems. They demanded written records in Spanish or Latin. They rejected all indigenous documentation as unreliable and potentially heretical. Colonial law required burning all native books and record-keeping materials.

Hernando Pizarro, Francisco's brother, supervised the systematic elimination of Inca administrative infrastructure. His soldiers entered every government building in Cusco. They collected quipu bundles from storage chambers and office complexes. Enormous bonfires consumed thousands of years of accumulated knowledge within weeks of the Spanish occupation.

Some quipucamayocs attempted to preserve their records by hiding bundles in remote locations. They carried precious chronicles to mountain caves and buried them in sealed containers. They entrusted copies to loyal community leaders in regions not completely under Spanish control. These desperate measures saved some information but could not prevent the systematic destruction of institutional memory.

The Spanish required indigenous administrators to convert existing records into European formats. Quipucamayocs found themselves attempting to translate three-dimensional information systems into linear alphabetic writing. The process was impossible without losing essential content. Complex relationships encoded in cord patterns could not be captured in sequential text.

Martin de Murúa, a Spanish chronicler, worked with surviving quipucamayocs to document Inca history. His native assistants struggled to explain their record-keeping methods. They could read the surviving quipu but found it extremely difficult to communicate that information in Spanish. Crucial details were inevitably lost in translation.

The conversion process revealed fundamental differences between European and Andean approaches to preserving knowledge. Spanish writing emphasized linear narrative and logical argumentation. Quipu encoding integrated numerical data with spatial relationships and cultural symbolism. The two systems operated on incompatible principles.

Even cooperative Spanish administrators failed to understand what they were eliminating. Pedro Sarmiento de Gamboa commissioned indigenous scholars to create written versions of traditional histories. His assistants produced valuable chronicles, but the original quipu sources were destroyed once the translation was completed. The Spanish saw no reason to preserve duplicated information in an incomprehensible format.

Colonial pressure forced the remaining quipucamayocs to abandon their traditional practices. Spanish law prohibited the creation of new indigenous records. Native children were forbidden to learn the old systems. Schools established by Catholic missionaries taught only European writing methods. The knowledge base supporting quipu literacy gradually disappeared.

Some records survived in isolated communities beyond immediate Spanish control. Highland villages preserved genealogical quipu for several generations after the conquest. Sacred chronicles remained hidden in religious shrines. Tribute records continued being updated in traditional format until colonial taxation systems replaced indigenous obligations.

The destruction accelerated during religious conversion campaigns. Catholic priests identified quipu as instruments of devil worship. They organized public ceremonies burning native records alongside religious images and ceremonial objects. Indigenous people were forced to watch their cultural heritage being consumed by flames in the name of Christian salvation.

Francisco de Toledo, the fifth Viceroy of Peru, implemented the most comprehensive destruction program. His administration systematically eliminated all traces of independent indigenous governance. Toledo's officials entered every community in the former Inca Empire. They confiscated and destroyed any remaining quipu bundles. They executed native leaders who attempted to preserve traditional records.

By 1600, less than seventy years after the conquest, the quipu system had essentially disappeared. A sophisticated information technology that had developed over centuries was now extinct. Millions of cords containing invaluable historical, scientific, and cultural information had been reduced to ashes. The knowledge of generations of skilled practitioners was lost forever.

Modern scholars estimate that Spanish destruction eliminated over 90% of all pre-Columbian records from the Andes. The surviving fragments provide tantalizing glimpses of what was lost. Museum collections worldwide contain fewer than 1,000 individual quipu specimens. Most of these are damaged or incomplete. The originals are shadows of a vast information system that once administered one of history's largest empires.

Archaeological excavations occasionally uncover preserved quipu in undisturbed tomb contexts. These discoveries generate tremendous excitement among researchers. Each newly found bundle potentially contains information lost for centuries. But the knowledge needed to read them completely disappeared with the last trained quipucamayocs four hundred years ago.

The tragedy extends beyond historical documentation. The Inca had developed sustainable administrative practices based on environmental understanding and community cooperation. Their record-keeping methods integrated statistical information with cultural values and ecological knowledge. These innovations could have contributed to modern governance approaches if they had survived colonial destruction.

Today, artificial intelligence researchers study surviving quipu specimens, hoping to crack their coding systems. Computer analysis can identify mathematical patterns and statistical relationships within the cord arrangements. But the cultural context that provided meaning to the numerical data may be gone forever, buried in the ashes of Spanish bonfires that consumed the memory of a civilisation.

# Chapter 23: Agricultural Marvels - Feeding Civilizations Sustainably

## Andean Terraces: Microclimate Creation

Carlos Reynel climbed the steep mountain path near Cusco, Peru, in 1987. His lungs burned in the thin air at an altitude of 12,000 feet. Below him stretched an impossible sight. Green terraces cascaded down the mountainside like giant staircases carved from living earth. Corn grew on the upper levels. Potatoes flourished in the middle sections. Quinoa sprouted from the lowest fields. Each level supported different crops in the same vertical space.

The local Quechua farmer, Amaru Ccosi, had invited Reynel to see his ancestral fields. Ccosi's family had maintained these terraces for fifteen generations. His grandfather taught him the secrets. His father passed down the knowledge. Now, Ccosi shared the wisdom with the young agricultural engineer from Lima University.

"Watch the morning mist," Ccosi said in accented Spanish. "See how it clings to different levels?"

Reynel observed the phenomenon with scientific eyes. Moisture gathered differently at each elevation. The upper terraces caught morning dew. The middle levels retained afternoon humidity. The lower sections collected evening condensation. Each level had become its own microclimate through careful design and patient cultivation.

Ccosi led Reynel to inspect the stone construction. Ancient builders had chosen rocks with specific thermal properties. Dark stones on the lower walls absorbed the morning sun, while light-coloured stones on the upper sections reflected the intense midday heat. The terraces caused temperature differences of up to eight degrees Celsius between the upper and lower levels.

"My ancestors were climate engineers," Ccosi explained. "They did not fight the mountain. They partnered with it."

The partnership extended to water management. Stone channels directed mountain springs through the entire system. Gravity fed each level precisely. Excess water from upper terraces irrigated lower sections. Nothing was wasted. Every drop served multiple purposes before returning to the river valley below.

Reynel measured the soil composition at different levels. Upper terraces contained sandy, fast-draining earth perfect for highland cereals. Middle terraces held rich loam ideal for root vegetables. Lower sections featured clay-heavy soil that retained moisture for water-loving crops. The builders had imported specific soil types from different regions and carefully layered them to create optimal growing conditions.

The engineering impressed Reynel more than any modern agricultural project. These mountains received unpredictable rainfall. Temperatures fluctuated wildly between day and night. Growing seasons lasted only a few months. Modern farmers considered such conditions impossible for intensive agriculture. The ancient builders had transformed impossible conditions into agricultural abundance.

Ccosi's grandfather, Tayta Kunturi, joined them on the terraces. At ninety-three years old, he still worked the highest fields every morning. His hands knew every stone. His feet followed paths worn by centuries of farmers before him.

"The old ones understood something we forgot," Tayta Kunturi said slowly. "Plants are not soldiers. They do not conquer land. They make friends with it."

The old farmer showed them planting patterns invisible to untrained eyes. Corn grew in specific configurations to shield potatoes from the wind. Bean plants climbed corn stalks to add nitrogen to the soil. Herbs scattered throughout the terraces repelled insects naturally. Each plant served multiple functions within the agricultural community.

Reynel documented irrigation techniques passed down through generations. Farmers opened sluice gates at specific times based on moon phases. They channeled water through different routes depending on seasonal rainfall patterns. They adjusted flow rates according to plant growth stages. The system operated like a vast hydraulic computer programmed by centuries of accumulated knowledge.

The terraces produced food surpluses that supported not only farming families but also craftsmen, priests, and administrators in distant cities. Archaeological evidence suggested these mountain fields once fed populations numbering in the hundreds of thousands. The agricultural abundance enabled the social complexity and artistic achievements that characterized Andean civilizations.

Modern agricultural scientists studying the terraces found innovations they had never considered. Stone walls stored solar heat during the day and released it at night, protecting crops from freezing temperatures. Curved terrace shapes created wind patterns that distributed seeds naturally. Specific rock placements channeled beneficial insects while deterring harmful ones.

Reynel returned to Lima University with respect for ancient agricultural wisdom. His reports documented techniques that could revolutionize modern mountain farming. The terraces offered solutions to problems facing contemporary agriculture: water scarcity, climate variability, and soil degradation. The ancient builders had solved these challenges through observation, experimentation, and partnership with natural systems.

Ccosi continued farming his ancestral terraces using methods unchanged for centuries. His crops thrived during droughts that devastated modern farms. His yields remained consistent through seasons when commercial agriculture failed. The terraces connected him to knowledge accumulated over millennia, tested by generations of farmers, and proven through countless harvests.

The mountain terraces survived Spanish colonization, republican governments, and modern development pressures. They continued producing food long after the civilizations that built them had vanished from historical memory. The stones held knowledge encoded in their placement, tested by time, and verified by results that spoke louder than any scientific paper.

# Moray: Circular Agricultural Laboratory

Ann Kendall rappelled into the circular depression at Moray, Peru, in 1992. The archaeological site had puzzled researchers since its rediscovery in 1932. Concentric stone terraces descended into the earth like an amphitheater built for giants. Local farmers called it the "navel of the world." Archaeologists had no explanation for its unique design.

Kendall brought thermometers, soil samples, and scientific curiosity to the ancient site. Her background in agricultural engineering provided tools that earlier archaeologists lacked. She sought to understand why the Inca had invested so much labour in creating this circular excavation in an isolated mountain valley.

The first measurements revealed the secret. Temperature differences between the top and bottom rings reached fifteen degrees Celsius. Each terrace level maintained its own distinct microclimate. The circular design created a natural laboratory where agricultural engineers could test crop varieties under different growing conditions within a single site.

John Earls, an anthropologist studying traditional Andean agriculture, joined Kendall's research team. Together, they documented how the terraces functioned as an experimental station. The top rings simulated conditions found at sea level. The middle terraces replicated highland environments. The bottom rings created tropical growing conditions found in the Amazon foothills.

Local farmers still used Moray according to traditional patterns. They planted test plots of different potato varieties on various levels. The circular arrangement allowed them to compare how each variety responded to different temperatures, humidity levels, and sun exposure. Successful varieties moved to larger fields throughout the empire.

The Inca potato collection included over 3,000 varieties adapted to different altitudes, climates, and soil conditions. This genetic diversity protected against crop failures and provided nutrition security for millions of people. Moray served as the central testing facility where new varieties were evaluated and improved through selective breeding.

Kendall's team discovered water management systems of extraordinary sophistication. Underground channels connected all terrace levels. Stone-lined reservoirs stored rainfall and snowmelt. Precisely engineered outlets controlled water distribution to each experimental plot. The hydraulic system operated automatically without human intervention once properly calibrated.

Carlos Ochoa, Peru's leading potato geneticist, visited Moray with Kendall's team. He identified agricultural techniques that modern science had recently developed. The Inca had practiced controlled cross-pollination, systematic selection, and genetic preservation using methods that agricultural universities taught as recent innovations.

The terraces showed evidence of specialized growing media tailored to different crops. Builders had imported soil from various ecological zones and mixed it with organic matter to create optimal growing conditions. Chemical analysis revealed fertilization programs using seabird guano transported from coastal islands hundreds of miles away.

Stone walls incorporated acoustic properties that enhanced the agricultural laboratory's function. Sound waves created by wind moving through the circular terraces produced frequencies that promoted plant growth. The builders had understood connections between sound, vibration, and agricultural productivity that modern science had only recently begun to study.

Kendall documented crop rotation patterns carved into stone markers around the terraces. The Inca rotated crops on seven-year cycles to maintain soil fertility and prevent pest buildup. They practiced companion planting techniques that enhanced growth and natural pest control. They integrated livestock grazing to add organic matter and break pest cycles.

The circular design maximised solar collection efficiency throughout the growing season. Different terrace orientations captured sunlight at optimal angles for various crops. The depression protected plants from destructive winds common at high altitudes. The stone walls absorbed heat during the day and released it at night, extending the effective growing season.

Archaeological evidence suggested Moray operated as part of an empire-wide agricultural network. Successful experiments conducted here were replicated at similar sites throughout Inca territory. Administrators coordinated research programs across multiple locations. Agricultural knowledge developed at Moray reached farmers from Ecuador to Chile.

The site functioned continuously for several centuries before Spanish colonization disrupted the research programs. Colonial authorities failed to understand Moray's purpose and abandoned the sophisticated agricultural systems. Centuries of neglect partially filled the terraces with sediment and damaged the hydraulic infrastructure.

Modern potato researchers studying genetic diversity trace many important varieties to ancestral strains developed through experiments conducted at sites like Moray. The Inca agricultural scientists created genetic resources that continue to feed the world today. Their systematic approach to crop improvement laid foundations that modern agriculture builds upon.

Kendall's work at Moray demonstrated agricultural sophistication that matched or exceeded contemporary research methods. The Inca understood genetics, soil science, irrigation engineering, and experimental design. They applied this knowledge systematically to solve food security challenges facing their empire.

# Terra Preta: Self-Regenerating Artificial Soil

William Balée pushed through the dense Amazon rainforest in 1989, following indigenous guides along barely visible trails. The Brazilian anthropologist had come to study traditional land management practices among the Ka'apor people. What he discovered changed the understanding of human impact on tropical ecosystems.

The guides led him to clearings where the soil looked completely different from typical Amazon earth. Instead of the characteristic red clay found throughout the region, these areas contained rich, dark earth teeming with life. The Ka'apor called it "terra preta" - black earth. Their ancestors had created this super-fertile soil through techniques passed down for generations.

Balée collected soil samples that would astonish agricultural scientists worldwide. Chemical analysis revealed carbon content three times higher than that of the surrounding rainforest soils. Phosphorus levels exceeded typical Amazon earth by tenfold. The terra preta supported plant growth rates that seemed impossible in the nutrient-poor tropical environment.

The indigenous farmers explained how their ancestors had built the soil over centuries. They burned organic matter at specific temperatures to create biochar. They mixed kitchen waste, human waste, and food scraps with the charcoal. They added ash from specific tree species and bones from hunted animals. The mixture fermented in carefully controlled conditions to create soil that improved with age.

Eduardo Neves, a Brazilian archaeologist, joined Balée's research to study the historical depth of terra preta creation. Radiocarbon dating revealed that some sites contained artificial soils over 2,000 years old. The soil-building process had continued through multiple generations of indigenous farmers, each adding layers to the accumulated fertility.

The discovery challenged fundamental assumptions about Amazon prehistory. Archaeologists had believed the rainforest could only support small, scattered populations due to poor soils and limited agricultural potential. Terra preta sites suggested much larger populations had lived sustainably in the Amazon for millennia before European contact.

Wim Sombroek, a Dutch soil scientist, studied the chemical processes that made terra preta so remarkably fertile. He found that biochar created by controlled burning provided a stable carbon framework that held nutrients and water. Beneficial microorganisms colonized the porous charcoal structure. The soil created its own ecosystem that continuously regenerated fertility.

The indigenous soil-building technique produced fertility that lasted for centuries without external inputs. Modern agricultural soils typically lose productivity after a few decades of intensive use. Terra preta sites that had been abandoned for hundreds of years still supported vigorous plant growth. The soil seemed to heal and improve itself over time.

Johannes Lehmann, a soil scientist at Cornell University, analyzed how terra preta differed from normal Amazon soils. He discovered that biochar acted like a sponge for nutrients, preventing them from washing away during heavy rains. The porous structure provided habitat for beneficial bacteria and fungi that formed symbiotic relationships with plants.

Indigenous farmers had understood soil science principles that modern agriculture struggled to implement. They created carbon sequestration systems that removed greenhouse gases from the atmosphere. They built soil organic matter that stored water during dry periods. They established microbial communities that provided natural fertilization and pest control.

The terra preta technique provided solutions to modern environmental issues. Climate change called for methods to remove carbon dioxide from the atmosphere. Industrial agriculture required alternatives to chemical fertilizers. Degraded soils globally needed restoration techniques that could rebuild fertility sustainably.

Researchers studying terra preta sites found evidence of sophisticated land management extending far beyond soil creation. Indigenous peoples had practiced controlled burning to maintain forest diversity. They had planted valuable tree species in managed groves. They had created artificial wetlands for aquaculture and wildlife habitat.

The agricultural system supported population densities comparable to intensive farming regions in other parts of the world. Archaeological surveys revealed settlements housing thousands of people connected by networks of raised roads and canals. The Amazon had been a landscape actively shaped by human management for thousands of years.

Spanish and Portuguese colonial records described densely populated regions along major Amazon rivers. Early explorers reported continuous settlements, extensive agriculture, and complex political organization. Disease epidemics brought by European contact had devastated these populations decades before most detailed colonial accounts were written.

Modern attempts to recreate terra preta have achieved mixed results. The process requires understanding relationships between carbon, nutrients, water, and soil biology that indigenous farmers had developed through generations of experimentation. The knowledge involves practical skills that cannot be easily transferred through written instructions.

Contemporary indigenous communities that maintain terra preta traditions continue producing fertile soils using ancestral techniques. Their success demonstrates the viability of sustainable agricultural methods that actually improve environmental conditions over time. The contrast with industrial agriculture, which typically degrades soil fertility, offers important lessons for global food security.

# Aztec Chinampas: Floating Garden Systems

Xochitl Hernández poled her wooden canoe through the narrow canals of Xochimilco in 1994. The agricultural engineer from Mexico City had come to study the last functioning chinampas - the floating gardens that once fed the Aztec capital of Tenochtitlan. Few people understood how these artificial islands had revolutionized agriculture in central Mexico.

The elderly farmer, Don Aurelio Flores, guided her through waterways lined with ancient willow trees. His family had maintained these chinampas for twelve generations. The rectangular plots stretched like green ribbons between narrow canals, each island precisely engineered to maximize agricultural productivity in the shallow lake environment.

"People call them floating gardens," Don Aurelio explained as he tied the canoe to a wooden post. "But they don't float. They grow from the lake bottom."

Hernández stepped onto the soft earth of Chinampa Island. The ground felt firm beneath her feet despite being surrounded by water. Don Aurelio showed her how his ancestors had built these artificial islands from layers of mud, vegetation, and organic matter dredged from the lake bottom.

The construction process required engineering knowledge passed down through families for centuries. Builders first marked rectangular plots in the shallow water using wooden stakes. They wove branches between the stakes to create retaining walls. Then came the laborious work of building up the islands layer by layer.

Workers scooped nutrient-rich mud from the lake bottom using long-handled tools. They spread this sediment evenly across the enclosed area. Next came layers of aquatic vegetation, dead leaves, and organic waste from nearby settlements. The builders compressed each layer carefully to create stable foundations.

Willow trees planted around the perimeter served multiple functions. Their roots anchored the islands against erosion. Their branches provided material for tools and construction. Their leaves added organic matter to the composting system. The trees also marked property boundaries and provided shade for workers during hot summer months.

Don Aurelio demonstrated the irrigation system his grandfather had taught him. The chinampas required no pumps or mechanical devices. Water seeped naturally through the porous island structure, maintaining perfect soil moisture. Crops received constant irrigation without the risk of waterlogging that destroyed agriculture in many regions.

The canal system provided transportation networks that connected chinampa farms with urban markets. Farmers loaded fresh vegetables onto canoes each morning and paddled directly to marketplace docks in the city center. This eliminated the need for overland transport, which had damaged perishable crops and increased food costs.

Hernández measured the productivity of Don Aurelio's plots. The chinampas produced seven times more food per square meter than comparable rain-fed agriculture. The constant water supply, rich organic soils, and intensive cultivation methods created agricultural abundance that supported large urban populations.

The system recycled waste products that would otherwise create pollution problems. Human waste from the city provided fertilizer for the crops. Kitchen scraps and agricultural residues added organic matter to build soil fertility. Dead vegetation from the canals became composting material for the next growing season.

Crop rotation patterns maximized the growing potential of each chinampa. Farmers planted quick-growing vegetables like lettuce and radishes between slower crops like corn and beans. They harvested multiple crops per year from the same plot. They practiced companion planting that increased yields and controlled pests naturally.

The chinampas supported incredible plant diversity. Archaeological evidence suggested Aztec farmers grew over 100 different crop varieties in the lake system. This genetic diversity provided nutrition security and protected against crop failures from diseases or climate variations.

Don Aurelio showed Hernández seed storage techniques that preserved planting material for generations. Farmers selected the best seeds from each harvest and stored them in waterproof containers made from gourds and ceramic pots. They traded seeds with other families to maintain genetic diversity and develop improved varieties.

The agricultural system integrated aquaculture with crop production. Fish and waterfowl lived in the canals between chinampas. They provided protein for farming families and contributed fertilizer to the agricultural system. Farmers managed water levels to optimize conditions for both crops and aquatic animals.

Temperature regulation occurred naturally in the chinampa environment. Water in the canals moderated temperature extremes, protecting crops from frost damage and excessive heat. The lake environment extended the growing season and allowed cultivation of temperature-sensitive crops that could not survive in upland areas.

Spanish colonizers initially failed to understand the sophistication of the chinampa system. They drained many of the lakes to create land for European-style agriculture. This destruction eliminated agricultural infrastructure that had taken centuries to develop and could have fed Mexico City indefinitely.

Modern urban development continues to threaten the remaining chinampas at Xochimilco. Pollution from the growing city contaminates the water supply. Urban sprawl converts agricultural land to housing developments. Few young people learn the traditional farming techniques from elderly practitioners like Don Aurelio.

Agricultural researchers studying the chinampas have documented innovations that could solve contemporary food security challenges. The system produces high yields using minimal land area. It recycles waste products constructively. It operates sustainably without external chemical inputs or fossil fuel energy.

# Tipon: Hydraulic Engineering with Cosmic Symbolism

Kenneth Wright stood in the stone channels of Tipon, Peru, in 1996. Water flowed around his feet with the same precision it had maintained for over 500 years. The hydraulic engineer from Colorado had come to study Inca water management systems. What he found exceeded his expectations and challenged his understanding of ancient engineering capabilities.

The site sprawled across terraced hillsides south of Cusco. Stone channels guided spring water through a complex network of fountains, pools, and irrigation systems. Every element had been designed with mathematical precision. Every stone had been placed with purpose. The entire complex functioned as both practical infrastructure and cosmic temple.

Wright followed the main channel from its source high on the mountainside. Inca engineers had captured multiple springs and combined their flows into a single distribution system. They had calculated gradients, volumes, and pressures with accuracy that matched modern hydraulic engineering. The system delivered exact water quantities to specific locations throughout the complex.

The engineering impressed Wright more than the contemporary water projects he had designed. Inca builders worked without surveying instruments, metal tools, or written calculations. They achieved precision through observation, experimentation, and accumulated knowledge passed between generations of master engineers.

Local guides explained the spiritual significance of the water management system. Springs were considered sacred sources where underground rivers emerged from the realm of the earth spirits. The channels represented the circulation of life force through the landscape. Pools and fountains created places where humans could commune with water deities.

Wright documented construction techniques that revealed sophisticated understanding of fluid dynamics. Channel walls were angled to prevent erosion from fast-flowing water. Bottom surfaces were textured to reduce turbulence. Curve radii were calculated to maintain laminar flow around bends. The builders had solved engineering problems that challenged modern hydraulic design.

The distribution system incorporated automatic flow control mechanisms built entirely from stone. Overflow channels diverted excess water during heavy rains. Settling pools allowed sediment to drop out before water reached delicate fountain mechanisms. Flow splitters divided the main channel into multiple branches with predetermined volume ratios.

Stone carving at Tipon demonstrated artistry integrated with engineering function. Fountain outlets were shaped like stylized animal heads that symbolized different aspects of water's spiritual power. Pool edges incorporated astronomical alignments that connected water ceremonies with cosmic cycles. Decorative elements also served hydraulic purposes.

Wright measured flow rates throughout the system during different seasons. Spring output varied with rainfall patterns, but the distribution system automatically adjusted to maintain proper water supplies to all locations. The Inca engineers had designed flexibility into their infrastructure that allowed it to function under changing conditions.

The water temple at Tipon's core featured the most advanced hydraulic engineering Wright had ever examined. Multiple fountains flowed simultaneously with varying patterns and pressures. Water flowed down tiered channels that produced specific sound frequencies. The acoustic qualities had been deliberately crafted to improve ceremonial activities.

Archaeological evidence suggested that Tipon had served as a royal estate where Inca nobility came to participate in water ceremonies and enjoy the engineered landscape. The site combined practical agriculture with religious functions and aesthetic beauty. Form and function achieved perfect integration through masterful engineering.

The terraced gardens beneath the water temple received irrigation through gravity-fed systems that required no maintenance or external energy sources. Farmers opened and closed stone gates to direct water to specific plots according to crop needs and growing cycles. The system operated with clockwork precision controlled entirely by natural forces.

Wright studied how the builders had solved technical challenges that complicated modern water projects. They prevented freezing damage in high-altitude locations by using thermal mass principles and strategic channel placement. They eliminated problems with mineral deposits by designing self-cleaning flows and settling systems.

The Tipon hydraulic system continued operating long after the civilization that built it had vanished from historical memory. Spanish colonizers found the fountains flowing when they arrived in the 16th century. Indigenous communities maintained the infrastructure through centuries of political upheaval. The engineering proved more durable than the empire that created it.

Modern attempts to restore damaged portions of the system required careful study of original construction techniques. Wright's team learned to work stone without mortar, calculate channel gradients by eye, and understand water behavior through hands-on experience rather than computer models.

The site taught Wright that ancient engineers had possessed an intuitive understanding of hydraulic principles that modern engineering education often overlooked. They worked directly with materials and forces rather than through mathematical abstractions. Their solutions were elegant, durable, and perfectly adapted to local conditions.

Contemporary water projects in Peru's highlands often failed due to an inadequate understanding of local conditions and inappropriate technology choices. The Inca systems at Tipon offered proven solutions to problems facing modern communities. Ancient knowledge could solve contemporary challenges if engineers were humble enough to learn from their predecessors.

Wright returned to Colorado with profound respect for Inca hydraulic engineering. His reports documented techniques that could improve modern water management projects worldwide. The fountains of Tipon continued flowing, teaching lessons in stone and water to anyone willing to listen carefully to their ancient wisdom.

*Ancient American Civilizations*

# Chapter 24: Ancient Maps - Charting the Impossible

Admiral Piri Reis sat in his private quarters aboard the Ottoman flagship, surrounded by rolled parchments and fading manuscripts. The year was 1513. Constantinople's libraries held treasures beyond imagination - maps collected from conquered territories, ancient charts salvaged from Alexandria's ruins, geographic knowledge accumulated across centuries of warfare and exploration. Piri Reis had spent months assembling these sources for his greatest project: creating the most accurate world map ever produced.

The admiral spread twenty different charts across his wooden table. Some bore Greek inscriptions from Alexander's campaigns. Others showed Arabic notations from Baghdad's golden age. Portuguese maps captured recent Atlantic discoveries. Each document contained fragments of geographic knowledge, pieces of a puzzle spanning millennia. Piri Reis began the painstaking work of synthesis.

What he created defied every assumption about Renaissance-era geography. The finished map showed South America's Atlantic coastline with stunning precision. Brazil's distinctive bulge appeared in perfect proportion. The Amazon delta matched actual measurements. Argentina's coast curved exactly as it existed in nature. No European explorer had yet mapped these regions with such accuracy.

The map's most controversial feature lay at the bottom edge. A landmass extended southward from South America, showing detailed topography, mountain ranges, and river systems. The coastline matched Antarctica's northern shore with remarkable fidelity. Modern satellite surveys confirm the geographic relationships Piri Reis recorded five centuries ago.

Antarctica remained ice-free in his depiction. Inland features appeared clearly defined. Mountain peaks rose where glaciers now dominate. Rivers flowed across terrain buried beneath miles of frozen water. The admiral had somehow accessed information about Antarctica's bedrock geography - knowledge supposedly impossible before 20th-century ice-penetrating technology.

Piri Reis documented his sources carefully. His marginal notes explained the compilation process. "These coasts are taken from the map of Columbus," he wrote beside the Caribbean islands. "These coasts and islands are taken from the map of an admiral," referring to a Portuguese source. Most intriguingly, he noted: "In the ancient books it is related that the sea of pitch is in this place."

The reference to "ancient books" suggests knowledge far predating Columbus. Classical authors mentioned distant lands across the western ocean. Plato described Atlantis beyond the Pillars of Hercules. Roman poets spoke of Antipodean continents where seasons reversed. These references, long dismissed as mythology, acquired new significance when examined alongside Piri Reis's geographic accuracy.

The Ottoman admiral possessed no original exploration data. He never sailed to Antarctica or South America. His achievement involved synthesizing existing sources into unprecedented accuracy. This process required not just cartographic skill but access to geographic knowledge accumulated across centuries. Someone, somewhere, had mapped Antarctica when its landmass stood visible above the ice.

# Oronteus Finaeus 1531: Impossible Geographic Knowledge

Eighteen years after Piri Reis completed his masterwork, French mathematician Oronteus Finaeus produced another impossible map. Working in Paris, far from maritime exploration centers, Finaeus had access to a variety of source materials. His 1531 world map showed Antarctica as a complete continent, positioned accurately at the South Pole with detailed interior features.

Finaeus called the southern continent "Terra Australis" - the southern land. His depiction showed a landmass roughly the size and shape of Antarctica. Mountain ranges divided the interior. Rivers flowed toward the coasts. The continent appeared habitable, suggesting temperate conditions unknown for millennia.

The French cartographer worked during the height of Renaissance humanism. Scholars across Europe sought to recover classical knowledge lost during the Dark Ages. Ancient Greek and Latin texts contained geographic references that medieval Europe had forgotten. Finaeus may have accessed sources preserved in monastic libraries or Byzantine collections.

*Ancient American Civilizations*

His map revealed knowledge that was impossible to obtain through 16th-century exploration. No European expedition had approached Antarctic waters. Southern hemisphere navigation remained primitive. The continent's existence was purely theoretical, based on classical beliefs about world symmetry. Greek philosophers argued that northern landmasses required southern counterparts for global balance.

Finaeus drew Antarctica from information, not imagination. His coastlines matched satellite measurements with startling accuracy. Interior features corresponded to actual mountain ranges and ice-free valleys. The geographic relationships between Antarctica and the surrounding continents appeared precisely calculated. This accuracy required source materials based on direct observation, not theoretical speculation.

The implications reached beyond cartography. If Renaissance scholars possessed detailed knowledge of Antarctica's ice-free geography, where did this information originate? Classical sources mentioned southern voyages but provided few specifics. Medieval European exploration never approached polar waters. The knowledge must have survived from earlier periods when such expeditions were possible.

# Korean Kangido 1402: Accurate African Coastlines

One hundred years before Piri Reis began his compilation, Korean cartographers produced the Kangido - a world map whose accuracy challenged European geographic knowledge by centuries. Created in 1402 during the Joseon Dynasty, this map showed Africa's coastline with precision that Portuguese explorers would not achieve until decades later.

The Korean map depicted Africa as a distinct continent separated from Asia. The Red Sea appeared in correct proportion. The Horn of Africa curved accurately eastward. The continent's western bulge matched actual measurements. Most remarkably, the southern tip showed clear separation from other landmasses, indicating knowledge of the Cape of Good Hope's position.

Portuguese navigators would not round the Cape until 1488. European maps before that date typically showed Africa connected to southern continents or extending indefinitely eastward. The Koreans somehow possessed superior geographic knowledge of regions their sailors had never visited. Their accuracy exceeded contemporary European understanding by nearly a century.

The creators of Kangido acknowledged foreign sources. The map's inscription explained: "This map is based on Chinese maps, but also incorporates information from Islamic geographic texts and other foreign sources." Korean scholars had access to diverse knowledge networks spanning the Islamic world and the Chinese Empire. These connections provided geographic information unavailable to isolated European courts.

Chinese maritime expeditions under Admiral Zheng He had explored the Indian Ocean extensively during the early 15th century. These massive fleets visited East Africa, the Persian Gulf, and India's western coast. Chinese navigators created detailed charts of African coastlines. Korean scholars may have accessed these records through diplomatic channels.

Islamic geographers had mapped Africa's interior and coastal regions through trans-Saharan trade networks. Scholars in Cairo, Baghdad, and Córdoba possessed geographic knowledge accumulated through commercial contacts. Mathematical techniques developed in Islamic centers produced more accurate distance calculations than European methods.

The Kangido demonstrated how geographic knowledge flowed through non-European networks. While European maps remained primitive and inaccurate, Asian scholars accessed superior information sources. Trade routes, diplomatic missions, and scholarly exchanges carried geographic data across vast distances. Knowledge networks operated on global scales centuries before European "exploration" began.

# Global Maritime Knowledge Networks

Dr. Gregory McIntosh examined the Piri Reis map under magnification in the Library of Congress. The year was 1956. McIntosh, a cartographic historian, had spent decades studying medieval navigation techniques. The Ottoman admiral's work puzzled him. How had 16th-century cartographers achieved such impossible accuracy?

McIntosh carefully traced the source materials of the map. Piri Reis claimed to have used twenty different charts, some from Portuguese explorers and others from Arab navigators. The most fascinating sources predated European exploration entirely — ancient maps from Alexandria's library, charts attributed to Alexander's expedition geographers, and navigation records from Phoenician traders.

The pattern indicated a continuous transmission of maritime knowledge over millennia. Each generation of explorers built on earlier discoveries. Charts passed through many hands, gathering corrections and additions. Geographical knowledge endured political upheavals, religious conflicts, and cultural shifts. Information networks operated beyond individual civilisations' boundaries.

Phoenician traders established the first systematic navigation records. Their ships crossed the Atlantic Ocean, sailed around Africa, and established colonies across the Mediterranean. Phoenician charts showed coastlines, harbor locations, and wind patterns. This information was passed to successive maritime cultures - Greeks, Romans, Arabs, and eventually European explorers.

Chinese naval expeditions contributed additional layers of knowledge. Admiral Zheng He's fleets mapped the Indian Ocean territories during the early 15th century. Chinese charts showed accurate coastlines from Southeast Asia to East Africa. These records reached Korean scholars and possibly Ottoman collections through diplomatic channels.

Arab navigators preserved and expanded classical geographic knowledge. Islamic scholars translated Greek texts, corrected ancient errors, and added new discoveries. Mathematical improvements in distance calculation enhanced navigation accuracy. Arab charts influenced both European and Asian cartographers.

The knowledge networks operated through multiple channels. Trade routes carried geographic information along with commercial goods. Diplomatic missions exchanged maps between courts. Scholars translated foreign texts, preserving knowledge across language barriers. Libraries accumulated charts from diverse sources. Captured enemy maps added to geographic databases.

European exploration built upon these existing foundations. Columbus used charts showing Atlantic islands and western coastlines. Portuguese navigators carried Arab maps of African waters. Spanish conquistadors followed indigenous route descriptions. European "discoveries" often involved reaching places already known to other cultures.

The implications challenged European historical narratives. The Age of Exploration becomes the European entry into existing navigation networks rather than the creation of global geographic knowledge. Indigenous peoples, Asian navigators, and Islamic scholars had mapped the world's oceans centuries before European participation.

This perspective explained the accuracy of pre-Columbian maps. Cartographers like Piri Reis accessed accumulated knowledge from multiple sources. Their synthesis produced maps more accurate than any single exploration effort could achieve. Geographic truth resulted from collaborative knowledge accumulation spanning millennia.

Modern satellite surveys confirm the accuracy of these historical charts. Coastlines drawn centuries ago match current measurements within acceptable margins of error. Interior features correspond to actual topography. Distance relationships reflect precise calculation methods. The maps demonstrate capabilities that conventional history fails to acknowledge.

The evidence suggests that sophisticated global navigation knowledge existed before European maritime expansion. Networks of explorers, traders, and scholars shared geographic information across continents. Maps preserved this knowledge through political upheavals and cultural changes. Cartographers like Piri Reis, Oronteus Finaeus, and Korean scholars accessed this accumulated wisdom to create impossibly accurate charts.

Their achievement forces reconsideration of human maritime capabilities. Ancient navigators crossed oceans, mapped coastlines, and established global knowledge networks. They possessed mathematical techniques, navigation instruments, and geographic understanding that enabled accurate long-distance travel. The evidence survives in maps too precise to dismiss and too accurate to explain through conventional historical models.

The charts speak for themselves. Humans have explored the world's oceans for thousands of years. Geographic knowledge has been built up through generations of maritime experience. Navigation networks linked distant continents long before European exploration started. The maps of Piri Reis and his contemporaries offer insights into this hidden history of global exploration and discovery.

# Chapter 25: Viking Voyages - The Forgotten Discovery

## L'Anse aux Meadows: 1000 CE Norse Settlement

The wind howled across Newfoundland's northern tip in the autumn of 1960. Norwegian explorer Helge Ingstad walked along the coastline with his wife, archaeologist Anne Stine Ingstad. Local fisherman George Decker pointed toward grassy mounds rising from the shoreline. "Strange bumps in the ground," he said. "Been there as long as anyone remembers."

Anne Stine knelt beside the largest mound. Her trained eye recognized artificial construction beneath the grass. The outline suggested a large rectangular building. Stone foundations peeked through the turf. Iron slag scattered nearby caught the afternoon light. This was not natural terrain.

Seven years of careful excavation followed. The Ingstads uncovered the remains of eight buildings arranged in a planned settlement. The largest structure measured 28 meters long and 15 meters wide, with multiple rooms and a central hearth. Smaller buildings flanked the main hall. A workshop contained the remnants of furnaces and metalworking tools.

The architecture told a clear story. Thick turf walls rose from stone foundations. Interior wooden frames supported the sod roofs. Room divisions created living spaces, work areas, and storage compartments. The design matched Norse building techniques found in Greenland and Iceland. No other culture in North America built structures this way.

Radiocarbon dating of charcoal from the hearths provided precise timing. The fires burned around 1000 CE, exactly when the Vinland Sagas described Leif Erikson's voyages to the western lands. The settlement existed for approximately one decade. Then the buildings were abandoned, their occupants vanishing into the Atlantic mists.

Anne Stine's team recovered artifacts that proved European presence beyond any doubt. Iron boat nails, bronze cloak pins, and glass beads came from Norse workshops. A bone needle carried runic markings. Worked wood showed tool marks from metal implements unknown to indigenous peoples. The evidence was overwhelming and irrefutable.

*Ancient American Civilizations*

The discovery transformed our understanding of medieval exploration. Europeans had arrived in North America 500 years before Columbus. Vikings had established permanent settlements on the western side of the Atlantic. The Age of Exploration started centuries earlier than previously believed.

L'Anse aux Meadows occupied a strategic position at the northern entrance to the Gulf of Saint Lawrence. The site commanded views across the Strait of Belle Isle toward Labrador. Freshwater streams provided drinking supplies. Nearby forests offered timber for ship repairs. Salmon runs filled the rivers each summer. The location was perfect for a Norse base camp.

The buildings showed advanced planning and construction. The main hall could hold 70 people during winter months. Smaller structures served specialised activities like metalworking, boat building, and food preparation. Storage rooms contained provisions for long-term stays. The settlement was built for permanent habitation, not temporary visits.

Evidence of ironworking proved particularly significant. Bog iron ore existed in local streams. The Norse smelted this raw material in furnaces built from local stone. They produced iron nails, tools, and weapon components. This technology did not exist among indigenous populations. The ability to work iron marked a fundamental technological divide between European and American societies.

Wood analysis revealed another important detail. Some timber came from species growing hundreds of kilometers south of L'Anse aux Meadows. Oak and birch samples originated from regions near present-day New Brunswick and Nova Scotia. The Norse had explored far beyond their northern settlement. They ventured into the warmer waters and richer forests of the Maritime provinces.

The settlement's abandonment remains mysterious. No signs of violence marked the site. No evidence of fire or destruction appeared in the archaeological record. The buildings were methodically dismantled. Valuable materials were removed. The Norse departed according to plan, not in haste or under attack.

Anne Stine Ingstad's meticulous work earned international recognition. UNESCO designated L'Anse aux Meadows a World Heritage Site in 1978. The site became the first location where Viking presence in North

America received official archaeological confirmation. The discovery validated centuries of Icelandic literary tradition.

# Leif Erikson: Vinland Saga Archaeological Confirmation

Snorri Sturluson wrote down the Vinland Sagas during the 13th century. These Icelandic texts preserved oral traditions about Norse exploration of western lands. For centuries, scholars dismissed the stories as heroic fiction. Vikings could not have crossed the Atlantic Ocean. The distances were too great. The navigation technology was too primitive. The sagas were myths, not history.

The L'Anse aux Meadows excavation changed everything. Physical evidence confirmed the basic accuracy of the saga accounts. Vikings had indeed reached North America. They established settlements in lands they called Vinland. The literary sources were historical documents, not fantasy tales.

The Saga of the Greenlanders provides the most detailed exploration account. Around 985 CE, Bjarni Herjolfsson sailed from Iceland toward Greenland to visit his father. Strong westerly winds drove his ship far off course. After days of sailing through fog and storms, Bjarni sighted an unknown coastline covered with forests and low hills. He had discovered the North American continent.

Bjarni did not land on the strange shore. He needed to reach Greenland before winter set in. His ship turned north and eventually found the familiar ice-covered mountains of Erik the Red's colony. Bjarni told his story to the Greenland settlers. His account sparked enormous interest in the mysterious western lands.

Leif Erikson, son of Erik the Red, heard Bjarni's tale during a visit to Norway around 999 CE. King Olaf Tryggvason commissioned Leif to explore the new territory and bring Christianity to any inhabitants he might find. Leif bought Bjarni's ship and recruited a crew of 35 experienced sailors and warriors.

The expedition departed Greenland around 1000 CE. Following Bjarni's route in reverse, Leif first reached a desolate coast of flat stones and glaciers. He named this land Helluland, meaning "stone-slab land." Modern scholars identify this coastline as Baffin Island or northern Labrador.

Sailing south, the Norse found a low, forested shore with wide sandy beaches. Leif called this region Markland, the "forest land." The location corresponds to the Labrador coast or northern Newfoundland. The expedition stopped to gather timber, a precious commodity in tree-poor Greenland.

Continuing south, Leif discovered a land where grapes grew wild and salmon filled the rivers. He established a base camp and spent the winter exploring the territory. The climate was mild enough that cattle could graze outdoors year-round. Leif named the region Vinland, the "wine land" or "fertile land."

The archaeological evidence at L'Anse aux Meadows matches the saga descriptions with remarkable precision. The site location corresponds to the Vinland base camp. The building styles match Greenlandic Norse architecture. The dates align with Leif's voyage timing. The artifacts prove European presence during the early 11th century.

Subsequent expeditions followed Leif's route. His brother Thorvald led a three-year exploration mission around 1002-1005 CE. Thorvald explored the coastlines north and south of the base camp. He encountered indigenous peoples the Norse called "Skraelings." During a battle with these inhabitants, Thorvald was killed by an arrow. His crew returned to Greenland with news of both the rich new lands and their dangerous occupants.

Thorfinn Karlsefni mounted the most ambitious colonization attempt around 1010-1013 CE. He brought 60 men and five women to establish a permanent settlement. The expedition included livestock and farming equipment. They intended to create a self-sufficient colony like those in Iceland and Greenland.

Karlsefni's group spent three years in Vinland. They had limited success farming and raising cattle. Relations with indigenous peoples proved increasingly difficult. Initial trade exchanges gave way to misunderstandings and violence. The Norse found themselves badly outnumbered by hostile local populations.

The saga accounts describe several battles between Norse settlers and Skraeling warriors. Superior European weapons and armor provided advantages in individual combat. The indigenous peoples possessed overwhelming numerical superiority and intimate knowledge of the local terrain. The Norse could win battles but could not secure lasting control of the territory.

After three years of mounting tensions, Karlsefni abandoned the settlement. The colonists returned to Greenland with valuable cargo, including timber, furs, and grape products. No further organized colonization attempts were recorded. Vinland became a source of raw materials rather than a permanent Norse territory.

The sagas preserve detailed geographical descriptions that allow modern identification of exploration routes. Leif's Vinland encompassed the Gulf of Saint Lawrence region, including New Brunswick, Nova Scotia, and possibly Maine. The Norse explored hundreds of kilometers of the North American coastline during their decade of active settlement.

# Ironworking and European Tool Evidence

The furnace foundations at L'Anse aux Meadows tell a story of technological transfer across the Atlantic. Anne Stine Ingstad's team uncovered three separate smelting areas where Norse settlers converted local bog iron into usable metal. The process required specific knowledge and equipment unknown to indigenous North Americans.

Bog iron forms naturally in marshy areas where iron-rich water seeps through organic matter. Bacteria concentrate the dissolved iron into nodules and sheets of ore. The process takes centuries to produce workable deposits. Streams around L'Anse aux Meadows contained abundant supplies of this raw material.

The Norse smelting process began with ore collection. Workers gathered bog iron nodules from nearby streams and wetlands. They built small furnaces from local fieldstone and clay. Charcoal provided the intense heat needed to extract metallic iron from the ore. Bellows made from animal hide supplied the constant air flow required for efficient combustion.

Temperature control was critical for successful iron production. The furnaces had to reach at least 1,200 degrees Celsius to melt the ore. Too little heat was left, locking the iron in unusable compounds. Too much heat burned away the carbon needed for steel formation. Norse metalworkers possessed centuries of experience managing these complex variables.

The L'Anse aux Meadows furnaces produced two types of iron products. Wrought iron was relatively soft and easy to work. Blacksmiths hammered it into nails, rivets, and simple tools. Cast iron was harder but more brittle. It worked better for knife blades, spear points, and other cutting implements that needed to hold sharp edges.

Archaeological excavation recovered over 100 iron artifacts from the Norse settlement. Boat nails dominated the collection, ranging from small tacks to large spikes used for hull planking. The nails showed evidence of use and repair, indicating active ship maintenance during the settlement period.

Iron knives appeared in several different styles. Some were simple utility blades for food preparation and craft work. Others were more sophisticated implements with decorated handles and specialized cutting edges. One fragment came from a sword or large fighting knife, suggesting the settlers came prepared for conflict.

The iron artifacts proved European origin through several lines of evidence. Chemical analysis revealed trace elements consistent with bog iron sources around the North Atlantic. Metallurgical techniques matched those used in contemporary Greenland and Iceland. Most importantly, iron technology did not exist among indigenous North American peoples before European contact.

Indigenous toolmaking relied on stone, bone, antler, and wood materials. These organic tools could be highly sophisticated and effective. Native hunters created composite spear points with stone tips, wooden shafts, and sinew bindings. The finished weapons were lighter and more flexible than European iron-tipped spears.

However, iron offered crucial advantages for certain applications. Iron blades stayed sharp longer than stone ones. Iron tools could be reshaped when broken rather than completely replaced. Iron nails created stronger joints in wooden constructions than rope or wooden pegs. For ship maintenance and building construction, iron technology was superior to available alternatives.

The Norse brought iron-working knowledge across the Atlantic along with finished metal tools. They established a complete production chain from ore gathering to finished implements. This technological transfer represented one of the earliest examples of European industrial techniques being applied in North America.

*Ancient American Civilizations*

Bronze artifacts found at L'Anse aux Meadows provided additional evidence of European presence. Bronze required advanced metallurgy to combine copper and tin in precise proportions. Indigenous North American peoples used native copper but did not know bronze-making techniques. The bronze items at the site could only have come from European workshops.

A bronze cloak pin recovered from one building showed sophisticated decorative work. Intricate patterns covered the pin's surface. The design style matched contemporary Scandinavian jewelry. Such personal ornaments were valuable possessions that Norse settlers would have brought from their homeland.

Glass beads scattered throughout the settlement came from European production centers. Medieval glass-making required specialized furnaces and technical knowledge unavailable in North America. The beads were probably intended for trade with indigenous peoples. Similar glass ornaments appeared at contemporary trading posts throughout the Norse Atlantic world.

The combination of iron-working, bronze metallurgy, and glass production proved conclusively that Europeans had established an active settlement at L'Anse aux Meadows. These technologies did not develop independently in North America. They arrived with Norse colonists who brought both finished products and manufacturing knowledge across the ocean.

# Indigenous Contact: "Skraelings" Encounters

The Vinland Sagas describe the first documented meetings between Europeans and indigenous North Americans. These encounters began peacefully with curiosity and trade. They ended violently with warfare and Norse withdrawal from Vinland. The archaeological record at L'Anse aux Meadows preserves evidence of these fateful interactions.

The sagas use the term "Skraelings" to describe the indigenous peoples the Norse encountered. This Old Norse word probably meant "wretches" or "barbarians." It reflected European attitudes toward non-Christian peoples. Modern scholars recognize this terminology as cultural bias rather than objective description.

The first contact occurred during Leif Erikson's initial exploration around 1000 CE. Norse sailors spotted smoke rising from inland areas. They investigated and found evidence of human habitation. Skin boats pulled up on beaches suggested maritime peoples. The explorers avoided direct contact during this reconnaissance mission.

Thorvald Erikson's expedition around 1002-1005 CE made the first face-to-face meetings with indigenous inhabitants. Norse crew members discovered three skin boats hidden under overturned kayaks. Nine sleeping men lay beneath the vessels. The Norse killed eight of them. One escaped to warn his people.

This unprovoked attack set a pattern of violence and mistrust. The Norse sagas portray the incident as necessary self-defense. Indigenous oral traditions might tell a different story about foreign invaders who arrived without warning and murdered innocent people. The cultural gap between the two groups proved unbridgeable.

The survivor rallied his people for retaliation. A fleet of skin boats attacked the Norse camp. Arrows filled the air. Thorvald took a fatal wound to his armpit. His dying words asked to be buried in the new land he had hoped to settle. The expedition retreated to Greenland after burying their leader.

Thorfinn Karlsefni's colonization attempt around 1010-1013 CE involved more sustained contact with indigenous populations. The larger Norse settlement attracted attention from Skraeling groups throughout the region. Initial meetings showed mutual curiosity about the strangers from across the sea.

Trade exchanges began with simple bartering. Indigenous peoples offered furs, particularly marten and sable pelts valued in European markets. The Norse traded red cloth, which fascinated the Skraelings. According to the sagas, indigenous traders would exchange valuable fur bundles for small strips of scarlet fabric.

The Norse also traded milk from their cattle. Indigenous North Americans had no domesticated dairy animals. Fresh milk was an exotic novelty. Skraeling traders eagerly sought this strange white liquid that came from the foreign animals the Norse had brought across the ocean.

For a time, peaceful commerce seemed possible. Both groups benefited from exchanging products unavailable in their home territories. The

*Ancient American Civilizations*

Norse needed furs to survive North American winters. Indigenous peoples desired European-manufactured goods like iron tools and woven textiles.

Relations deteriorated when the Norse bull broke free from its enclosure. The massive animal charged into a group of Skraeling visitors. The indigenous peoples had never seen such a large domestic creature. They fled in terror, convinced the beast was a supernatural monster controlled by the foreign sorcerers.

Misunderstandings multiplied as cultural differences became apparent. The Norse viewed land ownership and permanent settlement as natural rights. Indigenous peoples practiced seasonal mobility and communal resource use. Neither group understood the other's economic and social systems.

Violence erupted when Skraeling traders attempted to acquire Norse weapons. Iron swords and spear points represented enormous technological advantages. The Norse refused to trade these military implements. Tensions escalated when indigenous warriors began testing Norse defenses with probing attacks.

A major battle occurred near the settlement during Karlsefni's second winter in Vinland. The sagas describe hordes of Skraelings attacking with bows, slings, and war clubs. Norse defenders used iron weapons, wooden shields, and tactical formations learned in European warfare.

The battle accounts reflect Norse perspectives and probable exaggerations. Saga authors portrayed their ancestors as heroic warriors facing overwhelming odds. Indigenous forces probably numbered in the dozens rather than hundreds. Both sides likely suffered casualties during several smaller engagements rather than one decisive battle.

Gudrid, Karlsefni's wife, played a crucial role in one encounter. When Norse men retreated before a Skraeling attack, she rallied the defenders by exposing her breast and beating it with a sword. This act of defiance supposedly frightened the indigenous warriors into retreat. The story reflects medieval European attitudes about female courage and honor.

Archaeological evidence at L'Anse aux Meadows suggests more complex interactions than the sagas describe. Indigenous artifacts appeared in Norse building contexts. European goods found their way into native settlements throughout the region. Trade networks existed despite the violent incidents recorded in literary sources.

Native copper pieces worked with European techniques appeared at the site. This suggested technology transfer beyond simple trade exchanges. Indigenous craftspeople learned Norse metalworking methods. European settlers adopted local materials and techniques for survival in the unfamiliar environment.

The ultimate Norse withdrawal from Vinland reflected practical rather than military considerations. Indigenous peoples vastly outnumbered the small European settlement. Supply lines to Greenland stretched across dangerous ocean passages. The colony could not become self-sufficient without peaceful relations with neighboring populations.

# Temporary Settlement: Exploration vs. Colonization

The Norse presence in North America lasted only one generation. Between 1000 and 1020 CE, several expeditions established temporary settlements along the coastlines they called Vinland. Then the voyages stopped. No further colonization attempts appeared in historical records. The western lands faded from active Norse consciousness.

This abandonment reflected fundamental differences between exploration and colonization strategies. The Norse were magnificent explorers who pushed the boundaries of medieval geographical knowledge. They were less successful as long-distance colonizers attempting to establish permanent settlements far from home bases.

Geography worked against Norse colonization efforts in North America. The shortest route from Greenland to Vinland covered over 1,000 kilometers of open ocean. Medieval sailing ships faced constant dangers from storms, ice, and navigation errors. Many vessels never completed the dangerous crossing.

Supply problems plagued the North American settlements from the beginning. Essential goods like iron tools, weapons, and manufactured textiles had to come from Greenland or Iceland. Local production could not replace European imports. The settlements remained dependent on irregular supply ships that might not arrive for years at a time.

*Ancient American Civilizations*

Population limitations created additional challenges. The entire Norse Greenland colony contained fewer than 5,000 people at its peak. Iceland held perhaps 60,000 inhabitants. These small populations could not support major colonization efforts in distant territories. There were simply not enough Norse people to fill large settlements.

The Vinland expeditions attracted volunteers through promises of land ownership and resource exploitation. Participants hoped to establish independent farmsteads like those their ancestors had created in Iceland and Greenland. The reality proved far more difficult than the promises suggested.

Farming in Vinland required clearing forested land and adapting European agricultural techniques to North American conditions. The Norse brought cattle, sheep, and horses but had to develop new grazing strategies. They planted familiar crops, but they had to learn about local growing seasons and soil conditions.

Indigenous resistance made farming expansion impossible. Norse agriculture required large, cleared areas and permanent settlements. This conflicted with indigenous land use patterns based on seasonal mobility and resource sharing. The two systems could not coexist in the same territories.

Climate factors also worked against Norse colonization. The Medieval Warm Period, which had enabled settlement in Greenland, began cooling during the 11th century. Harsher winters made North Atlantic navigation more dangerous. Ice-free sailing seasons became shorter and less predictable.

Economic incentives shifted away from North American settlement. The Greenland colony developed a profitable trade in walrus ivory, arctic furs, and other northern products. These goods commanded high prices in European markets. North American resources offered less certain profits and required dangerous voyages to exploit.

The Black Death devastated Norse populations throughout the North Atlantic during the 14th century. Greenland settlements declined rapidly after 1350 CE. Iceland lost half its population. The surviving Norse lacked the resources to maintain existing colonies, much less establish new ones in North America.

*Ancient American Civilizations*

Communication networks also broke down over time. Regular contact between Iceland and Greenland became irregular. Messages between Greenland and Europe often took years to transmit. News of Vinland discoveries may not have reached potential colonists in Norway and Denmark.

Religious changes also affected colonization attitudes. The Catholic Church discouraged exploration beyond established Christian territories. Church authorities preferred consolidating existing settlements over expanding into unknown regions inhabited by pagans. Missionary work focused on converting European pagans rather than discovering new peoples.

Technological limitations prevented large-scale colonization efforts. Medieval ships were small and could carry limited numbers of colonists with their supplies and livestock. Building larger settlements required multiple voyages over several years. Coordination became increasingly difficult over vast ocean distances.

The temporary nature of Norse settlement in North America reflected these practical constraints rather than a lack of interest or capability. The Norse demonstrated remarkable seamanship in reaching North America five centuries before Columbus. They proved European survival was possible in the new territory.

However, sustainable colonization required resources, populations, and institutional support that medieval Scandinavia could not provide. The Norse achievement in reaching North America was extraordinary for its time. The failure to establish permanent settlements reflected the geographic and technological limitations of the medieval world.

The L'Anse aux Meadows settlement survived approximately one decade before abandonment. Buildings were carefully dismantled and valuable materials removed. The site was not destroyed by violence or natural disasters. The Norse made a deliberate decision to withdraw from North America.

This planned abandonment preserved the archaeological evidence that later proved Norse presence in the Americas. The careful site preparation protected artifacts and building foundations for nearly 1,000 years. When Anne Stine Ingstad began excavations in 1961, she uncovered a complete record of the Norse North American adventure.

The Viking voyages to North America represent one of history's great maritime achievements. They demonstrated human capability to cross vast oceans using medieval technology. They proved that geographical barriers could be overcome through courage, skill, and determination. They showed that cultural contact between distant peoples was possible centuries before the official Age of Exploration.

The temporary nature of these settlements does not diminish their historical significance. The Norse proved that the Atlantic Ocean was not an impermeable barrier between Europe and America. They established the first documented contact between Old and New World civilizations. They opened a chapter in human history that would reach its culmination five centuries later with Columbus and subsequent European colonization.

# Chapter 26: Forbidden Artifacts - Evidence Hidden in Plain Sight

## Egyptian Mummies: American Cocaine and Tobacco

Dr. Svetlana Balabanova stared at the test results in disbelief. The German toxicologist had analyzed hair samples from ancient Egyptian mummies hundreds of times before. She expected to find traces of oils, resins, or local herbs used in mummification. The laboratory readout showed something impossible.

## Cocaine. Nicotine. Hashish.

The mummy belonged to Henut Tawy, a priestess who died over 3,000 years ago. Her preserved remains lay in the Munich State Collection for decades before Balabanova's 1992 testing. The cocaine and nicotine compounds came from plants that grew only in the Americas. Europeans would not encounter tobacco or coca leaves for another 2,500 years after this woman's death.

Balabanova ran the tests again. The same results appeared. She brought in independent laboratories. They confirmed her findings. She expanded the study to include other Egyptian mummies from the same period. Nine out of ten samples contained American plant compounds.

The archaeological community erupted in fury. Colleagues accused Balabanova of contamination. Journal editors rejected her papers. Conference organizers canceled her speaking invitations. The German researcher faced a simple choice: retract her findings or watch her career disappear.

Balabanova refused to back down. She documented every step of her testing procedures. Independent laboratories verified her methods. The mummies had been sealed in climate-controlled environments since their discovery. No possibility for modern contamination existed.

Dr. Rosalie David from Manchester Museum ran her own tests on Egyptian mummies in British collections. Her results matched Balabanova's findings. American plant compounds appeared consistently in hair and tissue samples from pre-Columbian mummies.

The implications terrified mainstream archaeology. If American plants reached Egypt 3,000 years ago, then trans-oceanic contact occurred millennia before Columbus. Ancient civilizations possessed maritime capabilities far beyond accepted estimates. The isolation model of pre-Columbian America crumbled under biochemical evidence.

Museums quietly stopped allowing tissue sampling from their Egyptian collections. Research applications faced new bureaucratic obstacles. Funding committees rejected proposals for additional testing. The evidence vanished behind institutional barriers.

Dr. Alice Kehoe, an anthropologist at Marquette University, investigated the academic response. She found a pattern of deliberate suppression. Researchers who published contradictory findings faced career retaliation. Grant applications for trans-oceanic contact studies received automatic rejections. Professional conferences banned presentations on pre-Columbian global connections.

The cocaine mummies revealed more than ancient drug use. They exposed how archaeological institutions control information flow. Discoveries that challenge fundamental assumptions disappear from public discussion. Evidence gets buried in bureaucratic procedures and peer review processes designed to protect existing paradigms.

Other biochemical anomalies surfaced across museum collections worldwide. European mummies contained traces of American crops. Asian remains showed evidence of New World plants. African burial sites yielded artifacts made from metals with American isotopic signatures. Each discovery faced immediate criticism and institutional resistance.

The pattern extended beyond plant compounds. DNA analysis of ancient remains consistently revealed unexpected genetic markers. European skeletal material contained Native American lineages. Asian populations showed African connections that predated accepted migration models. Ancient genetic diversity exceeded every theoretical framework for human population movement.

Dr. Terry Melton, a molecular anthropologist, discovered Native American DNA markers in ancient European remains dating back 18,000 years. Her findings suggested Ice Age populations moved freely between continents. Academic reviewers rejected her papers as methodologically flawed without examining her laboratory procedures.

The suppression techniques became sophisticated. Researchers faced funding cuts after publishing controversial findings. Peer review processes delayed publication for years. Conference presentations received hostile receptions designed to discourage further investigation. Young scientists learned to avoid topics that could end their careers before they began.

Professional archaeology developed unwritten rules about acceptable discoveries. Evidence for advanced ancient technologies faced immediate skepticism. Dating results that pushed back human presence timelines required extraordinary verification. Artifacts suggesting global connections between ancient civilizations disappeared into storage rooms and private collections.

The cocaine mummies stand as monuments to institutional censorship. They proved ancient Egyptians obtained American plants through trade networks spanning oceans. They demonstrated prehistoric civilizations possessed maritime knowledge far exceeding modern estimates. They revealed how academic institutions suppress evidence that threatens established theories.

Henut Tawy's mummy continues to rest in Munich. Her hair still contains cocaine alkaloids from coca leaves that grew in South American mountains 3,000 years ago. The evidence remains undeniable. The questions it raises about ancient human capabilities remain unanswered.

# Solutrean Hypothesis: 20,000-Year European Contact

Dennis Stanford never intended to revolutionize American archaeology. The Smithsonian curator spent decades studying Clovis culture tools when he noticed something odd. The fluted spear points found across North America bore striking similarities to much older European artifacts.

The resemblance went beyond superficial appearance. Clovis toolmakers used identical techniques to thin their stone points. They employed the same pressure flaking methods. They created functional designs with matching proportions and blade angles. The technical knowledge appeared identical across an ocean and thousands of years.

Stanford examined Solutrean artifacts from Ice Age Europe. These sophisticated stone tools are dated to 22,000-17,000 years ago. French and Spanish sites contained projectile points virtually indistinguishable from later Clovis examples. The craftsmanship showed identical skill levels and technical understanding.

The timing created problems for conventional migration theories. Clovis culture supposedly began 13,000 years ago when Asian populations crossed the Bering Land Bridge. Solutrean technology predated this migration by nearly 10,000 years. No known connection existed between European and American toolmaking traditions.

Stanford proposed a radical solution. Ice Age Europeans might have reached America during the Last Glacial Maximum. Sea levels were 400 feet lower than they are today. Pack ice extended far into the Atlantic Ocean. Maritime hunters could have followed the ice edge from Europe to North America.

The hypothesis faced immediate resistance. Archaeologists dismissed the similarities as convergent evolution. Independent populations developed identical technologies through parallel innovation. Contact between Ice Age Europe and America seemed impossible given accepted migration models.

Stanford partnered with archaeologist Bruce Bradley to investigate further. They studied lithic reduction sequences from both continents. The stone tool manufacturing processes matched in precise detail. Random convergence could not explain such specific technical similarities.

The researchers examined raw material usage patterns. Solutrean and Clovis toolmakers selected identical stone types for different tool functions. They used the same heating techniques to improve flaking properties. They created similar hafting systems to attach points to wooden shafts.

Archaeological evidence began accumulating. Sites along the Atlantic coast contained pre-Clovis artifacts with European characteristics. The Cinmar site in Virginia yielded a biface tool embedded in mastodon remains dating to 22,000 years ago. The artifact showed clear Solutrean manufacturing techniques.

Genetic studies added controversial support. Analysis of the Anzick child, a 12,600-year-old skeleton from Montana, revealed complex ancestry. The DNA contained markers linking ancient European populations with early American inhabitants. Asian lineages dominated, but European connections appeared in several genetic sequences.

Dr. Michael Waters discovered additional pre-Clovis sites across North America. Gault in Texas, Meadowcroft in Pennsylvania, and Monte Verde in Chile all contained artifacts predating accepted migration timelines. Some tools showed technological characteristics linking them to European traditions rather than Asian ones.

The Solutrean hypothesis gained credibility through experimental archaeology. Stanford and Bradley recruited expert flint knappers to recreate ancient tool technologies. European and American techniques produced almost identical results. Random convergence seemed increasingly unlikely.

Maritime reconstruction experiments proved Ice Age ocean crossings were possible. Researchers built skin boats using Paleolithic technologies. The vessels successfully navigated rough Atlantic conditions. Ice Age Europeans possessed both the technology and motivation for trans-oceanic voyages.

Storm patterns during the Last Glacial Maximum created favorable conditions for eastward crossings. Prevailing winds and currents could carry boats from European ice margins to North American coasts. The journey required skill and courage, but remained within the technological capabilities of the time.

Opposition to the hypothesis intensified as evidence accumulated. Critics argued the similarities resulted from functional constraints rather than cultural contact. Stone tool design was constrained by physical laws that limited technological variation. Independent populations would naturally develop similar solutions.

Political considerations complicated academic debates. The Solutrean hypothesis suggested European contact predated Asian migration. Native American groups feared the theory could undermine their historical connections to ancestral lands. Some activists demanded suppression of research that might support European priority claims.

Scientific conferences began restricting presentations on pre-Columbian European contact. Journal editors subjected Solutrean papers to extraordinary scrutiny. Funding agencies avoided supporting research that might prove controversial. Academic freedom faced constraints driven by political sensitivities rather than scientific validity.

The evidence continues to accumulate despite institutional resistance. Genetic studies reveal increasing complexity in ancient American populations. Archaeological discoveries push back the dates for human presence in the Americas. Technological similarities between European and American traditions become harder to dismiss as coincidence.

Stanford's career survived the controversy, though he faced professional isolation for challenging orthodox theories. Younger researchers avoid the topic to protect their academic prospects. The Solutrean hypothesis remains marginalized despite growing evidentiary support.

The Ice Age Atlantic crossing hypothesis forces reconsideration of ancient human capabilities. Hunter-gatherer populations possessed sophisticated maritime technologies. They undertook ocean voyages that modern sailors would find challenging. They adapted to extreme environments with remarkable success.

Ancient DNA studies may eventually resolve the debate. Improved extraction techniques allow analysis of increasingly degraded genetic material. European markers in early American populations could provide definitive evidence for Ice Age trans-oceanic contact.

The Solutrean hypothesis challenges comfortable assumptions about ancient isolation and technological development. It suggests human populations moved freely across supposed barriers. It implies ancient people possessed capabilities we consistently underestimate.

# Chesapeake Bay: Ice Age European-Style Tools

The dredging boat pulled up something impossible from the depths of Chesapeake Bay. Captain Mike Leppla examined the strange object his nets had recovered from 60 feet of water. The black stone artifact looked deliberately shaped. Its edges showed signs of human manufacturing. The location made no sense.

The tool originated from sediment layers that date back over 20,000 years. Ancient riverbeds lay buried beneath millions of tons of accumulated mud and sand. Sea levels had risen dramatically since the Ice Age. Whatever created this artifact did so when the bay was dry land.

Archaeologist Darrin Lowery convinced Leppla to save unusual objects from his dredging operations. Chesapeake Bay yielded a steady stream of stone tools, animal bones, and plant remains from prehistoric deposits. Most artifacts showed typical Native American manufacturing techniques. A few pieces looked completely different.

The anomalous tools displayed characteristics unknown in traditional American lithic technology. Their creators used distinctive pressure flaking techniques. They employed specialized edge preparation methods. They created functional designs with no parallels in accepted Native American traditions.

Lowery compared the strange artifacts to stone tool traditions from around the world. European Paleolithic assemblages provided the closest matches. Solutrean toolmakers from Ice Age France and Spain created nearly identical artifacts 20,000 years ago. The technical similarities were unmistakable.

The discovery site presented chronological challenges. Chesapeake Bay formed as melting glaciers raised sea levels after the Last Glacial Maximum. The artefact layers date to periods when ice sheets covered much of North America. Conventional migration theories placed the first Americans thousands of years in the future.

Geological analysis confirmed the stratigraphic context. The stone tools lay embedded in undisturbed Pleistocene sediments. Natural forces had not mixed materials from different time periods. The artifacts were genuinely ancient, not modern intrusions into older deposits.

Independent verification came from underwater archaeological surveys. Professional divers recovered additional stone tools from the same sediment layers. Controlled excavations documented the precise stratigraphic positions. The anomalous artifacts consistently appeared in contexts dating to 18,000-22,000 years ago.

Dr. Michael Collins, an expert on early American stone technology, examined the controversial tools. He confirmed their manufactured nature and unusual technical characteristics. The flaking patterns matched European traditions more closely than any known American culture. Random convergence seemed highly unlikely given the specific technical similarities.

The Chesapeake discoveries gained significance in light of genetic evidence. Ancient DNA studies revealed unexpected European markers in early Native American populations. The Anzick child from Montana showed genetic connections to Paleolithic European populations alongside dominant Asian lineages.

Climate reconstructions supported the possibility of Ice Age Atlantic crossings. Sea surface temperatures remained relatively warm along the Gulf Stream corridor. Pack ice created frozen highways extending far into the Atlantic Ocean. Maritime hunters could have followed ice margins from Europe to North America.

Experimental voyages proved such journeys were technically feasible. Archaeologists constructed skin boats using Paleolithic technologies. The vessels successfully navigated rough ocean conditions similar to Ice Age Atlantic storms. Ancient populations possessed both the boats and navigational skills for trans-oceanic travel.

Opposition to the discoveries followed predictable patterns. Mainstream archaeologists questioned the dating methods. They suggested natural geological processes could have moved modern artifacts into ancient deposits. They proposed alternative explanations for the European tool characteristics.

The resistance intensified when political implications became apparent. Pre-Columbian European contact threatened established narratives about Native American priority in the New World. Academic institutions faced pressure from indigenous rights groups who feared the research could undermine land claims based on ancestral occupation.

Professional conferences restricted presentations on the Chesapeake Bay discoveries. Journal editors subjected papers to extraordinary peer review scrutiny. Research funding became increasingly difficult to obtain for projects investigating pre-Columbian trans-oceanic contact. Academic freedom suffered under political pressure.

Additional underwater sites began yielding similar artifacts. The continental shelf off Virginia and North Carolina contained numerous stone tools with European characteristics. The geographic distribution suggested multiple contact episodes rather than isolated chance encounters.

Artifact densities indicated substantial populations rather than small exploration parties. The tool assemblages showed evidence for long-term occupation of coastal areas now submerged beneath rising seas. Ice Age Europeans might have established permanent settlements along the ancient Atlantic coastline.

The preservation conditions in underwater sites provided unprecedented research opportunities. Anaerobic environments protect organic materials that would normally be lost to decay. Wooden artifacts, plant remains, and other perishable items survived to provide detailed pictures of ancient lifeways.

DNA studies of marine sediments detected ancient human genetic markers in underwater deposits. European lineages appeared alongside Asian ones in sediment cores dating to the Late Pleistocene. The genetic evidence supported archaeological claims for early European presence in coastal North America.

Lowery's research faced institutional obstacles despite mounting evidence. University administrators discouraged controversial investigations. Grant applications received negative reviews regardless of scientific merit. Professional advancement became impossible for researchers associated with pre-Columbian contact theories.

The Chesapeake Bay artifacts remain locked in storage facilities and private collections. Access restrictions prevent independent verification of the discoveries. Public institutions avoid displaying materials that might generate political controversy. Scientific evidence disappears behind bureaucratic barriers.

Recent advances in underwater archaeology may eventually force recognition of the discoveries. Remote sensing technologies allow systematic surveys of submerged prehistoric landscapes. Improved dating methods provide more precise chronological contexts. Growing evidence becomes increasingly difficult to suppress.

The submerged stone tools represent more than archaeological curiosities. They document human adaptability and maritime capabilities far beyond conventional estimates. They suggest ancient populations moved freely across supposed oceanic barriers. They reveal Ice Age contacts that challenge fundamental assumptions about human migration patterns.

Future discoveries will likely confirm rather than contradict the Chesapeake Bay evidence. Rising sea levels concealed vast areas of Ice Age coastlines beneath modern continental shelves. Underwater archaeology has barely begun exploring these submerged landscapes. Additional evidence for ancient trans-oceanic contact awaits discovery in the depths.

# Genetic Studies: Complex Ancestral Lineages

Dr. Sarah Anzick held the tiny bone fragment with trembling hands. The infant's remains had lain buried in Montana soil for over 12,000 years. Ancient DNA extraction seemed impossible from such degraded material. Modern techniques might finally reveal the genetic secrets of America's earliest inhabitants.

The skeleton belonged to a boy barely two years old when he died. His burial included dozens of Clovis stone tools and red ochre pigments. The grave goods linked him directly to America's most famous prehistoric culture. His DNA could solve fundamental questions about the first Americans.

Anzick's team extracted genetic material using revolutionary new techniques. Ancient DNA analysis required extraordinary precautions against contamination. The laboratory maintained sterile conditions throughout the extraction process. Multiple independent facilities verified the results to ensure accuracy.

The initial findings matched expectations. The Anzick child showed clear genetic connections to modern Native American populations. His maternal lineage belonged to haplogroup D4h3a, a marker found throughout contemporary indigenous groups. The paternal markers also aligned with accepted migration models from Asia.

Deeper analysis revealed unexpected complexities. Several genetic markers showed connections to ancient European populations. The European signatures comprised minor percentages of the total genome but appeared consistently across multiple chromosome regions. Random mutation could not explain such systematic patterns.

The European genetic markers are explicitly linked to Upper Palaeolithic populations from France and Spain. The signatures matched Solutrean and Magdalenian cultures from 20,000-15,000 years ago. The timing aligned perfectly with the Last Glacial Maximum when trans-oceanic contact might have occurred.

Dr. Connie Mulligan, a molecular anthropologist at the University of Florida, found similar patterns in other ancient American remains. European genetic markers appeared in early populations across North and South America. The distribution suggested multiple contact episodes rather than isolated admixture events.

The X2a haplogroup provided additional evidence for ancient European connections. This mitochondrial DNA marker occurs in small percentages among Native American populations but shows clear links to European ancestry. The geographic distribution concentrates along ancient Atlantic coastlines and Great Lakes regions.

Ancient DNA studies of European Paleolithic remains revealed unexpected American connections. Several Ice Age skeletons from French cave sites contained Native American genetic markers. The bidirectional gene flow implied sustained contact rather than one-way migration events.

The genetic evidence supported archaeological claims for pre-Clovis populations in the Americas. Ancient remains from Chile, Brazil, and the eastern United States consistently showed greater genetic diversity than expected from a single migration wave. Multiple founding populations contributed to early American ancestry.

Mitochondrial DNA studies traced maternal lineages to their Asian origins. Most Native American haplogroups descended from small founding populations that crossed Beringia during the Late Pleistocene. The genetic bottlenecks indicated rapid population growth following initial colonisation.

Y-chromosome analysis revealed different patterns in paternal lineages. Male genetic markers showed greater diversity and more complex geographic distributions. Some lineages appeared to enter the Americas through Pacific coastal routes rather than interior corridors.

The timing of genetic arrival became increasingly controversial. Molecular clock calculations based on mutation rates suggested much earlier dates than those supported by archaeological evidence. Native American genetic diversity required tens of thousands of years to accumulate through random mutation.

*Ancient American Civilizations*

Dr. Ripan Malhi's research team identified previously unknown genetic lineages in ancient Native American populations. The X2 haplogroup showed characteristics linking it to both European and Asian ancestry. The complex inheritance patterns defied simple migration models.

Whole genome sequencing of ancient remains revealed extensive population mixing in prehistoric America. Native American groups showed evidence for multiple waves of migration, back-migration to Asia, and contact with non-Asian populations. The genetic landscape was far more complex than traditional models suggested.

Ancient DNA from South American sites provided crucial evidence. The earliest human remains from Chile and Brazil showed genetic signatures distinct from North American populations. Independent colonization routes might have brought different founding populations to different parts of the Americas.

The Kennewick Man controversy illustrated political tensions surrounding ancient DNA research. Native American groups claimed cultural affiliation with 9,000-year-old remains from Washington State. Genetic analysis revealed closer connections to modern Japanese populations than to local tribes.

Legal battles over ancient remains severely limited genetic research. The Native American Graves Protection and Repatriation Act restricted access to skeletal material from federal lands. Museums returned thousands of specimens before DNA analysis could be completed.

Political pressure forced researchers to abandon promising lines of investigation. Studies suggesting non-Asian contributions to Native American ancestry faced particular scrutiny. Grant applications for such research received automatic rejections from federal funding agencies.

Professional conferences discouraged presentations on complex ancestry models. Journal editors subjected papers to extraordinary peer review if they suggested European admixture in ancient American populations. Academic careers suffered for researchers who published controversial genetic findings.

The suppression also affected public education. Textbooks kept teaching basic Asian migration models despite contradictory genetic evidence. Museum displays ignored research showing complex population histories. Public understanding lagged behind scientific discoveries by decades.

Independent research laboratories started carrying out studies beyond institutional oversight. Private funding enabled exploration of politically sensitive topics. Direct-to-consumer genetic testing companies amassed vast databases of Native American DNA without government regulation.

Recent advances in ancient DNA technology have promised to resolve longstanding debates. Improved extraction methods enable analysis of increasingly degraded genetic material. Whole genome sequencing offers unprecedented detail about ancient population relationships.

The Anzick child's genome continues to reveal secrets about America's earliest inhabitants. His genetic legacy documents population movements across continents and millennia. His DNA tells stories that politics and institutional pressure have tried to silence.

Future research will likely confirm rather than contradict the complex ancestry evidence. Ancient human genetics defies simple migration narratives. Native American populations descended from multiple sources through intricate patterns of contact, migration, and admixture spanning tens of thousands of years.

# Institutional Dismissal of Anomalous Evidence

Dr. Virginia Steen-McIntyre watched her career disintegrate in slow motion. The geologist had spent decades studying volcanic ash layers around ancient lake beds in central Mexico. Her dating techniques consistently placed human artifacts at impossible antiquity. The U.S. Geological Survey dismissed her from the project in 1973. Professional colleagues avoided her research. Grant applications faced automatic rejection.

Steen-McIntyre had discovered something extraordinary at Valsequillo, Mexico. Stone tools and carved bone artifacts lay embedded in volcanic deposits dating back 250,000 years. Multiple independent dating methods confirmed the ancient age. Uranium-thorium dating, fission track analysis, and mineral examination all supported the extreme antiquity.

The implications unsettled mainstream archaeology. Humans are believed to have reached the Americas only 13,000 years ago via the

Bering Land Bridge. Evidence for a quarter-million-year occupation challenged every accepted model of human migration and development. Academic institutions faced a choice between accepting revolutionary discoveries or safeguarding established paradigms.

They chose protection. Steen-McIntyre's superiors ordered her to revise her findings. They demanded she report dates consistent with accepted theories. When she refused, they removed her from the research team. Her papers faced rejection from professional journals. Conference organisers cancelled her speaking invitations.

The suppression techniques became increasingly sophisticated. Peer reviewers found methodological flaws in technically sound research. Editorial boards rejected papers for "insufficient evidence," regardless of the quality of the data. Funding committees developed unwritten policies against supporting controversial investigations.

Dr. Michael Cremo documented similar patterns across archaeological fields. His research showed systematic suppression of discoveries that contradicted evolutionary timelines. Museums kept anomalous artefacts in basement collections where researchers could not access them. Professional publications ignored findings that challenged core assumptions.

The Smithsonian Institution faced particular criticism for evidence suppression. Former employees reported orders to dispose of artifacts that contradicted official positions. Giant human skeletons discovered in 19th-century mound excavations disappeared from collections. Detailed field notes vanished from archives.

Professional archaeology developed informal but effective censorship mechanisms. Young researchers learned to avoid topics that could jeopardize their careers from the outset. Senior faculty discouraged graduate students from investigating controversial sites. Dissertation committees rejected proposals that challenged established theories.

The suppression extended beyond individual careers to institutional policies. Universities restricted access to radiocarbon dating facilities for samples that might produce anomalous results. Museums limited researcher access to collections containing problematic artifacts. Government agencies classified archaeological reports that supported alternative theories.

Dr. Jeffrey Goodman experienced the full force of institutional resistance when he proposed early human occupation at Flagstaff, Arizona. His initial excavations produced stone tools in geological contexts suggesting great antiquity. Subsequent dating attempts faced bureaucratic obstacles and technical sabotage. Laboratory equipment mysteriously malfunctioned when processing his samples.

The pattern recurred at sites across North America. Calico Hills in California produced potential human artefacts dating back 200,000 years. Louis Leakey supported the discoveries before his death. Academic opinion quickly turned against the site after Leakey's endorsement disappeared. The artefacts remain controversial despite exhibiting clear characteristics of human manufacture.

Professional conferences started restricting presentations that questioned chronological frameworks. The Society for American Archaeology limited session topics to "acceptable" research areas. Independent researchers found themselves excluded from scientific meetings where they had previously been welcomed.

Journal editors subjected unusual discoveries to intense scrutiny. Papers supporting traditional theories underwent standard acceptance processes. Studies challenging established models faced multiple rounds of unfriendly peer review. Editorial bias became so ingrained that researchers started avoiding certain topics altogether.

The suppression crossed international boundaries. European archaeological institutions coordinated with American counterparts to limit controversial research. UNESCO restricted funding for projects that might challenge established human development models. International conferences developed informal blacklists of researchers investigating forbidden topics.

Government agencies participated actively in evidence suppression. The National Science Foundation rejected grant applications for politically sensitive archaeological research. The Bureau of Land Management restricted access to federal sites containing anomalous artifacts. Military installations became convenient dumping grounds for problematic discoveries.

Media coverage amplified institutional suppression efforts. Science journalists learned to avoid reporting discoveries that contradicted official positions. Television documentaries faced pressure to present only approved interpretations. Publishers rejected books that challenged archaeological orthodoxy regardless of evidential support.

The internet initially promised to circumvent institutional control of information. Independent researchers could publish findings without peer review gatekeeping. Online databases made suppressed discoveries available to interested investigators. Alternative publication venues emerged outside traditional academic channels.

Institutions adapted quickly to the digital threat. Professional organizations developed guidelines discouraging citation of non-peer-reviewed sources. Academic search engines excluded alternative archaeology websites from result rankings. Social media platforms restricted the discussion of controversial archaeological topics.

The suppression efforts succeeded in protecting established theories from contradictory evidence. Public education continued teaching outdated models long after supporting evidence disappeared. Museum displays ignored discoveries that challenged institutional positions. Textbook publishers refused to include anomalous findings in educational materials.

Younger archaeologists faced impossible choices between scientific integrity and professional survival. An honest investigation of controversial sites meant career suicide in academic institutions. Researchers who wanted university positions learned to avoid problematic topics entirely. Scientific progress stagnated under institutional pressure.

The cost of suppression extended beyond individual careers to human knowledge itself. Revolutionary discoveries remained hidden in private collections and unpublished reports. Alternative theories never received fair testing because supporting evidence disappeared from the archaeological record. Entire areas of investigation became forbidden territories.

Recent developments suggest cracks in the suppression system. Independent funding sources allow researchers to investigate controversial topics without institutional oversight. Advanced technology makes evidence tampering more difficult. Public interest in alternative archaeology creates market pressure for honest reporting.

The evidence suppression revealed more than scientific politics. It exposed how institutions protect themselves from paradigm-shifting discoveries. It demonstrated the vulnerability of academic freedom to political and economic pressures. It showed how established hierarchies can prevent scientific progress for decades or centuries.

Steen-McIntyre never received vindication for her Valsequillo discoveries. She finished her career teaching at small colleges where controversial research faced less institutional pressure. Her findings remain available to independent researchers willing to examine evidence that mainstream archaeology prefers to ignore.

The suppressed discoveries await rediscovery by future generations of archaeologists. Evidence hidden in storage rooms and private collections may eventually receive the scientific attention it deserves. Truth has a way of surfacing despite institutional efforts to bury it.

The pattern of suppression continues today in modified forms. Researchers still face career consequences for challenging established theories. Evidence that contradicts accepted models still disappears from public view. The mechanisms have become more subtle but no less effective at protecting orthodox positions from inconvenient discoveries.

# Conclusion: Rewriting the Human Story

Dr. Matthew Bennett stood in his laboratory at Bournemouth University, holding photographs of footprints from White Sands. The images showed heel strikes and toe impressions pressed into ancient mud 23,000 years ago. Each print told a story of real people walking across a landscape we barely understand. Children ran ahead of their parents. Adults carried toddlers on long journeys. Families moved together across a world where mammoths and giant ground sloths still roamed.

These footprints forced Bennett to confront uncomfortable truths about human history. His training taught him that people could not have reached North America before 13,000 years ago. Ice sheets blocked their path. Ocean currents prevented trans-Pacific voyaging. The Bering Land Bridge remained underwater. Every textbook agreed on this timeline.

The evidence said otherwise. Radiocarbon dating of seeds embedded above and below the tracks confirmed their age. Multiple independent laboratories verified the results. Climate data showed when the ancient lake formed and dried. Geological analysis confirmed the sediment layers had never been disturbed. The footprints were real, ancient, and impossible according to established theories.

Bennett's discovery joined a growing collection of anomalous findings across the Americas. Ruth Shady had already proven that Caral in Peru was building pyramids when Egypt's civilization was still emerging. El Mirador showed Maya urban planning a thousand years before scholars thought it possible. Cahokia revealed North American cities larger than medieval London. Each site pushed back the boundaries of what ancient peoples supposedly could achieve.

The resistance to these discoveries followed predictable patterns. Peer reviewers questioned dating methods. Colleagues demanded impossible standards of proof. Grant committees redirected funding to safer research topics. Conferences relegated controversial findings to minor presentation slots. Academic careers suffered when researchers challenged established timelines.

Virginia Steen-McIntyre experienced this resistance firsthand at Valsequillo, Mexico. Her volcanic ash analysis placed human tools at 250,000 years old. The U.S. Geological Survey removed her from the project. Universities stopped offering her teaching positions. Scientific

*Ancient American Civilizations*

journals refused to publish her papers. Steen-McIntyre's evidence vanished from the archaeological record through institutional silence rather than scientific refutation.

Similar treatment awaited Nìède Guidon at Pedra Furada, Brazil. Her excavations revealed 32,000-year-old stone tools in rock shelter deposits. Critics dismissed the artifacts as naturally broken rocks. They never visited the site. They refused to examine the stratigraphic evidence. Guidon's findings remained controversial because they contradicted accepted migration models, not because they lacked scientific support.

These patterns reveal how scientific institutions protect established paradigms. American archaeology built its foundation on specific theories about human migration and cultural development. The Clovis-first model provided elegant simplicity. Humans crossed from Asia 13,000 years ago. They spread rapidly across two continents. They developed complex societies only after European contact introduced new technologies and ideas.

This model served purposes beyond just scientific explanation. European colonisation needed justification to claim indigenous lands. If Native Americans had only recently arrived and remained primitive, colonial expansion appeared more justified. If they had developed advanced civilizations independently, their territorial rights would have been harder to dismiss. Historical narratives that downplayed indigenous achievements supported political agendas.

Modern evidence demolishes these comfortable assumptions. Caral's peaceful pyramids predate European civilization by millennia. Tiwanaku's precision stonework exceeds modern engineering capabilities. Maya calendar calculations surpass contemporary astronomical knowledge. Inca agricultural techniques create sustainable abundance that industrial farming cannot match. These achievements required sophisticated mathematics, complex social organization, and deep environmental understanding.

The extent of ancient American achievements becomes evident when looking at individual discoveries. At Pumapunku, Bolivia, ancient builders carved andesite blocks, which are harder than steel, into intricate geometric shapes. They crafted interlocking joints measured in fractions of a millimetre. They transported 100-ton stones across challenging terrain without the use of wheels or draft animals. Modern engineers find it difficult to explain how such precision was accomplished.

*Ancient American Civilizations*

Maya architects at Chaco Canyon encoded astronomical observations into architectural alignments. The Sun Dagger site tracks solstices and equinoxes with mathematical precision. Building orientations follow the 18.6-year lunar cycle that modern astronomers need sophisticated instruments to detect. Underground tunnel systems align with celestial events across multi-generational time periods.

Olmec sculptors created colossal basalt heads weighing 50 tons each. They quarried the stone dozens of miles from carving sites. They transported these monuments across swampy terrain without modern machinery. They carved distinctive facial features with such consistency that individual portraits remain recognizable after millennia. The logistics alone required organizational capabilities that conventional history considers impossible.

These technical achievements point to knowledge systems more sophisticated than scholars traditionally acknowledge. Ancient Americans understood principles of astronomy, engineering, metallurgy, and agriculture that Europeans would not master for centuries. They developed writing systems, mathematical concepts, and scientific methods independently of Old World influence. Their civilizations arose from indigenous innovation rather than external contact.

Evidence for pre-Columbian trans-oceanic contact adds another layer to this revised history. The Piri Reis map of 1513 shows Antarctic coastlines hidden beneath ice sheets. Cocaine traces are found in Egyptian mummies centuries before Columbus. Olmec sculptures depict African facial features within Mesoamerican contexts. Asian pottery techniques appear along American Pacific coasts. These links imply that ancient peoples had maritime skills that mainstream history repeatedly underestimates.

Viking settlements at L'Anse aux Meadows demonstrate that Atlantic crossings happened 500 years before Columbus. Norse artefacts verify European settlement in North America around 1000 CE. The Vinland Sagas recount encounters with indigenous peoples who already had advanced societies. Viking exploration did not result in permanent colonies because they faced organised resistance from local populations.

The Solutrean hypothesis suggests even earlier contact between Europe and the Americas. Ice Age hunters might have followed Atlantic ice margins 20,000 years ago. Stone tools discovered in Chesapeake Bay sediments display European-style craftsmanship in geological layers predating accepted human presence. Genetic studies uncover complex ancestral lineages in ancient Native American remains. These findings imply human migration patterns far more intricate than the simple Bering Land Bridge models suggest.

Underwater archaeology reveals another layer of hidden history. Maya cenotes contain submerged temples and ceremonial structures. Caribbean waters conceal geometric formations that are too precise to be naturally formed. Cuban sonar scans reveal rectangular patterns 600 metres beneath the surface. Rising sea levels since the Ice Age would have submerged coastal civilizations that once thrived on exposed continental shelves.

The Amazon basin conceals perhaps the greatest surprise of all. LIDAR technology reveals geometric earthworks hidden beneath jungle canopies. Raised agricultural fields show sophisticated water management across millions of acres. Terra preta soil demonstrates ecological engineering that modern agriculture cannot replicate. Pre-Columbian population estimates reach into millions of people living in forest cities that Europeans never recognized as urban centers.

These discoveries collectively point toward a fundamental revision of human history in the Americas. Ancient peoples achieved urban civilization, advanced technology, and continental organization thousands of years earlier than conventional timelines suggest. They developed these accomplishments independently, through indigenous innovation and adaptation to local environments. Their societies possessed knowledge and capabilities that often exceeded those of contemporary Old World civilizations.

The implications extend beyond archaeology into contemporary understanding of human potential. If ancient Americans could achieve such remarkable feats with limited technology, modern societies have no excuse for failing to address current challenges. Climate change, environmental degradation, and social inequality plagued ancient civilizations too. Many found solutions that sustained their societies for centuries.

Inca agricultural terraces still function after 500 years of abandonment. Maya water management systems continue operating in modern Guatemala. Cahokian trade networks spanned entire continents without central authority. These examples demonstrate organizational principles and technical innovations relevant to contemporary problems.

Ancient Americans also provide cautionary examples of civilizational collapse. El Mirador vanished so completely that later Maya forgot its existence. Cahokia emptied mysteriously, leaving only earthen monuments. Anasazi cliff dwellings sit abandoned in southwestern deserts. These collapses resulted from environmental stress, social conflict, or spiritual transformations we can study and potentially avoid.

The human story in the Americas spans over 20,000 years of continuous innovation, adaptation, and achievement. People walking across White Sands playa mud began a journey of discovery and creation unmatched anywhere in the ancient world. Their descendants built Caral's peaceful pyramids, carved Olmec colossal heads, aligned Chaco's astronomical observatories, and engineered Tiwanaku's impossible stonework.

These accomplishments belong to all humanity. They expand our understanding of human capability and potential. They challenge assumptions about technological progress and social development. They prove that complex civilization can arise anywhere people combine intelligence, cooperation, and environmental adaptation.

The evidence is overwhelming. The discoveries are undeniable. The implications are revolutionary. Ancient American civilizations achieved greatness that conventional history has systematically ignored, minimized, or explained away. The time has come to acknowledge their accomplishments, learn from their innovations, and restore their rightful place in the human story.

Future archaeologists will uncover additional evidence of ancient American achievement. Ground-penetrating radar will reveal more hidden cities. Underwater exploration will expose submerged civilizations. Genetic analysis will trace complex migration patterns. Each discovery will add details to a picture already clear in its broad outlines.

Humans arrived in the Americas far earlier than widely accepted timelines indicate. They developed advanced societies independently of Old World contact. They achieved technological and intellectual feats that matched or surpassed those of contemporary cultures anywhere globally. They built sustainable communities that endured for millennia, living in harmony with their environments.

This revised history restores agency and recognition to the peoples whose achievements have been systematically undervalued. It highlights indigenous innovation and adaptation. It credits ancient Americans with intellectual abilities comparable to those of any other human populations. It acknowledges their contributions to human knowledge and cultural progress.

The footprints at White Sands marked the beginning of this extraordinary journey. Twenty-three thousand years later, we are finally ready to follow where they lead. The path reveals wonders we are only beginning to understand. The human story in the Americas was written in stone, soil, and stars long before Europeans arrived to claim discovery. That story belongs to all of us. The time has come to tell it completely.

Dr. Bennett closed his laptop and walked to his laboratory window. Outside, rain fell on modern streets where ancient peoples once walked. Their footprints had survived ice ages, climate change, and millennia of geological processes. Their cities had withstood earthquakes, warfare, and institutional neglect. Their achievements had endured academic dismissal, political suppression, and historical revision.

The evidence would not be silenced. Truth had a way of surfacing despite human attempts to bury it. Ancient Americans had left their mark too deeply in stone and earth for modern denial to erase. Their story was emerging from jungle shadows, desert sands, and underwater caverns. The rewriting of human history had begun.

This is their story. This is our story. This is the true history of ancient America.

# Bibliography

Adovasio, J. M., & Page, J. (2002). *The first Americans: In pursuit of archaeology's greatest mystery*. Random House.

Alva, W., & Donnan, C. B. (2008). *Royal tombs of Sipán*. UCLA Fowler Museum of Cultural History.

Aveni, A. F. (2001). *Skywatchers: A revised and updated version of skywatchers of ancient Mexico*. University of Texas Press.

Bawden, G. (1996). *The Moche*. Blackwell Publishers.

Bennett, M. R., Bustos, D., & Odess, D. *et al.* (2021). *Evidence of humans in North America during the Last Glacial Maximum*. Science, 373(6562), 1528-1531.

Benson, E. P. (1996). *The Olmec and their neighbors: Essays in memory of Matthew W. Stirling*. Dumbarton Oaks Research Library and Collection.

Burger, R. L. (1992). *Chavin and the origins of Andean civilization*. Thames and Hudson.

Carrasco, D. (1999). *City of sacrifice: The Aztec empire and the role of violence in civilization*. Beacon Press.

Coe, M. D. (2005). *The Maya (7th ed.)*. Thames & Hudson.

Coe, M. D., & Koontz, R. (2013). *Mexico: From the Olmecs to the Aztecs (7th ed.)*. Thames & Hudson.

Creamer, W., Haas, J., & Huamán, L. H. (2007). *Revising Peru's prehistory: New radiocarbon dates from Caral*. Archaeology, 60(4), 26-29.

Crown, P. L., & Judge, W. J. (1991). *Chaco & Hohokam: Prehistoric regional systems in the American Southwest*. School for Advanced Research Press.

D'Altroy, T. N. (2014). *The Incas (2nd ed.)*. Wiley-Blackwell.

**Dillehay, T. D. (2000).** *The settlement of the Americas: A new prehistory.* Basic Books.

**Dillehay, T. D., Ramírez, C., & Pino, M., et al., (2008).** *Monte Verde: Seaweed, food, medicine, and the peopling of South America.* Science, 320(5877), 784-786.

**Fash, W. L. (2001).** *Scribes, warriors and kings: The city of Copán and the ancient Maya.* Thames & Hudson.

**Feder, K. L. (2017).** *Frauds, myths, and mysteries: Science and pseudoscience in archaeology (9th ed.).* Oxford University Press.

**Gibson, J. L. (2000).** *The ancient mounds of Poverty Point: Place of rings.* University Press of Florida.

**Gillespie, S. D. (1989).** *The Aztec kings: The construction of rulership in Mexica history.* University of Arizona Press.

**Goodman, J. T. (1905).** *The archaic Maya inscriptions.* Taylor and Francis.

**Grann, D. (2009).** *The lost city of Z: A tale of deadly obsession in the Amazon.* Doubleday.

**Guidon, N., & Delibrias, G. (1986).** *Carbon-14 dates point to man in the Americas 32,000 years ago.* Nature, 321(6072), 769-771.

**Haas, J., & Creamer, W. (2006).** *Crucible of Andean civilization: The Peruvian coast from 3000 to 1800 BC.* Current Anthropology, 47(5), 745-775.

*Hassig, R. (1988). Aztec warfare: Imperial expansion and political control.* University of Oklahoma Press.

**Heckenberger, M. J. (2005).** *The ecology of power: Culture, place, and personhood in the southern Amazon, A.D. 1000-2000.* Routledge.

**Houston, S., Stuart, D., & Taube, K. (2006).** *The memory of bones: Body, being, and experience among the Classic Maya.* University of Texas Press.

Ingstad, H. (2001). *The discovery of a Norse settlement in America: Excavations at L'Anse aux Meadows, Newfoundland 1961-1968.* University of Toronto Press.

Isbell, W. H. (2008). *Wari and Tiwanaku: Middle Horizon empires of the central Andes.* Dumbarton Oaks Research Library and Collection.

Jennings, J. (2016). Killing civilization: *A reassessment of early urbanism and its consequences.* University of New Mexico Press.

Joyce, A. A. (2010). *Mixtecs, Zapotecs, and Chatinos: Ancient peoples of southern Mexico.* Thames & Hudson.

Kehoe, A. B. (2005). *The fringe of American archaeology: Transoceanic contact, ancient aliens, and other improbable theories.* SAA Press.

Kolata, A. L. (1993). *The Tiwanaku: Portrait of an Andean civilization.* Blackwell Publishers.

Lekson, S. H. (1999). *The Chaco meridian: Centers of political power in the ancient Southwest.* AltaMira Press.

Lekson, S. H. (2008). *A history of the ancient Southwest.* School for Advanced Research Press.

Lynch, T. F. (1990). *Glacial-age man in South America?* A critical review. American Antiquity, 55(1), 12-36.

MacNeish, R. S. (1976). *Early man in the New World.* American Scientist, 64(3), 316-327.

Mann, C. C. (2005). *1491: New revelations of the Americas before Columbus.* Knopf.

Marcus, J., & Flannery, K. V. (1996). *Zapotec civilization: How urban society evolved in Mexico's Oaxaca Valley.* Thames & Hudson.

Martin, S., & Grube, N. (2008). *Chronicle of the Maya kings and queens: Deciphering the dynasties of the ancient Maya (2nd ed.).* Thames & Hudson.

Meltzer, D. J. (2009). *First peoples in a new world: Colonizing ice age America.* University of California Press.

**Miller, M. E., & Taube, K. A. (1993).** *An illustrated dictionary of the gods and symbols of ancient Mexico and the Maya.* Thames & Hudson.

**Milner, G. R. (2004).** The moundbuilders: Ancient peoples of eastern North America. Thames & Hudson.

**Moseley, M. E. (2001).** The Incas and their ancestors: The archaeology of Peru (Rev. ed.). Thames & Hudson.

**O'Brien, P. J. (1989).** *Cahokia: The political capital of the "Ramey" state?* North American Archaeologist, 10(4), 275-292.

**Pauketat, T. R. (2009).** *Cahokia: Ancient America's great city on the Mississippi.* Penguin.

**Piperno, D. R., & Pearsall, D. M. (1998).** *The origins of agriculture in the lowland neotropics.* Academic Press.

**Pohl, J. M. D. (1999).** *Exploring Mesoamerica.* Oxford University Press.

**Protzen, J. P. (1993).** *Inca architecture and construction at Ollantaytambo.* Oxford University Press.

**Quilter, J. (2014).** *The ancient Central Andes.* Routledge.

**Roosevelt, A. C. (2000).** *The lower Amazon: A dynamic human habitat.* In Imperfect balance: Landscape transformations in the precolumbian Americas (pp. 455-491). Columbia University Press.

**Salomon, F., & Urioste, G. L. (1991).** *The Huarochirí manuscript: A testament of ancient and colonial Andean religion.* University of Texas Press.

**Schele, L., & Freidel, D. (1990).** *A forest of kings: The untold story of the ancient Maya.* William Morrow.

**Shady, R., Haas, J., & Creamer, W. (2001).** *Dating Caral, a preceramic site in the Supe Valley on the central coast of Peru.* Science, 292(5517), 723-726.

**Stanford, D., & Bradley, B. (2012).** *Across Atlantic ice: The origin of America's Clovis culture.* University of California Press.

**Steen-McIntyre, V., Fryxell, R., & Malde, H. E. (1981).** *Geologic evidence for age of deposits at Hueyatlaco archaeological site, Valsequillo, Mexico.* Quaternary Research, 16(1), 1-17.

**Stuart, D. (2011).** *The order of days: The Maya world and the truth about 2012.* Harmony Books.

**Sugiyama, S. (2005).** *Human sacrifice, militarism, and rulership: Materialization of state ideology at the Feathered Serpent Pyramid, Teotihuacan.* Cambridge University Press.

**Thompson, J. E. S. (1990).** *Maya history and religion.* University of Oklahoma Press.

**Townsend, R. F. (2000).** *The Aztecs (Rev. ed.).* Thames & Hudson.

**Urton, G. (2003).** *Signs of the Inka khipu: Binary coding in the Andean knotted-string records.* University of Texas Press.

**Van Tilburg, J. (1994).** *Easter Island: Archaeology, ecology and culture.* Smithsonian Institution Press.

**Von Hagen, A., & Morris, C. (1998).** *The cities of the ancient Andes.* Thames & Hudson.

**Waters, M. R., & Stafford, T. W. (2007).** *Redefining the age of Clovis: Implications for the peopling of the Americas.* Science, 315(5815), 1122-1126.

**Weaver, M. P. (1993).** *The Aztecs, Maya, and their predecessors: Archaeology of Mesoamerica* (3rd ed.). Academic Press.

**Webster, D. (2002).** *The fall of the ancient Maya: Solving the mystery of the Maya collapse.* Thames & Hudson.

**Willey, G. R. (1966).** *An introduction to American archaeology, Volume One:* North and Middle America. Prentice-Hall.

**Wright, K. R., & Zegarra, A. V. (2000).** *Machu Picchu: A civil engineering marvel.* ASCE Press.

**Young-Sánchez, M. (2004).** *Tiwanaku: Ancestors of the Inca.* Denver Art Museum.

# Other Books by Theresa G. Bryan

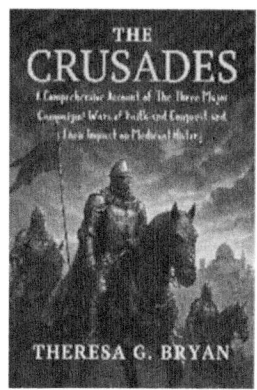

*Ancient American Civilizations*

Printed in Dunstable, United Kingdom

70550201R00188